THE EFFECTIVE ENGINEER

THE EFFECTIVE ENGINEER

How to Leverage Your Efforts in Software Engineering
to Make a Disproportionate and Meaningful Impact

Edmond Lau

The Effective Bookshelf
Palo Alto, CA

THE EFFECTIVE ENGINEER.

Published by The Effective Bookshelf, Palo Alto, CA.

For more information, please contact: support@theeffectiveengineer.com.

Printed in the United States of America.

978-0996128100 (ISBN 13)

TO MY PARENTS

whose hard work and sacrifices made my opportunities possible

Table of Contents

Foreword

My first job out of Stanford's Computer Science program was as a Product Manager at Google. It was an amazing first job. I shared offices with engineers who had written the textbooks I used in college. I helped create Google Maps, which is still my proudest achievement as a product designer and engineer. And I learned how to be effective on large scale software projects. By the time I left Google to start my first company, FriendFeed, I had worked on so many projects at scale, I felt extremely confident I could start one myself.

However, being a product manager at a large company is different than founding a startup. For one, you are judged differently. While, in theory, product managers are judged on the success of the products they work on, in practice, large companies also judge product managers on their ability to manage all the people and departments that have a stake in a product's outcome. Did you engage the PR team enough time before launch? Did you integrate your product with the CEO's pet project? Did you convince the competing executive of your product direction before the big executive review? At software companies that aren't as enlightened as Google, product managers are judged more on these political issues than they are on any aspect of the products they work on.

That's why so many engineers and product managers that come out of larger companies have trouble with the concept of *leverage* that Edmond Lau talks about in *The Effective Engineer*. They are effectively trained to care about low leverage activities because the bureaucracy that trained them values and rewards them. The most successful engineers I've worked with in my career were the few that were able to see past these bureaucratic idiosyncrasies and recognize the one or two things that would really impact their product's success. The engineer that taught me the most about leverage is, without question, Paul Buchheit.

Paul was one of the co-founders of FriendFeed. He had previously created Gmail, and while we hadn't worked together much at Google, we had enough mutual respect to join forces with Jim Norris and Sanjeev Singh to start a company together in mid-2007. More than any person I've ever met, Paul was willing to challenge conventional thinking, and he completely changed my perspective on engineering and product management.

Whenever we would encounter a challenging technical problem, I would ask "How should we do this?" Paul would respond, often obnoxiously, "Why do we need to do it at all?" Instead of trying to solve impossible problems, he would more often challenge the assumptions so we could simply work around them. At times, it almost seemed like Paul was lazy—given any sufficiently hard project, Paul would question the purpose of the project. But he was almost always right. Unless the project was destined to make or break our nascent company, why spend our precious engineering resources on it?

Working with Paul proved to me through experience that engineering was much more about leverage than programming ability, and I've tried to apply that lesson to all my subsequent jobs. When I became the Chief Technology Officer of Facebook after the company acquired FriendFeed, I spent as much time canceling projects as creating them. At Quip, the company I founded with Kevin Gibbs in 2012, we felt so strongly that effective engineering was not correlated with hours of effort that we have proudly embraced a "nine-to-five" culture unheard of at Silicon Valley companies.

I love the culture of Silicon Valley. I love that young engineers have as much of an impact on our industry as veterans, and I love how our industry redefines itself every decade. But I also think the culture of working endless hours is unnecessary and abused by ineffective managers around our industry. In addition to being unnecessary, that aspect of our culture is one of the main things that prevents people from choosing long term careers in software engineering—it is unsustainable for people with families, and it creates a homogeneous, immature atmosphere at the companies where it is ubiquitous.

I'm happy Edmond chose to write this book because I think Silicon Valley would be a much better place for both managers and engineers if people embraced "working smart" rather than "working hard." It's neither counterintuitive nor hard in practice, but very few people do it, and I hope more people embrace Edmond's philosophy and techniques to make their companies and careers more successful.

— Bret Taylor, CEO of Quip

Introduction

MY FIRST FEW YEARS WORKING AT STARTUPS STAND OUT AS SOME OF the longest in my career. They were a relentless grind punctuated with intense personal growth and countless emotional roller coasters. My team almost never worked fewer than 60 hours each week, and months would go by where we would toil away for 70 to 80 hours. I'd start my work day in the office; I'd regularly spend lunch consulting with my team; and then I'd continue to work from home after dinner—or sometimes even stay in the office until midnight. Even while visiting family over the holidays, I'd still squeeze in time to code and to respond to emails on my laptop.

After all, the nature of startups meant that we were the underdogs fighting formidable competitors. The harder we worked, the more value we could produce, and the more likely it was that our startup would succeed. Or so I thought.

A few experiences forced me to reconsider this assumption. There was the custom analytics module that I spent two weeks building—and that the customer never used. There were the new tools to improve content quality that we spent months tweaking and perfecting before launch—and that never got the user adoption we wanted. There were the weekly traffic spikes—followed by hours spent spinning up and winding down extra servers. There was the time when I was hiking up the Mauna Loa volcano in Hawaii—and I got a text message saying that the infrastructure generating analytics reports for customers was down, and could I please take a look.

I worked the long hours because I wanted to make a meaningful impact, but I couldn't help but wonder: Was putting in 70- to 80-hour weeks really the most effective way of ensuring our startup's success? Our intentions were sound, but could we have worked smarter? Could we have reduced some of that effort and achieved the same impact, or possibly even more?

In the ensuing years, I've come to learn that working more hours isn't the most effective way to increase output. In fact, working too many hours leads to decreased productivity and burnout. Output may even turn out to be negative when it's necessary to repair the mistakes made by overworked and fatigued engineers.

To be effective engineers, we need to be able to identify which activities produce more impact with smaller time investments. Not all work is created equal. Not all efforts, however well-intentioned, translate into impact.

What Makes an Effective Engineer?

How do you measure an engineer's effectiveness? Is it by the number of hours she works? The amount of effort he applies? The number of tasks she completes? At the end of the day, a hard-working engineer who pours his energy into a feature whose schedule slips and that no one uses isn't that effective. I've been that engineer before, as have many talented people I know.

For over a decade, I've worked as a software engineer at many technology companies, including Microsoft, Google, Ooyala, Quora, and Quip. Throughout this time, the question of what makes an effective engineer has always been on my mind. I wanted to increase my impact, but working 70 to 80 hours per week to do it wasn't sustainable. And so I searched for an answer that would let me work less and accomplish more.

Others have asked this question, too, particularly in the context of hiring. I've had the good fortune of participating in various aspects of growing an engineering team. Through that experience, I've screened thousands of resumes, interviewed over five hundred candidates, and debated their merits in hiring committees. At the end of each debate, we ultimately needed to decide: Will this individual grow into a strong contributor on the team and effectively get things done?

I've also created onboarding and mentoring programs and have trained dozens of new engineering hires. The people I mentor inevitably ask me how they can be more effective. Understanding what makes one engineer more effective than another, to the point where I can then teach that effectiveness to others, has been a holy grail of mine. In my quest to find the answer, I've had conversations with dozens of engineering leaders. I spent the last few years consuming shelves of productivity, team-building, personal psychology, business, and self-help books. Even though most of them weren't targeted at engineers, I found ways to experiment with and apply their lessons in an engineering context.

There will always be more effectiveness techniques to learn. But what I've developed on my journey is a powerful framework for reasoning about effectiveness that can be applied to any activity. I'm excited to share this framework with you in *The Effective Engineer*. This book examines and describes what it means to be an effective engineer, and it distills the key lessons that I've learned. More importantly, it supplements the framework with actionable and tested strategies that you can use right away to become more effective.

So what makes an effective engineer? Intuitively, we have some notion of which engineers we consider to be effective. They're the people who get things done. They're the ones who ship products that users love, launch features that customers pay for, build tools that boost team productivity, and deploy systems that help companies scale. Effective engineers produce results.

But if they took too long to accomplish these tasks, then we might hesitate to call them effective. They might be hard-working, but we would consider someone who produced the same results in less time and with fewer resources to be more effective. Effective engineers, therefore, also get things done efficiently.

Efficiency alone doesn't guarantee effectiveness, however. An engineer who efficiently builds infrastructure that can scale to millions of requests for an internal tool that would be used by at most a hundred people isn't effective. Nor is someone who builds a feature that only 0.1% of users adopt, when other features could reach 10% adoption—unless that 0.1% generates disproportionately more business value. Effective engineers focus on value and impact—they know how to choose *which* results to deliver.

An effective engineer, therefore, is defined by the rate at which he or she produces value per unit of time worked. This is exactly what leverage—a concept that we'll introduce in Chapter 1 and revisit throughout this book—captures.

What You'll Learn from Reading This Book

Despite being a book for software engineers, you won't find a single line of code in *The Effective Engineer*. Books and articles abound on different technologies, programming languages, software frameworks, and system architectures. Technical knowledge, however, represents only a fraction of the skills that engineers need to learn in order to be effective.

More important for effectiveness, but often overlooked by engineers, are the meta-skills. These skills help you determine where to focus your time and energy so that more of your effort translates into impact. *The Effective Engineer* teaches you these meta-skills. My promise to you is that after reading this book, you'll have a useful framework, called *leverage*, for analyzing the effectiveness of different activities. You'll be equipped with actionable tools to increase your impact, and you'll develop insights into the common engineering pitfalls that sap precious time and energy.

I learned some of these skills through my own experiences, from conversations with other engineers, and by applying lessons from scientific research in productivity and psychology. But you'll find much more than just my own stories in this book. I've also interviewed senior engineers, managers, directors, and VPs at technology companies around Silicon Valley to distill their secrets for effectiveness. You'll find their stories about the most valuable practices they've adopted, as well as the costliest mistakes they've made. And even though everyone's narrative was different, many common themes emerged.

In Chapter 1, you'll learn why leverage is the yardstick for measuring an engineer's effectiveness. In each subsequent chapter, you'll find a high-leverage habit—accompanied by research, stories, and examples—that effective engineers use. You'll learn what key engineering principles Instagram's co-founder Mike Krieger followed to enable a small team of 13 to scale effectively and support a product with over 40 million users. You'll learn about key habits that former Facebook director Bobby Johnson fostered in his infrastructure team as the social network grew to over a billion users. And you'll hear many more stories from people at Google, Facebook, Dropbox, Box, Etsy, and other top technology companies, as they share their philosophies on how to be more effective individual contributors as well as leaders. Ignoring these habits often led to hard-learned lessons, and you'll find some war stories here, as well.

The themes of this book are organized into three parts. Part 1 describes the mindsets that allow us to reason more rigorously about and increase our effectiveness. We begin by outlining the mindset of leverage (Chapter 1), and then move on to show how both optimizing for learning (Chapter 2) and regular prioritization (Chapter 3) let us accelerate our growth and make the most of our time. Much of engineering revolves around execution, and Part 2 takes a deep dive into the key strategies we need to consistently execute and make progress on the tasks we're faced with: iterating quickly (Chapter 4), validating ideas early and often (Chapter 6), measuring what we want to improve (Chapter 5), and developing our project estimation skills (Chapter 7). Effective engineers aren't short-term investors, and so in Part 3, we'll shift gears and look into approaches for building long-term value. We'll learn how to balance quality with pragmatism (Chapter 8), minimize operational burden (Chapter 9), and invest in our team's growth (Chapter 10).

Whether you want to increase your impact on the world, get promoted more quickly, waste less time grinding away at mindless tasks, or work fewer hours without sacrificing results, *The Effective Engineer* gives you the tools you need. This book is not a comprehensive guide for everything that can help you grow, but it provides you with a consistent framework—leverage—for navigating which skills might be good investments of your time. Teaching and mentoring are passions of mine, and I'm excited to share what I've learned with you.

Part 1: Adopt the Right Mindsets

1

Focus on High-Leverage Activities

In the span of three months, Quora's engineering team doubled. Our startup had an ambitious mission: to build a question-and-answer platform that would share and grow the world's knowledge. To achieve that internet-scale Library of Alexandria, we needed more engineers. And so, during the summer of 2012, 14 new engineering hires crammed into our small office on the second floor of 261 Hamilton Avenue in downtown Palo Alto, California. Even after construction crews knocked down three sets of walls to expand our office space, we could still barely accommodate everyone's desks.

I had met many times with Charlie Cheever, one of Quora's two co-founders, to prepare for the influx of people. I had volunteered to be directly responsible for onboarding new engineering hires, and so I needed to design the team's plan to ramp everyone up quickly. How would we ensure that the product wouldn't break all the time, especially since we deployed code to production multiple times a day? How would we keep code quality high with so many new people unfamiliar with the design and conventions in the codebase? How would we make sure new hires were productive and not blocked on what to do next? Figuring out these answers would be a marked departure from my regular duties of writing software, but I was excited because I knew that onboarding the new hires effectively would have a larger impact than any code I could produce. It would directly affect how much work half of the engineering team would get done during their first few months.

I researched onboarding and mentoring programs at other companies and talked with their engineers to learn what worked and what didn't. With support from the rest of my team, I formalized a mentoring program at Quora for new engineering hires. Each new engineer was paired up with a mentor for two to three months, and the mentor was responsible for the new hire's success. Mentoring activities included everything from reviewing code, outlining technical skills to learn, and pair programming, to discussing engineering tradeoffs, explaining how to prioritize better, and offering guidance on how to work well with different team members. Mentors also planned a sequence of starter tasks and projects to increase the new hires' mastery of our systems.

To ensure that our hires started on a common foundation, I also created an onboarding program with a series of 10 recurring tech talks and 10 *codelabs*. Codelabs, an idea I borrowed from Google, were documents that explained why we designed core abstractions, described how to use them, walked through the relevant code, and provided exercises to validate understanding. Through tech talks and codelabs, we gave our hires an overview of the codebase and the engineering focus areas, and taught them how to use our development and debugging tools.

As a result of these efforts, many of our hires that summer were able to successfully deploy their first bug fix or small product feature to users by the end of their first week, and others deployed their first changes soon after. During those months, we launched a new Android application, an internal analytics system, better in-product recommendations, improvements to our product's news feed, and much more. Code quality stayed high, and mentors met regularly to share thoughts on how to make the onboarding process even smoother. Even after I moved on from the company, dozens of new engineers have continued to go through these onboarding and mentoring programs. [1] They were two of the highest-leverage investments that we made on the engineering team.

In this chapter, we'll define what leverage is and explain why it's the yardstick for measuring our effectiveness. Then we'll go over three ways of reasoning about how to increase the leverage of our activities. And finally, we'll discuss why directing energy toward our leverage points, as opposed to easy wins, is key to increasing our impact.

Use Leverage as Your Yardstick for Effectiveness

Why did Quora engineers spend so much energy on mentoring and onboarding new engineers? We all had hundreds of other things that we could have worked on—ideas to prototype, features to build, products to launch, bugs to fix, and teams to run. Why didn't we focus on these instead? More generally, given the hundreds or more tasks that we all could be doing in our jobs right now, how should we decide what to actually work on in order to more effectively achieve our goals?

The key to answering these questions and prioritizing these different activities is assessing their *leverage*. *Leverage* is defined by a simple equation. It's the value, or impact, produced per time invested:

$$\text{Leverage} = \frac{\text{Impact Produced}}{\text{Time Invested}}$$

Put another way, leverage is the return on investment (ROI) for the effort that's put in. Effective engineers aren't the ones trying to get more things done by working more hours. They're the ones who get things done efficiently—and who focus their limited time on the tasks that produce the most value. They try to increase the numerator in that equation while keeping the denominator small. Leverage, therefore, is the yardstick for measuring how effective your activities are.

Leverage is critical because time is your most limited resource. Unlike other resources, time cannot be stored, extended, or replaced. [2] The limitations of time are inescapable, regardless of your goals. You might be a product engineer deciding what to tackle to maximize your impact on users. Or you might be an infrastructure engineer figuring out what scaling issue to focus on next. You might be a workaholic who loves to code 60 to 70 hours per week at the office. Or you might be a subscriber to Timothy Ferris's *4-Hour Work Week* philosophy and only want to put in the minimal hours per week required to sustain your lifestyle business. No matter who you are, at some point in your career you'll realize that there's more work to be done than time available, and you'll need to start prioritizing.

Another way of thinking about leverage is the commonly-mentioned Pareto principle, or 80–20 rule—the notion that for many activities, 80% of the impact comes from 20% of the work. [3] That 20% comprises the high-leverage activities, activities that produce a disproportionately high impact for a relatively small time investment.

Effective engineers use this simple equation as their central, guiding metric for determining how and where to spend their time. Greek mathematician and engineer Archimedes once declared, "Give me a place to stand, and a lever long enough, and I shall move the world." [4] It can be hard to move a huge boulder by yourself, but with a powerful enough lever, you can move almost anything. High-leverage activities behave similarly, letting you amplify your limited time and effort to produce much more impact.

Based on the principle of leverage, it's clear why our engineering team focused on mentoring and training new engineers. Mentoring is a prime example of a high-ROI activity. In a single year, a typical engineer works between 1,880 and 2,820 hours. [5] Devoting even 1 hour every day for the first month (20 hours) to mentor or train a new hire may seem like a large investment; yet it represents only about 1% of the total time the new hire will spend working during her first year. Creating reusable resources like codelabs paid off even higher dividends and required little upkeep after an upfront investment.

Moreover, that 1% time investment can have an outsized influence on the productivity and effectiveness of the other 99% of work hours. Pointing out a useful UNIX command could save minutes or hours on basic tasks. Walking through debugging tools could drastically reduce development time for every new feature. Reviewing code early and thoroughly to catch common errors could remove the need to re-address similar issues later and prevent bad habits from forming. Teaching a new hire how to prioritize different projects to complete or skills to learn could easily increase his productivity. Planning good starter projects that teach core abstractions and fundamental concepts could improve her software designs and reduce future maintenance requirements.

Since the success of our startup depended more on the success of the entire team than on what any one engineer could accomplish, investing in programs to ramp up new engineers as quickly and as seamlessly as possible was one of the highest-leverage activities that we could have done.

Increase Your Leverage in Three Ways

In his book *High Output Management*, Former Intel CEO Andrew Grove explains that by definition, your overall leverage—the amount of value that you produce per unit time—can only be increased in three ways: [6]

1. By reducing the time it takes to complete a certain activity.
2. By increasing the output of a particular activity.
3. By shifting to higher-leverage activities.

These three ways naturally translate into three questions we can ask ourselves about any activity we're working on:

1. How can I complete this activity in a shorter amount of time?
2. How can I increase the value produced by this activity?
3. Is there something else that I could spend my time on that would produce more value?

Your output as an engineer is measured in a variety of ways, including the numbers of products launched, bugs fixed, users acquired, and engineers hired, along with ranking quality improved, revenue generated, and many other metrics. Your total output is the sum of the output of your individual activities. In a typical work day, these activities might include attending meetings, responding to emails, investigating bugs, refactoring old code, developing new features, reviewing changes, monitoring metrics, maintaining production systems, interviewing potential hires, and more.

However, spending your work day going through the motions of these different activities does not necessarily mean that you're producing value the entire time. As Figure 1 shows, each individual daily activity has its own leverage, measured by the activity's output divided by the time it takes to complete that activity. Some activities, like implementing a feature request, learning a new testing framework, or fixing an important bug, have high leverage; others, like surfing the web or responding to email, might take up just as much time but have lower leverage because they don't generate as much value.

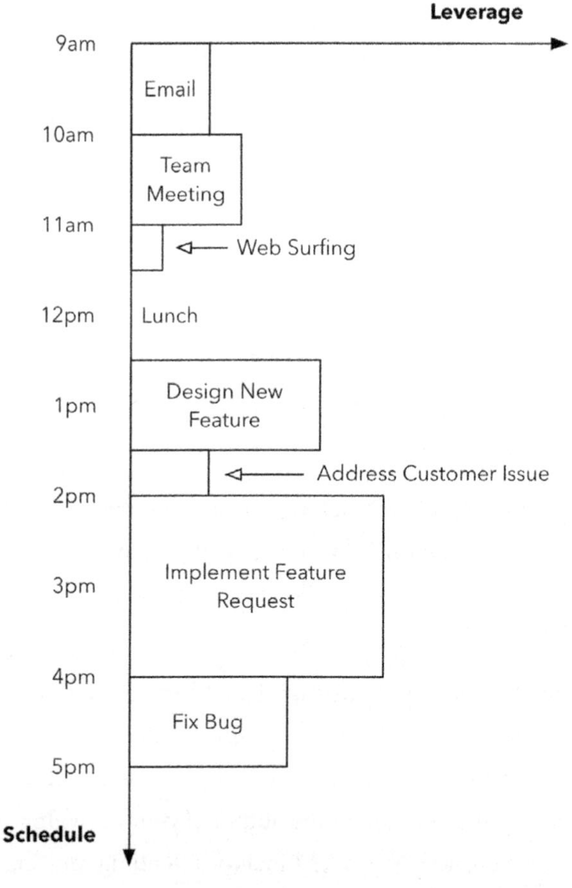

Figure 1: Leverage of different activities during a typical workday.

To increase the leverage of each activity, ask yourself the previous three questions, each of which leads to a different avenue of potential improvements. For example, you might have a one-hour meeting that you've scheduled with your team to review their progress on a project. You can increase the meeting's leverage by:

1. Defaulting to a half-hour meeting instead of a one-hour meeting to get the same amount done in less time.
2. Preparing an agenda and a set of goals for the meeting and circulating them to attendees beforehand so that the meeting is focused and more productive.
3. If an in-person discussion isn't actually necessary, replacing the meeting with a email discussion and spending the time building an important feature instead.

Or perhaps you're a product engineer, ready to start working on a new customer-facing feature for your company's flagship product. You might increase the leverage of your development time by:

1. Automating parts of the development or testing process that have thus far been done manually, so that you can iterate more quickly.
2. Prioritizing tasks based on how critical they are for launch so that you maximize the value of what you finally ship.
3. Talking with the customer support team to gain insights into the customers' biggest pain points, and using that knowledge to understand whether there's another feature you could be working on that would produce even more value with less development effort.

Or suppose that you're a performance engineer identifying and fixing the bottlenecks in a web application. The application might slow down as the product teams launch new products and features, and it's your job to ensure that it stays fast. Some approaches you might consider to increase your leverage include:

1. Learning to effectively use a profiling tool so that you can reduce the time it takes to identify each bottleneck.
2. Measuring both the performance and visit frequency of each web page so that you can address the bottlenecks that affect the most traffic first, thereby increasing the impact of each fix you make.

3. Working with product teams to design performant software from the outset, so that application speed is prioritized as a feature during product development rather than treated as a bug to be fixed.

As these examples illustrate, for any given activity, there are three approaches you can take to increase the leverage of your time spent. When you successfully shorten the time required for an activity, increase its impact, or shift to a higher-leverage activity, you become a more effective engineer.

Direct Energy Toward Leverage Points, Not Just Easy Wins

We have a limited amount of time and a large number of possible activities. As you make your way through this book, constantly keep one lesson in mind: *focus on high-leverage activities.* This is the single most valuable lesson that I've learned in my professional life.

Don't confuse high-leverage activities with easy wins, however. Just as a lever lets you apply a small amount of force over a long distance to generate a much larger force, so too do many high-leverage activities require consistent applications of effort over long time periods to achieve high impact. Yishan Wong, an early director of engineering at Facebook and a former CEO of Reddit, shared a story with me of his proudest accomplishment at Facebook that underscores this point. [7]

Facebook has a strong hiring culture. Employees view themselves as the guardians of high standards, and hiring is a top priority for both managers and engineers. But it wasn't always this way. When Wong first entered into a management position at Facebook in late 2006, engineers viewed recruiting and interviews as distractions from getting their work done [8]—an attitude that's common to engineers at many companies. Everyone knew on some level that hiring was important, but translating it into action was another matter.

Wong had to gradually apply pressure to change the prevailing mindset to one where people considered the hiring process an art form to be mastered. When engineers asked him how the company would ensure that the people being hired were strong engineers, Wong would tell them that this was *their* job. And because hiring was a top priority, engineers didn't skip interviews to do other work. They were expected to submit feedback immediately, as opposed to deferring it for hours or days. When recruiters needed to schedule interviews with candidates, Wong would push them to schedule the conversations in the "first humanly-possible time slot." [9] Can't meet until tomorrow? How about 8am? Not free until the afternoon? What about 1pm? Wong built a culture where even rejected candidates would leave interviews wanting to work at Facebook. And over his four years at the company, an obsession with speed and quality in hiring became one of Facebook's competitive advantages. While slower-moving companies dilly-dallied, Facebook closed candidates.

Building a strong hiring culture wasn't a quick and easy fix; it was a high-leverage activity that required consistent effort over many years. Once strong people joined the company, however, it became easier to attract more strong people. It's clear that Facebook could not have become a massively successful $220+ billion company with over 9,000 employees without its emphasis on the hiring process. [10]

Our own work might not be on as grand a scale, but the concept of leverage is as powerful of a framework for us as it is for Facebook. Moreover, leverage is used not just by effective engineers, but also by the world's most successful people. Bill Gates, for example, after retiring as the CEO of Microsoft, started focusing his time and energy on how to best invest his billions of dollars in philanthropy. While the $40.2 billion managed by the Bill & Melinda Gates Foundation may be a lot of money, it's still not nearly enough to solve all of the world's problems. [11] "[I]n a global economy worth tens of trillions of dollars, any philanthropic effort is relatively small," writes Gates in a November 2013 *Wired* essay. "If you want to have a big impact, you need a leverage point—a way to put in a dollar of funding or an hour of effort and benefit society by a hundred or a thousand times as much." For Gates, those leverage points include funding measles and malaria vaccines that cost less than 25 cents each but that save millions of lives. [12]

Similarly, engineering has its own set of leverage points. This book won't be a substitute for mindful reflection, but it can help shortcut your path to finding these points. In each subsequent chapter, you'll find a high-leverage habit of effective engineers—reinforced by scientific research, stories from industry, and concrete examples. You'll read about why the leverage of each habit justifies its time investment, and you'll also find concrete and actionable tips for incorporating each habit into your own craft. Doubling down on these leverage points will help you transform the time and effort you spend as an engineer into meaningful impact.

Key Takeaways

- **Use leverage to measure your engineering effectiveness.** Focus on what generates the highest return on investment for your time spent.
- **Systematically increase the leverage of your time.** Find ways to get an activity done more quickly, to increase the impact of an activity, or to shift to activities with higher leverage.
- **Focus your effort on leverage points.** Time is your most limited asset. Identify the habits that produce disproportionately high impact for the time you invest.

2

Optimize for Learning

A Tyrannosaurus rex skeleton stands guard over the Googleplex, Google's Silicon Valley headquarters. It's right next to the company's sand volleyball court and a building that houses a replica of SpaceShipOne, the plane that completed the first manned, private flight to space. Scattered around the rest of the campus are foosball and ping-pong tables, video arcade machines, climbing walls, tennis courts, a bowling alley, and even a brightly colored ball pit. Carefully placed mini-kitchens stocked with drinks and snacks, and 18 cafes serving a variety of cuisines, all ensure that employees stay well-fed.

In the summer of 2006, right after graduating from MIT, I landed a job at Google's Search Quality team and found myself in this corporate playground. For a curious and motivated 22-year-old, the fun didn't stop with the amazing facilities. Google turned out to be an intellectual playground as well.

Exciting new things to learn were everywhere, and I hungered to soak in all the knowledge I could get my hands on. I raced through codelabs, the documents that explained why core software abstractions like Protocol Buffers,[1] BigTable,[2] and MapReduce[3] were developed and described how they all worked. I read internal wikis and design documents to learn about the rationale for and the internals behind Google's state-of-the-art search, indexing, and storage systems. I studied programming guides for C++, Python, and JavaScript, in which veteran engineers had distilled decades of collective experience and best practices into easily digestible forms. I dug around in the source code of libraries written by early Google legends like Jeff Dean and Sanjay Ghemawat. I attended tech talks given by renowned architects like Joshua Bloch, who designed core Java libraries, and Guido van Rossum, the creator of the Python programming language.

Writing software at Google proved to be an exhilarating adventure. My two teammates and I built and launched query suggestions on google.com, helping tens to hundreds of millions of people every day refine their search queries and find better search results. Empowered by Google's massive data centers, we orchestrated MapReduce jobs over thousands of machines to build data models. One night, just before a meeting with then-VP of Search Products Marissa Mayer, the three of us hacked together a working demo to get initial approval for our first experiment on live traffic. Another surge of adrenaline rushed through the team weeks later, when we presented our metrics and our feature to Google's co-founders, Larry Page and Sergey Brin, for their final approval. And for our small team to build and launch the entire feature in just five months made the experience all the more memorable.

The other perks were hard to beat, too. In addition to the free food, the campus gym, and the on-site massages, Google engineers went on annual company trips to places like Squaw Valley Ski Resort and Disneyland. My search team even received an all-expenses-paid trip to Maui. Life was grand.

And yet, despite all this, I left Google after two years.

I left when I realized that Google was no longer the optimal place for me to learn. After two years, my learning curve had plateaued, and I knew I could be learning more somewhere else. I had consumed most of the training materials and design documents that I had cared to read, and the exciting five-month timeline for launching a new end-to-end feature turned out to be the exception rather than the rule. When I projected what I could accomplish with an additional year at the company, I felt unsatisfied. I knew it was time for my next adventure.

After Google, I spent my next five years at Ooyala and Quora, two fast-paced startups in Silicon Valley. And with each transition, I've optimized for learning and found myself growing, both professionally and personally, more than I could ever have done if I had stayed within the comforts of the Googleplex. Google might be one of the few places where you can work on large-scale machine learning, self-driving cars, and wearable computers, and these projects attract many talented engineers. But since leaving, I've found unique opportunities to work with amazingly talented people, help grow great engineering teams, shape company culture, and build products used by millions of people from the ground up—opportunities that would have been much harder to find had I stayed at Google. The mantra of optimizing for learning has guided much of what I do, and I've never regretted my decision.

Optimizing for learning is a high-leverage activity for the effective engineer, and in this chapter, we'll examine why. We'll walk through how adopting a growth mindset is a prerequisite for improving our abilities. We'll discuss the compounding effects of learning and why it's important to invest in your rate of learning. We'll identify six key elements about a work environment that you should consider when looking for jobs or switching teams. We'll cover actionable tips for taking advantage of learning opportunities on the job. And finally, we'll close with some strategies for how you can always be learning, even outside of the workplace.

Adopt a Growth Mindset

Several years after graduating, I still mostly hung out with a few close college friends. I'm an introvert, and even though I would've been much happier with a larger social circle, meeting new people and making small talk weren't my strong suits. I much preferred the conversational comfort of people I knew well. I turned down coffee meetings with people I didn't know, I stayed away from big parties, and I passed on networking events, all because they made me uncomfortable. Eventually, however, I realized that avoiding social events wasn't exactly conducive to meeting new people (what a surprise) and that the situation wouldn't improve on its own.

And so one year, like Jim Carrey's character in the movie *Yes Man,* I resolved to say yes to every social engagement that I was invited to or came across. I showed up to parties and meetups where I didn't know anyone, and I grabbed coffee with people who reached out to me online. Awkward silences and forced small talk punctuated many initial conversations. I would spend hours at some networking events and leave with no meaningful connections. But I kept at it. If I botched one conversation, I would think about wittier responses I could have given and try to improve on the next one. I practiced telling better stories. I held onto the belief that being an engaging conversationalist was a learnable skill and that I would get more comfortable with it over time. That year was a formative experience for me. Not only did I make a number of great friends and contacts—people I wouldn't have connected with otherwise—I also stretched the limits of my own comfort zone. I still have ample space to improve, but I learned that like many other skills, engaging in dialogue with strangers gets better with effort and practice.

This story might not seem like it has much to do with engineering, but it illustrates the power of the right mindset about any of our skills. How we view our own intelligence, character, and abilities profoundly affects how we lead our lives; it largely determines whether we remain stuck in our current situations or achieve what we value. That's what Stanford psychologist Carol Dweck concludes in her book *Mindset,* written after 20 years of researching people's self-perceptions and beliefs. [4] Dweck's findings are relevant to us engineers, because how we view our own effectiveness impacts how much effort we invest in improving it.

Dweck found that people adopt one of two mindsets, which in turn affects how they view effort and failure. People with a *fixed mindset* believe that "human qualities are carved in stone" and that they're born with a predetermined amount of intelligence—either they're smart or they're not. Failure indicates they're not, so they stick with the things they do well—things that validate their intelligence. They tend to give up early and easily, which enables them to point to a lack of effort rather than a lack of ability as causing failure. On the other hand, those with a *growth mindset* believe that they can cultivate and grow their intelligence and skills through effort. They may initially lack aptitude in certain areas, but they view challenges and failures as opportunities to learn. As a result, they're much less likely to give up on their paths to success. [5]

Mindset influences whether people take advantage of opportunities to improve their skills. In one study conducted in a Hong Kong university where all classes were taught in English, Dweck offered struggling English speakers the chance to enroll in a remedial language class. By asking if they agreed with statements like "You have a certain amount of intelligence, and you can't really do much to change it," she distinguished between the students with fixed and growth mindsets. Tellingly, 73% of students with a growth mindset enrolled in the class, compared with only 13% of the fixed mindset students. [6] This makes intuitive sense—after all, if you believe your level of intelligence to be set and unchangeable, why waste time and effort trying and failing to learn? Another study compared two groups of 7th graders in New York City public schools. The students who were taught about the nature of intelligence and how it could be increased through experience and hard work saw their math grades improve over the year. The math scores of the control group, who didn't receive the extra lesson, actually worsened. [7] Several other studies have confirmed the pattern: those with growth mindsets are willing to take steps to better themselves, whereas those with fixed mindsets are not. [8] [9]

This research reminds us that the mindset we adopt about our effectiveness as engineers drastically shapes whether we learn and grow or let our skills plateau and stagnate. Do we treat our abilities as fixed quantities outside of our control? Or do we direct our efforts and our energy toward improving ourselves?

So how *do* we build a growth mindset? One piece of advice that Tamar Bercovici, an engineering manager at Box, offers to new hires is "own your story." In just two years, Bercovici had risen to become a staff engineer and manager at a company that helps over 200,000 businesses share and manage content online. But prior to joining Box's 30-person engineering team in 2011, Bercovici hadn't even done any full-time web development. She came from a theoretical and math-heavy background at an Israeli university. Engineering interviewers assumed that she didn't enjoy coding, that her PhD provided few practical advantages, and that she didn't know enough about engineering to ramp up quickly.

Someone with a fixed mindset might have concluded from those assessments that she ought to stick with her strengths and do more theoretical work. But rather than let those preconceptions define her, Bercovici adopted a growth mindset and took control of the parts of her story that were within her sphere of influence. She studied new web technologies, distilled relevant engineering lessons from her PhD, and practiced for the whiteboard interviews common at many engineering companies—and she got the job. "It's not about apologizing for where your resume doesn't line up but rather telling *your* story—who you are, what skills you've built, what you're excited about doing next and why," Bercovici explained to me. By writing her own story instead of letting others define it, she ended up leading the distributed data systems team at one of Silicon Valley's hottest companies, which went public in January 2015.

Bercovici's story is a great illustration of what adopting a growth mindset looks like. It means accepting responsibility for each aspect of a situation that you can change—anything from improving your conversational skills to mastering a new engineering focus—rather than blaming failures and shortcomings on things outside your control. It means taking control of your own story. It means optimizing for experiences where you learn rather than for experiences where you effortlessly succeed. And it means investing in your rate of learning.

Invest in Your Rate of Learning

In school, we learn about the power of compound interest. Once interest gets added to the principal of a deposit, that interest gets put to work generating future interest, which in turn generates even more future interest. There are three important takeaways from that simple lesson:

1. Compounding leads to an exponential growth curve. As Figure 1 shows, an exponential growth curve looks like a hockey stick. It grows slowly at first, looking flat and almost linear; but then suddenly it transitions to rapid growth.

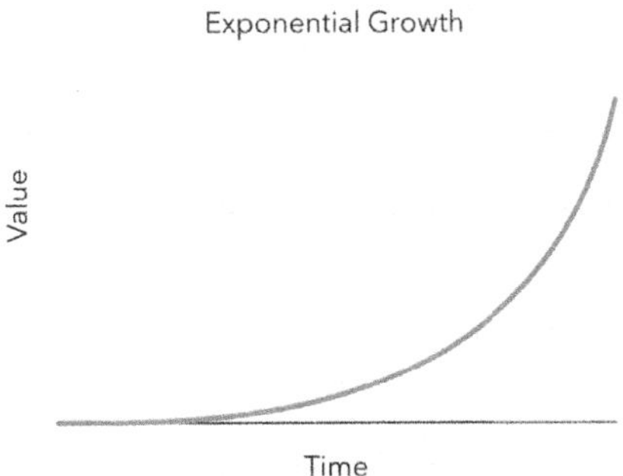

Figure 1: An exponential growth curve due to compounding.

2. The earlier compounding starts, the sooner you hit the region of rapid growth and the faster you can reap its benefits. That's why financial advisors suggest investing in retirement accounts like 401(k)s as early as possible: so you can take advantage of additional years of compounding.
3. Even small deltas in the interest rate can make massive differences in the long run. This is illustrated graphically in Figure 2(a), which compares two accounts that pay 4% and 5% interest respectively, compounded daily. The 5% account produces 49% higher returns after 40 years and 82% after 60. And if you manage to double the interest rate to 8% as in Figure 2(b), you end up with almost *5x* higher returns after 40 years and *11x* after 60.[10]

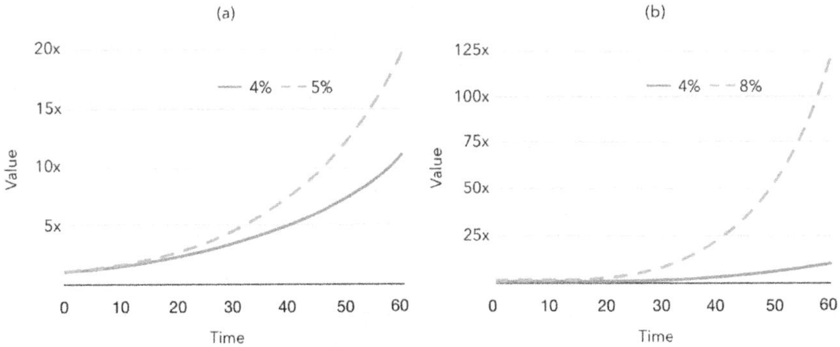

Figure 2: Growth of value over time in accounts that (a) pay 4% and 5% interest and that (b) pay 4% and 8% interest, compounded daily.

Learning, like interest, also compounds. Therefore, the same three takeaways apply:

1. Learning follows an exponential growth curve. Knowledge gives you a foundation, enabling you to gain more knowledge even faster. For example, an understanding of recursion provides the basis for many other concepts, like trees and graph searches, which in turn are necessary for understanding compilers and network topologies.
2. The earlier that you optimize for learning, the more time your learning has to compound. A good first job, for example, makes it easier to get a better second job, which then affects future career opportunities.
3. Due to compounding, even small deltas in your own learning rate make a big difference over the long run.

This last point about the compounding returns of intelligence is the least intuitive: we tend to drastically underestimate the impact of small changes on our growth rate. But when we spend our work hours on unchallenging tasks, we're not just boring ourselves and missing out on chances to learn—we're also paying a huge opportunity cost in terms of our future growth and learning. Stephen Cohen, the co-founder of Palantir, a technology company that powers the infrastructure of intelligence agencies like the CIA, FBI, and MI6, emphasized this point at a Stanford guest lecture. When companies pay you for cushy and unchallenging 9-to-5 jobs, Cohen argues, "what they are actually doing is paying you to accept a much lower intellectual growth rate. When you recognize that intelligence is compounding, the cost of that missing long-term compounding is enormous. They're not giving you the best opportunity of your life. Then a scary thing can happen: … [y]ou get complacent and stall." [11]

So how do we avoid complacency and instead shift ourselves toward a growth mindset? LinkedIn co-founder Reid Hoffman suggests treating yourself like a startup. In his book *The Startup of You,* he explains that startups initially prioritize learning over profitability to increase their chances of success. They launch beta versions of their product and then iterate and adapt as they learn what customers actually want. Similarly, setting yourself up for long-term success requires thinking of yourself as a startup or product in beta, a work-in-progress that needs to be invested in and iterated on every single day. [12]

Continuous iteration is also advocated by Zappos CEO Tony Hsieh, in his book *Delivering Happiness.* [13] Pursuing growth and learning is one of the ten core values at the online shoes and clothing company, which grew its revenue from zero to over $1.2 billion in ten years. Hsieh and his CFO, Alfred Lin, gave a standing challenge to all employees: "Think about what it means to improve just 1% per day and build upon that every single day. Doing so has a dramatic effect and will make us 37x better, not 365% (3.65x) better, at the end of the year." [14] [15]

What will you learn today to improve yourself by 1%? That 1% is a high-leverage investment to develop the skills and the knowledge to make use of future opportunities. Mutual funds and bank accounts build your financial capital, but learning builds your human and career capital. You would rather invest your financial assets in accounts that pay high interest rates, not low ones. Why would you treat your time—your most limited asset—any differently? Invest your time in activities with the highest learning rate. In the rest of the chapter, we'll give some concrete examples of how we can do that and improve ourselves by 1% per day.

Seek Work Environments Conducive to Learning

Because we spend so much of our time at work, one of the most powerful leverage points for increasing our learning rate is our choice of work environment. When starting a new job or joining a new team, there's a lot to learn up front. We pick up new programming languages, adopt new tools and frameworks, learn new paradigms for understanding the product, and gain insight into how the organization operates. But how do we ensure that beyond the initial learning curve, the work environment remains one where we can sustainably learn new things day after day?

Some work environments are more conducive than others for supporting a high personal and professional growth rate. Here are six major factors to consider when choosing a new job or team and the questions you should be asking for each of them:

1. **Fast growth.** When Sheryl Sandberg was deciding whether to join Google, CEO Eric Schmidt gave her a valuable piece of advice: "If you're offered a seat on a rocket ship, you don't ask what seat. You just get on."[16] That advice to focus on growth served her well: she rose to become a VP at Google, which opened the opportunity for her to later become Facebook's COO. At fast-growing teams and companies, the number of problems to solve exceeds available resources, providing ample opportunities to make a big impact and to increase your responsibilities. The growth also makes it easier to attract strong talent and build a strong team, which feeds back to generate even more growth. A lack of growth, on the other hand, leads to stagnation and politics. Employees might squabble over limited opportunities, and it becomes harder to find and retain talent.

> **Questions to consider**
>
> - What is the weekly or monthly growth rates of core business metrics (e.g., active users, annual recurring revenue, products sold, etc.)?
> - Are the particular initiatives that you'd be working on high priorities, with sufficient support and resources from the company to grow?
> - How aggressively has the company or team been hiring in the past year?
> - How quickly have the strongest team members grown into positions of leadership?

2. **Training.** Strong onboarding programs demonstrate that the organization prioritizes training new employees. Google, for example, invests significant resources in its engEDU program—a set of classes, professional seminars, design documents, and programming guides geared toward helping employees grow as engineers and leaders. Facebook has a six-week onboarding program called Bootcamp, where new engineers learn about the company's tools and focus areas and do their initial hands-on development.[17] A smaller company won't have the same volume of resources, but any team

that understands the value of ramping up new hires as quickly as possible will invest in creating similar programs—like our team did at Quora. Similarly, a solid mentorship program also indicates that the team prioritizes professional growth.

Questions to consider

- Is each new person expected to figure things out on his or her own, or is there a more formalized way of onboarding new engineers?
- Is there formal or informal mentorship?
- What steps has the company taken to ensure that team members continue to learn and grow?
- What new things have team members learned recently?

3. **Openness.** A growing organization isn't going to figure out the most effective product idea, engineering design, or organizational process on its first attempt. If it can continuously learn and adapt from past mistakes, however, then it stands a much better chance of success. That's more likely to happen if employees challenge each others' decisions and incorporate feedback into the future iterations. Look for a culture of curiosity, where everyone is encouraged to ask questions, coupled with a culture of openness, where feedback and information is shared proactively. Reflecting on failed projects, understanding what caused production outages, and reviewing the returns on different product investments all help the right lessons get internalized.

Questions to consider

- Do employees know what priorities different teams are working on?
- Do teams meet to reflect on whether product changes and feature launches were worth the effort? Do they conduct post-mortems after outages?
- How is knowledge documented and shared across the company?
- What are examples of lessons that the team has learned?

4. **Pace.** A work environment that iterates quickly provides a faster feedback cycle and enables you to learn at a faster rate. Lengthy release cycles, formalized product approvals, and indecisive leadership slow down iteration speed; automation tools, lightweight approval processes, and a willingness to experiment accelerate progress. Smaller teams and companies tend to have fewer bureaucratic barriers to getting things done than larger ones. While I was at Google, for example, any visible change (even experimental ones) to Google search had to go all the way up the management chain to a weekly user interface review with Marissa Mayer, the VP of Search Products and User Experience, which slowed the pace of experimentation. At startups, the aggressive risk-taking and oftentimes longer hours can contribute to an increased learning rate—as long as you don't burn out. Do push yourself, but also find a pace that's sustainable for you in the long run.

Questions to consider

- Is moving quickly reflected in the company or engineering values?
- What tools does the team use to increase iteration speed?
- How long does it take to go from an idea's conception to launch approval?
- What percentage of time is spent on maintenance versus developing new products and features?

5. **People.** Surrounding yourself with people who are smarter, more talented, and more creative than you means surrounding yourself with potential teachers and mentors. Who you work with can matter more than what you actually do, in terms of your career growth and work happiness. At smaller companies, you might be able to switch teams soon if you don't gel with your co-workers, but bigger companies generally recommend that you stay on a team for at least six months to a year to reduce switching costs and overhead. Meet with potential team members ahead of time before starting a new position. Don't leave getting assigned to a strong or subpar team to the luck of the draw.

Questions to consider

- Do the people who interviewed you seem smarter than you?
- Are there skills they can teach you?
- Were your interviews rigorous and comprehensive? Would you want to work with the types of people who would do well on them?
- Do people tend to work on one-person projects, or are teamwork and cooperation common themes?

6. **Autonomy.** The freedom to choose what to work on and how to do it drives our ability to learn—as long as we have the support that we need to use that freedom effectively. At established companies, employees tend to work on specialized projects, but they also have access to more coaching and structure. At smaller companies, you'll end up wielding significantly more autonomy over the total surface area of product features and responsibilities, but you'll also need to take more ownership of your own learning and growth. In my three years at Quora, for example, I had opportunities to work on a broad range of technical challenges (including experimentation tools, real-time analytics frameworks, site speed, infrastructure, recommendations, spam detection, and mobile development) as well as organizational challenges (including training interviewers, creating onboarding resources, building the mentoring program, and coordinating the internship program). It would have been difficult to work on such a diversity of projects at a larger company, where the problems might be tackled by specialized teams and where the processes might already be well-established.

Questions to consider

- Do people have the autonomy to choose what projects they work on and how they do them?
- How often do individuals switch teams or projects?
- What breadth of the codebase can an individual expect to work on over the course of a year?
- Do engineers participate in discussions on product design and influence product direction?

These six factors vary from company to company and from team to team, and their importance to you will also change during the course of your career. Onboarding and mentoring are more important earlier in your career, and autonomy matters more later on. When switching teams or jobs, make sure that you're asking the right questions: find out if they are a good fit and offer you ample learning opportunities.

Dedicate Time on the Job to Develop New Skills

It's easy to feel overwhelmed by how much you need to get done at work. People whom I've mentored, particularly ones who've recently started at a new job, often feel that their task list keeps growing and growing and that they're falling further and further behind. They spend all their energy trying to catch up and don't devote enough time to developing the skills that could actually help them work more effectively.

The solution is to borrow a lesson from Google. Google pioneered an idea called "20% time," where engineers spend the equivalent of one day a week on a side project to make the company better. Initially, 20% time was a controversial proposal; people doubted it would improve the company's bottom line. In fact, the investment empowered engineers to create and launch products like Gmail, Google News, and AdSense—which now comprise three of Google's core offerings. [18] Many other engineering companies have followed suit, adopting similar innovation policies. [19] [20]

To invest in your own growth, you should carve out your own 20% time. It's more effective to take it in one- or two-hour chunks each day rather than in one full day each week, because you can then make a daily habit out of improving your skills. Your productivity may decrease at first (or it might not change much if you're taking time away from web surfing or other distractions), but the goal is to make investments that will make you more effective in the long run.

So what should you do with that 20% time? You can develop a deeper understanding of areas you're already working on and tools that you already use. Or, you can gain experience in what Steven Sinofsky, the former head of Microsoft's Windows division, calls "adjacent disciplines."[21] These are the disciplines related to your core role and where increased familiarity can make you more self-sufficient and effective. If you're a product engineer, adjacent disciplines might include product management, user research, or even backend engineering. If you're an infrastructure engineer, they might include machine learning, database internals, or web development. If you're a growth engineer, adjacent disciplines might be data science, marketing, or behavioral psychology. Knowledge in adjacent disciplines will not only be useful, but you'll also be more likely to retain the information because you'll be actively practicing it.

Whichever route you decide, here are ten suggestions to take advantage of the resources available to you at work:

- **Study code for core abstractions written by the best engineers at your company.** Particularly if you're at a big technology company with a large, shared codebase, read through code in some of the core libraries written by early engineers. Start with ones that you've used before. Ask yourself if you would've written similar code and how you might learn from their examples. Understand why certain choices were made and how they were implemented, and see if earlier versions of code were rewritten to address shortcomings. You can also do the same with any well-designed, open source projects that your company uses or is considering using.
- **Write more code.** If you feel that programming is your weak point, shift time away from other activities like meetings and product design, and

spend more of it building and writing code. Over a decade of research on learning has shown that the more effort you expend when retrieving knowledge from memory, the better you'll learn and retain those ideas. [22] Since actively programming expends more effort than passively reading code, you'll find that practicing the craft is a high-leverage activity for improving your programming skills. Moreover, it's easy to *think* you understand something you've read, only to find large knowledge gaps when you actually set out to do it.

- **Go through any technical, educational material available internally.** Google, for instance, has a wide array of codelabs that teach core abstractions and guides of best practices for various languages, all written by veteran engineers. If your company maintains design documents or holds tech talks, use them as learning opportunities.
- **Master the programming languages that you use**. Read a good book or two on them. Focus on developing a solid grasp of the advanced concepts in that language, and gain familiarity with core language libraries. Make sure that at least one of your languages is a scripting language (e.g., Python or Ruby) that you can use as your Swiss army knife for quick tasks.
- **Send your code reviews to the harshest critics.** Optimize for getting good, thoughtful feedback rather than for lowering the barrier to getting your work checked in. Ask for a more detailed review on those implementations you're not as confident about. Discuss software designs with your company's best designers in order to avoid writing great code for a design that doesn't work well.
- **Enroll in classes on areas where you want to improve.** These could be courses offered on the company campus, at nearby universities, or online through educational initiatives like Coursera, edX, Udemy or Udacity. Online education is exploding; you can easily sign up for classes in machine learning, mobile development, computer networking, compilers, and more, many of them taught by professors from world-class institutions like Stanford or MIT. Many of the larger technology companies will even pay for your classes.

- **Participate in design discussions of projects you're interested in.** Don't wait for an invitation. Ask project leads if they'd mind you being a silent observer or even a participant in a design meeting. If mailing lists are open internally, add yourself or read through key conversations in the archives.
- **Work on a diversity of projects.** If you find yourself always doing similar tasks using similar methods, it's going to be hard to pick up new skills. Interleaving different projects can teach you what problems are common across projects and what might just be artifacts of your current one. Moreover, research on learning confirms that the *interleaved practice* of different skills is more effective than repeated, *massed practice* of a single skill at preparing people to tackle unfamiliar problems. [23]
- **Make sure you're on a team with at least a few senior engineers whom you can learn from.** If you're not, consider changing projects or teams. This will help increase your learning rate for the remaining 80% of your time.
- **Jump fearlessly into code you don't know.** After years of observation, Bobby Johnson, a former engineering director at Facebook, concluded that engineering success was highly correlated with "having no fear in jumping into code they didn't know." Fear of failure often holds us back, causing us to give up before we even try. But as Johnson explains, "in the practice of digging into things you don't know, you get better at coding." [24]

Create learning opportunities out of your 20% time, and you'll steadily improve your skills and productivity.

Always Be Learning

Learning opportunities aren't limited to the workplace. We should always be asking: How can I improve? How could I have done this better? What should I learn next to best prepare me for the future? These questions may not have anything to do with engineering—maybe you're interested in music, art, sports, writing, or crafts. Some skills we learn could be cross-functional and help our engineering work (increasing my comfort level in conversing with strangers, for example, helped me when meeting and interviewing other great engineers for this book). Other skills might not translate directly into engineering benefits, but the practice of adopting a growth mindset toward them still makes us better learners and more willing to stretch beyond our comfort zone. This itself is a high-leverage investment. Plus, there's a side benefit: research in positive psychology shows that continual learning is inextricably linked with increased happiness. [25]

There are many ways to learn and grow in whatever you love to do. Here are ten starting points to help inspire a habit of learning outside of the workplace:

- **Learn new programming languages and frameworks.** One of the most exciting aspects of working in software is that the technology landscape changes so rapidly. But this also means that if you're not continuously learning, your skills might get stale and outdated. Moreover, new skills can expand your mind and teach you how to think in different ways. Keep a running list of the programming languages, software tools, and frameworks that you want to learn, and set goals to spend time and master them.
- **Invest in skills that are in high demand.** If you're unsure about what types of skills you should be learning, see what's being included in job postings you find interesting, or evaluate the current industry trends and demand for skills. For example, as of 2014, 15% of Internet traffic now comes from mobile devices, [26] and global annual smartphone sales are triple that of consumer PCs. [27] As these trends continue, honing your expertise in mobile development can open up many other opportunities.
- **Read books.** Bill Gates reads a lot and mostly non-fiction, using books to discover how the world works. [28] Books offer a way for you to learn from the lessons and mistakes of others: you can re-apply that knowledge without having to start from scratch. This is such a high-leverage investment that I've actually trained myself to speed read. I can now read 2–3x faster, sharply increasing my rate of learning, and I read 1-2 books a week. You can find a list of non-fiction books that shaped my thinking on engineering effectiveness in the Appendix.
- **Join a discussion group.** In the eighteenth century, politician and inventor Benjamin Franklin organized a group of friends into a "club of mutual improvement." The club met every Friday evening to discuss and debate

"morals, politics, or natural philosophy," providing members with a structured opportunity to improve themselves. [29] I'm a part of a few book clubs and reading groups that meet regularly for discussion at cafes and apartments.

- **Attend talks, conferences, and meetups.** Growing technology companies often hold open tech talks, both to share knowledge and to help recruit new engineers. Google even shares many of its on-campus talks on YouTube. [30] [31] Conferences and meetups can be hit-or-miss in terms of quality, so ask around to see which ones are worth attending. Some conferences, like TED, provide high-quality recordings of inspiring ideas. [32] Attend targeted conferences to get more familiar with industry trends and to meet people who share your interests.
- **Build and maintain a strong network of relationships.** I used to avoid coffee meetings and meetups with people I didn't know. But I've since learned that the more people you meet, the more you'll find serendipitous opportunities. Richard Wiseman captures this idea in his book *The Luck Factor*, when he writes, "Lucky people dramatically increase the possibility of a lucky chance encounter by meeting a large number of people in their daily lives. The more people they meet, the greater opportunity they have of running into someone who could have a positive effect on their lives." [33]
- **Follow bloggers who teach.** Admittedly, social media and technology journalism sites can be online sources of distraction—but at the same time, many bloggers share thoughtful and useful lessons. Subscribe to their newsletters and learn ways to shortcut around the mistakes that they've made. You can find a starter list of engineering blogs in the Appendix.
- **Write to teach.** When you write to teach other people, you gain a deeper understanding of ideas you're already familiar with and pinpoint the details that you didn't fully understand. That's the technique that Physics Nobel Prize winner Richard Feynman used to learn faster. [34] Writing also provides an opportunity for mindful reflection on what you've learned. So start a blog and begin writing. These days, platforms like Blogger, Tumblr, Wordpress, Medium, and Quora make it easy. Presenting at conferences can have similar benefits.

- **Tinker on side projects.** Side projects, even ones not related to engineering, provide further opportunities to hone your skills, particularly in areas of interest that you don't typically engage in at work. Research suggests that creativity stems from combining existing and often disparate ideas in new ways. [35] Projects in seemingly orthogonal areas like drawing and writing can have benefits that flow over to help you be a better engineer.
- **Pursue what you love.** Replace passive time spent aimlessly surfing TV channels or the web with time actively spent doing what you love. The average American watches 34 hours of TV per week, [36] and psychology studies show that the average mood while watching TV highly is mildly depressed. [37] Spend time on what you're passionate about instead, and let that passion fuel your motivation to learn and to grow.

More important than any of these individual suggestions, however, is embracing a growth mindset in which you're motivated to learn about the things that excite you. Interviewers often ask candidates, "Where do you see yourself five years from now?" It's a tough question, and most people don't have an answer. But by adopting a growth mindset and optimizing for learning, you'll be best prepared to make the most of whatever opportunities do come your way.

Key Takeaways

- **Own your story.** Focus on changes that are within your sphere of influence rather than wasting energy on blaming the parts that you can't control. View failures and challenges through a growth mindset, and see them as opportunities to learn.
- **Don't shortchange your learning rate.** Learning compounds like interest. The more you learn, the easier it is to apply prior insights and lessons to learn new things. Optimize for learning, particularly early in your career, and you'll be best prepared for the opportunities that come your way.
- **Find work environments that can sustain your growth.** Interview the people at the team or company you're considering. Find out what opportunities they provide for onboarding and mentoring, how transparent they are internally, how fast they move, what your prospective co-workers are like, and how much autonomy you'll have.
- **Capitalize on opportunities at work to improve your technical skills.** Learn from your best co-workers. Study their code and their code reviews. Dive into any available educational material provided by your company, and look into classes or books that your workplace might be willing to subsidize.
- **Locate learning opportunities outside of the workplace.** Challenge yourself to become better by just 1% a day. Not all of your learning will necessarily relate to engineering skills, but being a happier and better learner will help you become a more effective engineer in the long run.

3

Prioritize Regularly

SUSTAINABLE AND SCALABLE STRATEGIES TO GROW A PRODUCT'S USER base are holy grails for startups. More engaged users drive more revenue, more venture capital, and higher startup valuations, and in recent years, teams dedicated to the art and science of user growth have proliferated. These teams focus on optimizing how users flow into and out of a product. [1] They live and breathe data and metrics, running endless user experiments and optimizing conversion rates in their mission to acquire users. They combine engineering, data, and product marketing to build their strategies, and they can be found at fast-growing companies ranging from Facebook, Twitter, and LinkedIn to Dropbox, Airbnb, Square, Uber, Lyft, Path, and many others.

Some of the problems that user growth teams tackle, like building experimentation frameworks and analyzing metrics, are similar to the ones solved by traditional engineering teams. What makes user growth especially challenging and exciting, however, is that the list of ideas for driving traffic and growth is extremely open-ended and spans virtually the entire product. Does the team:

- Optimize the conversion rate of the signup form on the home page?
- Buy traffic through Google, Facebook, or Twitter ads?
- Improve application speed to increase user engagement?
- Attempt to create viral content to spread through social media and email?

- Increase search referral traffic by improving search rankings?
- Invest in making the product simpler to learn, use, and adopt?
- Iterate on user engagement emails to improve open and click-through rates?
- Encourage users to refer their friends to the product?
- Optimize content ranking and people recommendations to increase the product's stickiness?
- Improve the mobile experience and increase distribution through the iOS and Android app stores?
- Internationalize the product to major languages and countries?
- Do something else entirely?

The right focus can significantly accelerate a product's growth rate. Even small 0.5% wins in key areas can compound like interest and add a million users down the line. But by the same token, the opportunity cost of working on the wrong ideas can set back growth by months or years.

I was the first engineer on Quora's user growth team and eventually became the engineering lead for the group. Our team developed a healthy cadence where we would prioritize ideas based on their estimated returns on investment, run a batch of experiments, learn from the data what worked and what didn't, and rinse and repeat. In a single year, our team grew Quora's monthly and daily active user base by over 3x. [2] And I learned through that experience that a successful user growth team rigorously and regularly prioritizes its work.

Prioritizing isn't only relevant to user growth, however. In any engineering discipline (and in life), there will always be more tasks to do than you have time for. Working on one task means not working on another. Therefore, regular prioritization is a high-leverage activity, because it determines the leverage of the rest of your time. After all, if you work for weeks on a project that has little impact and garners few lessons, how is that different for your business than not working at all?

Prioritization is hard work, and like most skills, it requires practice. The most effective engineers work persistently on improving their prioritization skills. You'll have days where you misallocate your time, but as long as you're retrospective, you'll continuously improve. You'll also have periods where you don't feel like prioritizing; perhaps it's your leisure time and you're not optimizing for anything other than curling up on the couch with a good book. That's perfectly fine! Everyone needs time to recharge. But when it comes to your personal and professional goals, taking the time and energy to prioritize will significantly increase your chances for success.

In this chapter, we'll walk through the strategies used to prioritize effectively. We'll start by explaining why it's important to track all our to-dos in a single and easily accessible list. From that list, we'll make pairwise comparisons between what we're doing and what we could be doing instead, in order to iteratively shift our time toward higher-leverage activities. To help us identify what's high-leverage, we'll discuss two simple heuristics: focusing on what directly produces value, and focusing on the important and non-urgent. Identifying high-priority tasks isn't enough, however; we also need to execute on them. So we'll cover how you can accomplish your priorities: first, by protecting your maker's schedule, and second, by limiting the amount of work you have in progress. We'll talk about creating *if-then plans* to help fight procrastination. Finally, since it's important to make a routine of prioritization, we'll end the chapter by walking through a sample implementation of a prioritization workflow, using all the strategies we've discussed.

Track To-Dos in a Single, Easily Accessible List

No matter how much of an expert you might be, a well-designed checklist can significantly improve your outcomes. In *The Checklist Manifesto*, Dr. Atul Gawande shows how the adoption of checklists has drastically reduced errors in field after field, even for the most seasoned experts working on routine tasks. Pilots who follow pre-flight checklists, surgeons who follow operation checklists, and construction managers who follow safety checklists all eliminate large classes of avoidable errors simply by writing steps down and tracking what needs to be done. [3]

Engineers can benefit from adopting checklists as well. The first step in effective prioritization is listing every task that you might need to do. As David

Allen explains in *Getting Things Done,* this is because the human brain is optimized for processing and not for storage. [4] The average brain can actively hold only 7 +/- 2 items—the number of digits in a phone number—in its working memory. This is a shockingly small number, and yet in experiments, once there are more than 7 items, people fail to repeat digits and words back in the correct order over half the time. [5] The only way that memory champions can memorize 67,890 digits of pi is by expending large amounts of mental resources. [6] [7] Research shows that expending effort on remembering things reduces our attention, [8] impairs our decision-making abilities, [9] and even hurts our physical performance. [10] For you and me, that brainpower is much better spent on prioritizing our work and solving engineering problems than on remembering everything we need to do.

When I started my software engineering career, I smugly dismissed to-do lists. I didn't think I needed the overhead, and I believed I could just keep track of tasks in my head. Within two years, I starting noticing tasks falling through the cracks. I knew I had to adopt to-do lists, and they've since become an integral part of my workflows. Given the vast body of research proving the value of to-do lists, it's a wonder I got much done at all before.

To-do lists should have two major properties: they should be a canonical representation of our work, and they should be easily accessible. A single master list is better than an assortment of sticky notes, sheets of paper, and emails, because these scattered alternatives are easily misplaced and make it harder for your brain to trust that they're comprehensive. Having the master list easily accessible allows you to quickly identify a task you can complete if you unexpectedly have a block of free time. Plus, if you think up a new task, you can add it directly to your list even when you're out and about, rather than investing mental energy in trying to remember it.

Your to-do list can take many forms. It can be a little notebook that you carry around, task management software that you use on the web, an application you access on your phone, or a Dropbox text file that you synchronize between your computer and your phone. When you consistently offload to-dos to your list, you reduce the number of tasks you need to remember down to just one—to check your single, master list—and you free your mind to focus on a higher-leverage activity: actually prioritizing your work.

If you could accurately compute the leverage of each task, then you could just sort all the tasks by leverage and work down your prioritized list. Unfortunately, estimating both the time required and the value produced by each task is incredibly hard. When I started working on user growth at Quora, our team brainstormed hundreds of ideas for how we might increase product usage and engagement. Huddled around a conference room table, we systematically went through every idea and estimated its percentage impact (0.1%, 1%, 10%, or 100%) on our growth metrics as well as the time it would take to implement (hours, days, weeks, or months). Not only were many of these estimates quite off because we had limited data, but every task we tackled inspired new tasks that we'd then insert into our to-do list—which in turn meant that we never got to most of the backlogged items on our ranked list. The net effect was that much of the estimation work we did to build that ranked list was wasted.

It's not actually that useful to know that the 100th task provides higher leverage than the 101st task. It's far easier and more efficient to compile a small number of goals that are important to complete, pick initial tasks toward those goals, and then make a pairwise comparison between what you're currently doing and what else is on your to-do list. Ask yourself on a recurring basis: *Is there something else I could be doing that's higher-leverage?* If not, continue on your current path. If yes, it's time to rethink what you're doing. The goal isn't to establish a total ordering of all your priorities, since any ordering you make will be based on imperfect information; instead, it's to continuously shift your top priorities toward the ones with the highest leverage, given the information you have.

So how do you determine if something else has higher leverage than what you're currently doing? The next two sections present two heuristics that can help: focusing on what directly produces value, and focusing on the important and non-urgent.

Focus on What Directly Produces Value

When measuring the leverage of different activities, an inevitable lesson learned is that the time and effort expended do not necessarily correlate with the value produced. Yishan Wong, based on his 4 years leading engineering teams at Facebook, explains that "activity is not necessarily production" and that many work activities "do not directly contribute towards useful output. Writing status reports, organizing things, creating organizational systems, recording things multiple times, going to meetings, and replying to low-priority communications are all examples of this." [11] These tasks only have a weak and indirect connection to creating value.

Therefore, the first heuristic for prioritizing high-leverage activities is to focus on what directly produces value. At the end of the day (or when it comes time for performance reviews), what matters is how much value you've created. That value is measured in terms of products shipped, users acquired, business metrics moved, or sales made, rather than in terms of hours worked, tasks completed, lines of code written, or meetings attended. Focus on tasks that directly bring a product closer to launch; that directly increase the number of users, customers or sales; or that directly impact the core business metric your team is responsible for. Write code for a necessary product feature, tackle roadblocks or secure necessary approvals that would hold back a launch, ensure your team members are working on the right tasks, address high-priority support issues, or do anything else that leads to results.

Once you're producing results, few people will complain about declined meetings, slow email response times, or even non-urgent bugs not being fixed, unless those other tasks are blocking even more valuable results from being delivered. When you get the important things right, the small things often don't matter. That's true in life as well. For example, if you're trying to save money, skipping the $3 Starbucks latte doesn't make much of a budgetary impact compared to investing an hour or two searching for cheaper plane tickets and saving a few hundred dollars on your next trip. Shopping for cheap tickets doesn't matter as much as investing a few extra hours in job negotiations to boost your annual salary by a few thousand dollars. And in the long run, even the job negotiations might not be as significant as adopting a healthy investment portfolio that can earn a few more percentage points in compounding returns per year. You may still decide to save money on that latte, of course. But make sure that the effort you invest is proportional to its expected impact.

After you ship a change that produces value, find the next task that will produce value. Prioritize the ones that produce the most value with the least amount of effort. Once you do this a few times, it becomes easier to recognize which tasks are the most valuable. As our user growth team at Quora ran more product experiments, we became significantly better at identifying which types of changes we could get done quickly and which activities would have higher payoffs.

The corollary to focusing on the activities that directly produce value is to defer and ignore the ones that don't. You only have a finite amount of time. When a co-worker schedules you for an unnecessary meeting, a manager assigns you a small bug, or a product manager comes into your office with a shiny new prototype, they're oftentimes not considering the opportunity cost of your time. Learn to say no. Don't treat every invitation to do something as an obligation. Explain how the meeting, bug, or project will detract from your other tasks, and discuss whether it should have higher priority. If not, you probably shouldn't be spending your time on it.

Don't try to get everything done. Focus on what matters—and what matters is what produces value.

Focus on the Important and Non-Urgent

We're inundated every day with urgent requests demanding our attention: meetings, emails, phone calls, bugs, pager duty alerts, the next deadline. Some of these requests are important; others aren't. If we're not careful, our default script is to respond immediately to whatever urgent issues come our way. We let life's daily interruptions, rather than our priorities, dictate our schedules.

Therefore, along with prioritizing the activities that directly produce value, we also need to prioritize the investments that increase our ability to be more effective and deliver more value in the future. Stated simply, the second heuristic is to focus on important and non-urgent activities.

In *The 7 Habits of Highly Effective People*, Stephen Covey explains that urgency should not be confused with importance. He advocates "putting first things first."[12] Covey partitions the activities that we do into four quadrants, based on whether they're urgent or non-urgent and important or unimportant. This is illustrated in Figure 1:

	Urgent	Not Urgent
Important	1 Crises Pressing Issues Deadlines	2 Planning and prevention Building relationships New opportunities Personal development
Not Important	3 Interruptions Most meetings Most emails and calls	4 Surfing the web Busy work Time wasters

Figure 1: Partitioning of activities based on urgency and importance.

When we let the urgent activities in Quadrant 1 (high-priority support issues or upcoming deadlines, for example) and in Quadrant 3 (most of our emails, phone calls, and meetings) determine how we spend our time, we neglect the non-urgent but important activities in Quadrant 2. Quadrant 2 activities include planning our career goals, building stronger relationships, reading books and articles for professional development, adopting new productivity and efficiency habits, building tools to improve our workflows, investing in useful abstractions, ensuring that infrastructure will continue to scale, learning new programming languages, speaking at conferences, and mentoring our teammates to help them be more productive.

Quadrant 2 investments don't have any natural deadlines and won't get prioritized as a result of urgency. But in the long run, they provide significant value because they help us to learn and to grow both personally and professionally. It's often easy to feel overwhelmed by the sheer volume of tasks that need to get done, especially if you're a new college graduate or an engineer joining a new company. One piece of advice that I consistently give my mentees is to carve out time to invest in skills development. Their productivity might slow down at first, but with time, the new tools and workflows that they learn will increase their effectiveness and easily compensate for the initial loss.

When I discussed prioritization techniques with Nimrod Hoofien, an engineering director at Facebook who's also run engineering teams at Amazon and Ooyala, he shared an exercise that he used to do. He would label everything on his to-do list from 1 through 4, based on which quadrant the activity fell under. The exercise "worked really well when what you're trying to do is to whittle down what you do to the important [and] not urgent," he explained. "It's a really good tool to get started."

Find which of your to-dos fall within Quadrant 2, and de-prioritize Quadrant 3 and 4 activities that aren't important. Be wary if you're spending too much time on Quadrant 1's important and urgent activities. A pager duty alert, a high-priority bug, a pressing deadline for a project, or any other type of firefighting all may be important and urgent, but assess whether you're simply addressing the symptoms of the problem and not its underlying cause. Oftentimes, the root cause is an underinvestment in a Quadrant 2 activity. Frequent pager duty alerts might indicate a need for automated recovery procedures. High-priority bugs might be a symptom of low test coverage. Constant deadlines might be caused by poor project estimation and planning. Investing in Quadrant 2 solutions can reduce urgent tasks and their associated stress.

The act of prioritization is itself a Quadrant 2 activity, one whose importance often gets overlooked because it's rarely urgent. Prioritize the act of prioritization, and you'll be on the road to dramatically increasing your effectiveness.

Protect Your Maker's Schedule

By now, you've identified some high-leverage tasks based on what directly produces value and what's important and non-urgent. The next step is to use your time to execute on those priorities.

Engineers need longer and more contiguous blocks of time to be productive than many other professionals. Productivity increases when we can maintain periods of what psychologist Mihály Csíkszentmihályi calls *flow*, described by people who experience it as "a state of effortless concentration so deep that they lose their sense of time, of themselves, of their problems." Csíkszentmihályi studied the state of flow in painters, violinists, chess masters, authors, and even motorcycle racers, and he called flow the "optimal experience" because of the spontaneous joy we feel when we're deeply focused. Flow requires focused attention; interruptions break flow. [13]

Unfortunately, the meeting schedules at many companies don't accommodate flow conditions for engineers. In his essay "Maker's Schedule, Manager's Schedule," programmer and venture capitalist Paul Graham discusses how managers have different schedules than the people who create and build things. Managers traditionally organize their time into one-hour blocks, but "people who make things, like programmers and writers[,] … generally prefer to use time in units of half a day at least. You can't write or program well in units of an hour. That's barely enough time to get started." [14] Empirical research highlights the cost of breaking the maker's schedule. A study from Microsoft Research found that employees take an average of 10 to 15 minutes to return to focused activity after handling email and instant messaging interruptions; [15] a study from UC Irvine put the number even higher, at 23 minutes. [16]

When possible, preserve larger blocks of focused time in your schedule. Schedule necessary meetings back-to-back or at the beginning or end of your work day, rather than scattering them throughout the day. If people ask you for help while you're in the middle of a focused activity, tell them that you'd be happy to do it before or after your breaks or during smaller chunks of your free time. Block off hours on your calendar (maybe even with a fake meeting) or schedule days like "No Meeting Wednesdays" to help consolidate chunks of time. Learn to say no to unimportant activities, such as meetings that don't require your attendance and other low-priority commitments that might fragment your schedule. Protect your time and your maker's schedule.

Limit the Amount of Work in Progress

After prioritizing our tasks and blocking off contiguous chunks of time, it can be tempting to try to tackle many things at once. When we fragment our attention too much, however, we end up reducing our overall productivity and hindering our ability to make substantive progress on any one thing.

David Rock, in his book *Your Brain at Work*, says that the brain's working memory is like a stage and its thoughts are like the actors. The part of our brain called the prefrontal cortex handles our planning, decision-making, and goal-setting, as well as all of our other conscious thoughts. The stage has a limited amount of space (for 7 ± 2 actors), but in order to make decisions, the prefrontal cortex needs to bring all the relevant actors onto the stage at once. [17] When we work on too many things simultaneously, we spend most of our brain's mental energy moving actors on and off the stage rather than paying attention to their performance.

I learned this lesson during my early days of working at Quora. I would find two or three major projects that sounded interesting and exciting and ambitiously volunteer for all of them. I put in the hours and alternated back and forth between projects. But because the progress on each project came in fits and starts, it was hard to build any momentum. I couldn't give each individual project and team the attention they deserved, so I didn't do an excellent job on any of them. Moreover, because the timeline of each project dragged out, psychologically, I felt less productive.

I later realized that the key—which Tonianne DeMaria Barry and Jim Benson describe in their book *Personal Kanban*—is to limit your work in progress. A juggler can keep three balls in the air with little effort but must concentrate significantly harder to keep track of six or seven. In the same way, there is a limit to how many things we can work on at once. "[T]he closer you get to reaching your capacity, the more [the] stress taxes your brain's resources and impacts your performance," Barry and Benson write. "[I]ncreasing work linearly increases the likelihood of failure exponentially." [18] Constant context switching hinders deep engagement in any one activity and reduces our overall chance of success.

Nowadays, I'm much more deliberate about limiting my work in progress. This means prioritizing and serializing different projects so that I can maintain strong momentum. The same principle applies to how teams tackle projects as well. When a small group of people fragment their efforts across too many tasks, they stop sharing the same context for design discussions or code reviews. Competing priorities divide the team, and momentum on any one activity slows down.

The number of projects that you can work on simultaneously varies from person to person. Use trial and error to figure out how many projects you can work on before quality and momentum drop, and resist the urge to work on too many projects at once.

Fight Procrastination with If-Then Plans

Sometimes, what hinders focus isn't a lack of contiguous time or too much context switching. Instead, many people do not have sufficient motivation to summon the activation energy required to start a difficult task. In the 1990s, Psychology Professor Peter Gollwitzer researched the science of motivation. He asked students on their way to final exams if they would volunteer to participate in a study; as part of the study, they would have to write an essay on how they spent their Christmas holidays. Students who agreed were told that they had to mail in their essays within two days of Christmas. Half of these students were also asked to specify when, where, and how they would write the essay. Of the students who articulated these "implementation intentions," 71% of them mailed in their essays. Only 32% of the other students did. A minor tweak in behavior resulted in over twice the completion rate. [19] [20]

Based on studies like Gollwitzer's, social psychologist Heidi Halvorson lays out a simple practice to help us overcome procrastination. In her book *Succeed*, Halvorson describes the *if-then plan*, in which we identify ahead of time a situation where we plan to do a certain task. Possible scenarios could be "*if* it's after my 3pm meeting, *then* I'll investigate this long-standing bug," or "*if* it's right after dinner, *then* I'll watch a lecture on Android development." Halvorson explains that the "planning creates a link between the situation or cue (the *if*) and the behavior that you should follow (the *then*)." When the cue triggers, the *then* behavior "follows *automatically* without any conscious intent." [21]

Subconscious followup is important because procrastination primarily stems from a reluctance to expend the initial activation energy on a task. This reluctance leads us to rationalize why it might be better to do something easier or more enjoyable, even if it has lower leverage. When we're in the moment, the short-term value that we get from procrastinating can often dominate our decision-making process. But when we make if-then plans and decide what to do ahead of time, we're more likely to consider the long-term benefits associated with a task. [22] Studies have shown that if-then planning increases goal completion rates for people like high school students studying for PSATs, dieters trying to lower their fat intake, smokers attempting to quit, people wanting to use public transportation more frequently, and many others. [23] If-then planning is a powerful tool to help you focus on your priorities.

The concept of if-then planning also can help fill in the small gaps in our maker's schedule. How many times have you had 20 minutes free before your next meeting, spent 10 of those minutes mulling over whether there's enough time to do anything, finally picked a short task, and then realized you don't have enough time left after all? An if-then plan that I've found to be effective is to make an "*if* I only have 20 minutes before my next activity, *then* I will do ______." I save a list of short tasks that I need to get done and that don't require a big chunk of uninterrupted time, and I use them to fill in the blank. Tasks that have worked well for me include finishing a code review, writing interview feedback, responding to emails, investigating a small bug, or writing an isolated unit test.

If-then plans made those college students more than twice as likely to complete their Christmas essays. Think about how much more effective you'd be if you could double the likelihood of completing something important you've been procrastinating on—whether it's picking up a new language, reading that book on your shelf, or something else. Make an if-then plan to do it.

Make a Routine of Prioritization

The strategies laid out so far help us to focus on the right things: the activities with the highest leverage. Once we're knee-deep working on those tasks, a common pitfall for many engineers is neglecting to revisit those priorities. As time passes, our current projects may no longer represent the best use of our time.

Why might that happen? Perhaps after working for two weeks on an infrastructure change that you initially estimated would take a month, you discover technical challenges or increased project requirements that bump the estimate up to three months. Is the project still worth completing? Or perhaps as you were building a new product feature, an older one starts triggering scalability issues or pager duty alerts that you need to spend an hour each day addressing. Would it be higher leverage to pause development of the new feature and develop a longer-term fix for the old one? Or perhaps during development you realize that you're spending a large portion of your time wrestling with a legacy codebase. Would it be worthwhile to refactor that code before continuing?

The answers to all these questions will vary from case to case. The key to answering these questions correctly is being retrospective and making a habit of revisiting your priorities.

Using the strategies presented in this chapter, you're ready to develop your own routine to manage and execute on your own priorities. Every productivity guru recommends a different set of workflow mechanics. David Allen, in *Getting Things Done*, suggests grouping to-do items by location-based contexts and then handling tasks based on your current context. [24] Tonianne DeMaria Barry and Jim Benson, in *Personal Kanban,* recommend creating a backlog of your work, transitioning tasks through various columns on a board (e.g., "backlog," "ready," "in progress," and "done"), and limiting the amount of work-in-progress according to your own bandwidth as determined by trial and error. [25] In *The Pomodoro Technique*, Francesco Cirillo uses a timer to track 25-minute focused sessions, called pomodoros; he works on a single task during each session. [26] Nick Cern, author of *Todoodlist,* is an advocate of the old-fashioned pencil and paper to track what you need to get done. [27] The suggestions are endless.

After experimenting with various systems and task management software, I've come to realize that there's no "best" prioritization workflow. Instead, take general principles, like the ones laid out in this chapter, and iteratively adapt your own system until you find something that works well for you. If you don't have a system, then reading productivity books or using another engineer's system can help provide a starting point. Just remember that the actual mechanics of how you review your priorities matter less than adopting the habit of doing it.

If you need a sample system to get started, however, I'll share what I currently do. As of this writing, I use a web product called Asana to manage my to-do list. From my perspective, Asana's key features are that it's fast, it supports keyboard shortcuts, it allows tasks to be tagged with projects and filtered by project, and it has both Android and iPhone apps so that I can update my to-do lists while I'm on the go. I maintain a backlog of all my personal and work tasks in Asana.

I have a "Current Priorities" project that I use to track the tasks that I want to accomplish in the current week. *If* it's the beginning of the week, *then* I add to the project the tasks that I want to accomplish during that week, pulling either from my backlog or from any unfinished work from the previous week. I prioritize tasks that directly produce value for whatever projects I'm working on and also some longer-term investments that I deem important. Because optimizing for learning is important and non-urgent, I generally include some tasks related to learning something new. Some of my current priorities include writing one thousand words per day on this book, learning about self-publishing, and making daily progress on tutorials for mobile development.

Project tasks can be sub-divided into sections in Asana. In my "Current Priorities" project, I borrow ideas from *Personal Kanban* and have sections for "This Week," "Today," and "Doing." Tasks start the week out under the "This Week" section. Every morning, I move a number of tasks from the "This Week" section into the "Today" section, based on their sizes and my availability. I like to do this in the mornings when I have more energy, because prioritizing is important but mentally taxing. Figure 2 shows what a sample task list under this scheme might look like.

Current Priorities

- [x] ~~[1] Review tasks for today.~~
- [x] ~~[1] Check with team on results from last week's UI experiments.~~

DOING

- [ ] [2] Investigate and fix bug where duplicate emails get sent.

TODAY

- [ ] [4] Instrument performance of signup flow.
- [ ] [6] Prototype experiment for streamlined new user experience.
- [ ] [2] Watch lecture 4 of Android development class.

THIS WEEK

- [ ] [4] Prepare starter tasks for new mentee.
- [ ] [4] Follow up with team on status of codelabs.
- [ ] [6] Write first draft of intro to "Invest in Iteration Speed."
- [ ] [1] Book tickets to New York.
- [ ] ...

Figure 2: A sample snapshot of tasks in my prioritized to-do list.

I estimate and annotate each task with the number of 25-minute pomodoros (there's no reason you couldn't use a differently-sized unit) that I think each will take, using a simple notation like "[4] Instrument performance of signup flow and add graphs to dashboard." This indicates that the task will take 4 chunks. On a typical day, I may have time for 10–15 chunks; the rest of the day tends to be spent dealing with meetings or other interruptions. I try to cluster meetings together to maximize my contiguous blocks of time.

An effective way to ensure that this morning prioritization happens is to make it part of your daily routine. While Quora was headquartered in Palo Alto, for example, I incorporated the practice into my walk to work. I would stop at a coffee shop along the way, where I would spend 5–10 minutes reviewing my to-dos while consuming my morning dose of caffeine. This helped me identify a small number of important tasks that I wanted to accomplish during the rest of the day. Moreover, whenever I didn't get something done that I had previously prioritized, the routine gave me an opportunity to review why: had I worked on something else more important, misprioritized, or simply procrastinated?

When I have free time during my day, I pick a task, move it from the "Today" to the "Doing" section, and work on it. Again, because I know I have more mental energy in the mornings, I use if-then plans to note that *if* it's in the morning, *then* I'll pick tasks requiring more mental effort and creativity. To increase my focus, I block off sites like Facebook, Twitter, etc. through my `/etc/hosts` file [28] and use a timer program called Focus Booster to time my 25-minute sessions. [29] Timing what I'm doing might seem like overkill (and in fact, I've only recently starting experimenting with it), but I've found that it increases my awareness of how much time I spend on a given task and makes me more accountable when distractions arise. I track how many 25-minute sessions I spend on a task, mainly to validate and learn about whether my initial estimates were accurate. In between those 25-minute sessions, I take a 5-minute break to stretch, check email, or surf the web before resuming.

When I complete a task, I check it off, and Asana takes care of archiving it and hiding it from my default project view. At the end of the day, I have a fairly clear idea of whether I've been productive or not, based on this system. I can count up the number of completed chunks and know whether it's on par with what I've done historically. I repeat this process throughout the week, and as new tasks and ideas come up, I add them to my "Today" or "This Week" section if they're urgent, or to my backlog if they're not.

I've also found that committing to an end-of-the-week 30-minute planning session helps ensure that I'm spending time on the right activities. On a Sunday afternoon or Monday morning, I review the priorities I've accomplished, examine the ones I had planned to finish but didn't so I can understand why, and scope out what I hope to accomplish in the following week. Asana makes it easy to define custom views, such as which tasks I finished in the past week, for this purpose.

Whereas my daily prioritization sessions typically result in small tweaks to what I'm currently working on, my weekly sessions provide opportunities to make larger course corrections. Is there something important and non-urgent that I should be spending more time on? Perhaps my team isn't iterating as quickly as it could be and would benefit from building better tools and abstractions. Or perhaps I had intended to brush up on mobile development but hadn't found the time the previous week. I might then resolve to work on the new priorities during the next week; I might even block off some time for this in my daily schedule. Periodically (about once a month), I do a larger planning session around my progress for the month and think about the things I'd like to change for the future.

This system works well for me right now, although it's likely that I'll still experiment with more tweaks in the future. The system that works for you may look quite different. What's important isn't to follow my mechanics, but to find *some* system that helps you support a habit of prioritizing regularly. This will allow you to reflect on whether you're spending time on your highest-leverage activities.

Prioritizing is difficult. It consumes time and energy, and sometimes it doesn't feel productive because you're not creating anything. Perhaps you won't want to do it during your downtime when you want to relax. That's okay—you don't have to always be prioritizing. But when you have certain personal or professional goals that you want to achieve, you'll find that prioritization has very high leverage. You'll see its outsized impact on your ability to get the right things done. And as you get more effective at it, you'll feel incentivized to prioritize more regularly.

Key Takeaways

- **Write down and review to-dos.** Spend your mental energy on prioritizing and processing your tasks rather than on trying to remember them. Treat your brain as a processor, not as a memory bank.
- **Work on what directly leads to value.** Don't try to do everything. Regularly ask yourself if there's something higher-leverage that you could be doing.
- **Work on the important and non-urgent.** Prioritize long-term investments that increase your effectiveness, even if they don't have a deadline.
- **Reduce context switches.** Protect large blocks of time for your creative output, and limit the number of ongoing projects so that you don't spend your cognitive energy actively juggling tasks.
- **Make if-then plans to combat procrastination.** Binding an intention to do something to a trigger significantly increases the likelihood that you'll get it done.
- **Make prioritization a habit.** Experiment to figure out a good workflow. Prioritize regularly, and it'll get easier to focus on and complete your highest-leverage activities.

Part 2: Execute, Execute, Execute

4

Invest in Iteration Speed

On any given day, our team at Quora might release new versions of the web product to users 40 to 50 times. [1] Using a practice called *continuous deployment*, we automatically shipped any new code we committed to production servers. On average, it took only seven minutes for each change to be vetted by thousands of tests and receive the green light to roll out to millions of users. This happened throughout every day, all without any human intervention. In contrast, most other software companies shipped new releases only weekly, monthly, or quarterly, and the mechanics of each release might take hours or even days.

For those who haven't used it before, continuous deployment may seem like a scary or unviable process. How did we manage to deploy software more frequently—orders of magnitude more frequently, in fact—than other teams, without sacrificing quality and reliability? Why would we even want to release software that often? Why not hire or contract a quality assurance team to sanity check each release? To be honest, when I first joined Quora back in August 2010, I had similar concerns. New engineers add themselves to the team page as one of their first tasks, and the notion that the code I wrote on my first day would so easily go into production was exhilarating—and frightening.

But now, after having used the process for three years, it's clear to me that continuous deployment played an instrumental role in helping our team grow the product. We increased new user registrations and user engagement metrics by over 3x during my last year at Quora. Continuous deployment, along with other investments in iteration speed, contributed in large part to that growth. [2]

A number of high-leverage investments in our infrastructure made this rapid release cycle possible. We built tools to automatically version and package our code. We developed a testing framework that parallelized thousands of unit and integration tests across a tier of worker machines. If all the tests passed, our release scripts tested the new build on web servers, called *canaries*, to further validate that everything behaved as expected, and then rolled out the software to production tiers. We invested in comprehensive dashboards and alerts that monitored our product's health, and we made tools to easily roll back changes in the event that some bad code had fallen through the cracks. Those investments eliminated the manual overhead associated with each deployment and gave us high confidence that each deployment was just business as usual.

Why is continuous deployment such a powerful tool? Fundamentally, it allows engineers to make and deploy small, incremental changes rather than the larger, batched changes typical at other companies. That shift in approach eliminates a significant amount of overhead associated with traditional release processes, making it easier to reason about changes and enabling engineers to iterate much more quickly.

If someone finds a bug, for instance, continuous deployment makes it possible to implement a fix, deploy it to production, and verify that it works—all in one sitting. With more traditional workflows, those three phases might be split over multiple days or weeks; the engineer has to make the fix, wait days for it to be packaged up with other bigger changes in the week's release, and then validate that fix along with a slew of other orthogonal changes. Much more context switching and mental overhead are required.

Or suppose you need to migrate an in-production database table from one schema to another. The standard process to change a live schema is: 1) create the new schema, 2) deploy code to write to both the old and new schemas, 3) copy existing data over from the old schema to the new schema, 4) deploy code to start reading from the new schema, and 5) remove the code that writes to the old schema. While each individual change might be straightforward, the changes need to happen sequentially over 4–5 releases. This can be quite laborious if each release takes a week. With continuous deployment, an engineer could perform the migration by deploying 4–5 times within a few hours and not have to think about it again in subsequent weeks.

Because changes come in smaller batches, it's also easier to debug problems when they're identified. When a bug surfaces or when a performance or business metric drops as a result of a release, teams with a weekly release cycle often have to dig through hundreds of changes from the past week in an attempt to figure out what went wrong. With continuous deployment, on the other hand, it generally is a straightforward task to isolate the culprit in the handful of code changes deployed in the past few hours.

Just because changes are deployed incrementally, however, doesn't mean that larger features aren't possible or that users see half-finished features. A large feature gets gated behind a configuration flag, which is disabled until the feature is ready. The same configuration flag often allows teams to selectively enable a feature for internal team members, beta users, or some fraction of production traffic until the feature is ready. In practice, this also means that changes get merged incrementally into the master code repository. Teams then avoid the intense coordination and "merge hell" that often accompanies longer release cycles as they scramble to integrate large chunks of new code and get them to work together correctly. [3]

Focusing on small, incremental changes also opens the door to new development techniques that aren't possible in traditional release workflows. Suppose that in a product discussion, we're debating whether we should keep a certain feature. Rather than letting opinions and politics dictate the feature's importance or waiting for the next release cycle to start gathering usage data, we could simply log the interaction we care about, deploy it, and start seeing the initial data trickle in within minutes. Or suppose we see a performance regression on one of our web pages. Rather than scanning through the code looking for regressions, we can spend a few minutes deploying a change to enable logging so that we can get a live breakdown of where time is being spent.

Our team at Quora wasn't alone in our strong emphasis on the importance of iterating quickly. Engineering teams at Etsy,[4] IMVU,[5] Wealthfront,[6] and GitHub,[7] as well as other companies,[8] have also incorporated continuous deployment (or a variant called *continuous delivery*, where engineers selectively determine which versions to deploy) into their workflows.

Effective engineers invest heavily in iteration speed. In this chapter, we'll find out why these investments are so high-leverage and how we can optimize for iteration speed. First, we'll discuss the benefits of iterating quickly: we can build more and learn faster. We'll then show why it's critical to invest in time-saving tools and how to increase both their adoption and your leeway. Since much of our engineering time is spent debugging and testing, we'll walk through the benefits of shortening our debugging and validation loops. Most of our core tools remain the same throughout our career, so we'll also review habits for mastering our programming environments. And lastly, because programming is but one element in the software development process, we'll look at why it's also important to identify the non-engineering bottlenecks in your work.

Move Fast to Learn Fast

In the hallways of Facebook's Menlo Park headquarters, posters proclaim in red caps: "MOVE FAST AND BREAK THINGS." This mantra enabled the social network to grow exponentially, acquiring over 1 billion users in just 8 years.[9] New employees are indoctrinated into the culture of moving fast during Bootcamp, Facebook's 6-week onboarding program.[10] Many new employees, including those who've never before used PHP, the website's primary programming language, ship code to production in their first few days. Facebook's culture emphasizes iterating quickly and focusing on impact rather than being conservative and minimizing mistakes. The company might not use continuous deployment in production, but it has managed to effectively scale its workflow so that over a thousand engineers are able to deploy code to facebook.com twice a day.[11] That's an impressive feat.

Facebook's growth illustrates why investing in iteration speed is such a high-leverage decision. The faster that you can iterate, the more that you can learn about what works and what doesn't work. You can build more things and try out more ideas. Not every change will produce positive value and growth, of course. One of Facebook's early advertising products, Beacon, automatically broadcasted a user's activity on external websites onto Facebook. The product caused an uproar and had to be shut down. [12] But with each iteration, you get a better sense of which changes will point you in the right direction, making your future efforts much more effective.

Facebook CEO Mark Zuckerberg captured the importance of moving fast in his letter that accompanied the company's initial public offering. "Moving fast enables us to build more things and learn faster," he wrote. "However, as most companies grow, they slow down too much because they're more afraid of making mistakes than they are of losing opportunities by moving too slowly … [I]f you never break anything, you're probably not moving fast enough." [13] A strong focus on maintaining a high iteration speed is a key ingredient for how Facebook got to where it is today.

Moving fast isn't just restricted to consumer web software, where users tend to more tolerant of downtime. And in actuality, the worst outage Facebook ever faced over a four-year period lasted only 2.5 hours—much shorter than outages experienced by larger, slower-moving companies. [14] Moving fast doesn't necessarily mean moving recklessly.

Consider Wealthfront, a financial advisory service whose offices are located in Palo Alto, CA. Wealthfront is a technology company whose mission is to provide access to the financial advice offered by major financial institutions and private wealth managers, at a low cost. They do this by replacing human advisors with software-based ones. As of June 2014, the company manages over a billion dollars in customer assets. [15] Any code breakage would be very costly—but despite this, Wealthfront has invested in continuous deployment and uses the system to ship new code to production over 30 times per day. [16] They're able to iterate quickly despite operating in a financial space that's heavily regulated by the Securities and Exchange Commission and other authorities. Pascal-Louis Perez, Wealthfront's former CTO, explained that continuous deployment's "primary advantage is risk reduction," as it lets the team focus on small batches of changes and "quickly pinpoint problems when they occur." [17]

Continuous deployment is but one of many powerful tools at your disposal for increasing iteration speed. Other options include investing in time-saving tools, improving your debugging loops, mastering your programming workflows, and, more generally, removing any bottlenecks that you identify. We'll spend the rest of the chapter discussing actionable steps for these strategies. All of these investments accomplish the same goal as continuous deployment: they help you move fast and learn quickly about what works and what doesn't. And remember: because learning compounds, the sooner you accelerate your iteration speed, the faster your learning rate will be.

Invest in Time-Saving Tools

When I ask engineering leaders which investments yield the highest returns, "tools" is the most common answer. Bobby Johnson, a former Facebook Director of Infrastructure Engineering, told me, "I've found that almost all successful people write a lot of tools ... [A] very good indicator of future success [was] if the first thing someone did on a problem was to write a tool." [18] Similarly, Raffi Krikorian, former VP of Platform Engineering at Twitter, shared with me that he'd constantly remind his team, "If you have to do something manually more than twice, then write a tool for the third time." [19] There are only a finite number of work hours in the day, so increasing your effort as a way to increase your impact fails to scale. Tools are the multipliers that allow you to scale your impact beyond the confines of the work day.

Consider two engineers, Mark and Sarah, working on two separate projects. Mark dives head first into his project and spends his next two months building and launching a number of features. Sarah, on the other hand, notices that her workflow isn't as fast it could be. She spends her first two weeks fixing her workflow—setting up incremental compilation of her code, configuring her web server to automatically reload newly compiled code, and writing a few automation scripts to make it easier to set up a test user's state on her development server. These improvements speed up her development cycles by 33%.

Mark was able to get more done initially, but after two months, Sarah catches up—and her remaining six weeks' worth of feature work is as productive as Mark's eight weeks. Moreover, Sarah continues to move 33% faster than Mark even after those first two months, producing significantly more work going forward.

The example is somewhat simplified. In reality, Sarah wouldn't actually front-load all that time into creating tools. Instead, she would iteratively identify her biggest bottlenecks and figure out what types of tools would let her iterate faster. But the principle still holds: time-saving tools pay off large dividends.

Two additional effects make Sarah's approach even more compelling. First, faster tools get used more often. If the only option for travel from San Francisco to New York was a week-long train ride, we wouldn't make the trip very often; but since the advent of passenger airlines in the 1950s, people can now make the trip multiple times per year. Similarly, when a tool halves the time it takes to complete a 20-minute activity that we perform 3 times a day, we save much more than 30 minutes per day—because we tend to use it more often. Second, faster tools can enable new development workflows that previously weren't possible. Together, these effects mean that 33% actually might be an *underestimate* of Sarah's speed advantage.

We've already seen this phenomenon illustrated by continuous deployment. A team with a traditional weekly software release process takes many hours to cut a new release, deploy the new version to a staging environment, have a quality assurance team test it, fix any blocking issues, and launch it to production. How much time would streamlining that release process save? Some might say a few hours each week, at most. But, as we saw with continuous deployment, getting that release time down to a few minutes means that the team can actually deploy software updates much more frequently, perhaps at a rate of 40–50 times per day. Moreover, the team can interactively investigate issues in production—posing a question and and deploying a change to answer it—an otherwise difficult task. Thus, the total time saved greatly exceeds a few hours per week.

Or consider compilation speed. When I first started working at Google back in 2006, compiling C++ code for the Google Web Server and its dependencies could take upwards of 20 minutes or more, even with distributed compilation. [20] When code takes that long to compile, engineers make a conscious decision not to compile very often—usually no more than a few times a day. They batch together large chunks of code for the compiler and try to fix multiple errors per development cycle. Since 2006, Google has made significant inroads into reducing compilation times for large programs, including some open source software that shorten compilation phases by 3–5x. [21]

When compile times drop from 20 minutes to, say, 2 minutes, engineering workflows change drastically. This means even an hour or two of time savings per day is a big underestimate. Engineers spend less time visually inspecting code for mistakes and errors and rely more heavily on the compiler to check it. Faster compile times also facilitate new workflows around iterative development, as it's simpler to iteratively reason about, write, and test smaller chunks of code. When compile times drop to seconds, incremental compilation—where saving a file automatically triggers a background task to start recompiling code—allows engineers to see compiler warnings and errors as they edit files, and makes programming significantly more interactive than before. And faster compile times mean that engineers will compile fifty or even hundreds of times per day, instead of ten or twenty. Productivity skyrockets.

Switching to languages with interactive programming environments can have a similar effect. In Java, testing out a small expression or function entails a batch workflow of writing, compiling, and running an entire program. One advantage that languages like Scala or Clojure, two languages that run on the Java Virtual Machine, have over Java itself is their ability to evaluate expressions quickly and interactively within a read-eval-print loop, or REPL. This doesn't save time just because the read-eval-print loop is faster than the edit-compile-run-debug loop; it also saves time because you end up interactively evaluating and testing many more small expressions or functions that you wouldn't have done before.

There are plenty of other examples of tools that compound their time savings by leading to new workflows. Hot code reloads, where a server or application can automatically swap in new versions of the code without doing a full restart, encourages a workflow with more incremental changes. Continuous integration, where every commit fires off a process to rebuild the codebase and run the entire test suite, makes it easy to pinpoint which change broke the code so that you don't have to waste time searching for it.

The time-saving properties of tools also scale with team adoption. A tool that saves you one hour per day saves 10 times as much when you get 10 people on your team to use it. That's why companies like Google, Facebook, Dropbox, and Cloudera have entire teams devoted to improving internal development tools; reducing the build time by one minute, when multiplied over a team of 1,000 engineers who build code a dozen times a day, translates to nearly one person-year in engineering time saved every week! Therefore, it's not sufficient to find or build a time-saving tool. To maximize its benefits, you also need to increase its adoption across your team. The best way to accomplish that is by proving that the tool actually saves time.

When I was working on the Search Quality team at Google, most people who wanted to prototype new user interfaces for Google's search result pages would write them in C++. C++ was a great language choice for the high performance needed in production, but its slow compile cycles and verbosity made it a poor vehicle for prototyping new features and testing out new user interactions.

And so, during my 20% time, I built a framework in Python that let engineers prototype new search features. Once my immediate teammates and I started churning out prototypes of feature after feature and demoing them at meetings, it didn't take very long for others to realize that they could also be much more productive building on top of our framework, even if it meant porting over their existing work.

Sometimes, the time-saving tool that you built might be objectively superior to the existing one, but the switching costs discourage other engineers from actually changing their workflow and learning your tool. In these situations, it's worth investing the additional effort to lower the switching cost and to find a smoother way to integrate the tool into existing workflows. Perhaps you can enable other engineers to switch to the new behavior with only a small configuration change.

When we were building our online video player at Ooyala, for example, everyone on the team used an Eclipse plugin to compile their ActionScript code, the language used for Flash applications. Unfortunately, the plugin was unreliable and sometimes failed to recompile a change. Unless you carefully watched what was being compiled, you wouldn't discover that your changes were missing until you actually interacted with the video player. This led to frequent confusion and slower development. I ended up creating a new command-line based build system that would produce reliable builds. Initially, because it required changing their build workflow off from Eclipse, only a few team members adopted my system. And so, to increase adoption, I spent some additional time and hooked the build process into Eclipse. That reduced the switching costs sufficiently to convince others on the team to change systems.

One side benefit of proving to people that your tool saves time is that it also earns you leeway with your manager and your peers to explore more ideas in the future. It can be difficult to convince others that an idea that you believe in is actually worth doing. Did the new Erlang deployment system that Joe rewrote in one week for fun actually produce any business value? Or is it just an unmaintainable liability? Compared with other projects, time-saving tools provide measurable benefits—so you can use data to objectively prove that your time investment garnered a positive return (or, conversely, to prove to yourself that your investment wasn't worth it). If your team spends 3 hours a week responding to server crashes, for example, and you spend 12 hours building a tool to automatically restart crashed servers, it's clear that your investment will break even after a month and pay dividends going forward.

At work, we can easily fall into an endless cycle of hitting the next deadline: getting the next thing done, shipping the next new feature, clearing the next bug in our backlog, and responding to the next issue in the never-ending stream of customer requests. We might have ideas for tools we could build to make our lives a bit easier, but the long-term value of those tools is hard to quantify. On the other hand, the short-term costs of a slipped deadline or a product manager breathing down our necks and asking when something will get done are fairly concrete.

So start small. Find an area where a tool could save time, build it, and demonstrate its value. You'll earn leeway to explore more ambitious avenues, and you'll find the tools you build empowering you to be more effective on future tasks. Don't let the pressure to constantly ship new features cause the important but non-urgent task of building time-saving tools to fall by the wayside.

Shorten Your Debugging and Validation Loops

It's wishful thinking to believe that all the code we write will be bug-free and work the first time. In actuality, much of our engineering time is spent either debugging issues or validating that what we're building behaves as expected. The sooner we internalize this reality, the sooner we will start to consciously invest in our iteration speed in debugging and validation loops.

Creating the right workflows in this area can be just as important as investing in time-saving tools. Many of us are familiar with the concept of a minimal, reproducible test case. This refers to the simplest possible test case that exercises a bug or demonstrates a problem. A minimal, reproducible test case removes all unnecessary distractions so that more time and energy can be spent on the core issue, and it creates a tight feedback loop so that we can iterate quickly. Isolating that test case might involve removing every unnecessary line of code from a short program or unit test, or identifying the shortest sequence of steps a user must take to reproduce an issue. Few of us, however, extend this mentality more broadly and create minimal workflows while we're iterating on a bug or a feature.

As engineers, we can shortcut around normal system behaviors and user interactions when we're testing our products. With some effort, we can programmatically build much simpler custom workflows. Suppose, for example, you're working on a social networking application for iOS, and you find a bug in the flow for sending an invite to a friend. You could navigate through the same three interactions that every normal user goes through: switching to the friends tab, choosing someone from your contacts, and then crafting an invite message. Or, you could create a much shorter workflow by spending a few minutes wiring up the application so that you're dropped into the buggy part of the invitation flow every time the application launches.

Or suppose you're working on an analytics web application where you need to iterate on an advanced report that is multiple clicks away from the home screen. Perhaps you also need to configure certain filters and customize the date range to pull the report you're testing. Rather than going through the normal user flow, you can shorten your workflow by adding the ability to specify the configuration through URL parameters so that you immediately jump into the relevant report. Or, you can even build a test harness that specifically loads the reporting widget you care about.

As a third example, perhaps you're building an A/B test for a web product that shows a random feature variant to users, depending on their browser cookie. To test the variants, you might hard code the conditional statement that chooses between the different variants, and keep changing what gets hard coded to switch between variants. Depending on the language you're using, this might require recompiling your code each time. Or, you can shorten your workflow by building an internal tool that lets you set your cookie to a value that can reliably trigger a certain variant during testing.

These optimizations for shortening a debugging loop seem obvious, now that we've spelled them out. But these examples are based on real scenarios that engineers at top tech companies have faced—and in some cases, they spent months using the slower workflow before realizing that they could shorten it with a little time investment. When they finally made the change and were able to iterate much more quickly, they scratched their heads, wondering why they didn't think to do it earlier.

When you're fully engaged with a bug you're testing or a new feature you're building, the last thing you want to do is to add more work. When you're already using a workflow that works, albeit with a few extra steps, it's easy to get complacent and not expend the mental cycles on devising a shorter one. Don't fall into this trap! The extra investment in setting up a minimal debugging workflow can help you fix an annoying bug sooner and with less headache.

Effective engineers know that debugging is a large part of software development. Almost instinctively, they know when to make upfront investments to shorten their debugging loops rather than pay a tax on their time for every iteration. That instinct comes from being mindful of what steps they're taking to reproduce issues and reflecting on which steps they might be able to short circuit. "Effective engineers have an obsessive ability to create tight feedback loops for what they're testing," Mike Krieger, co-founder and CTO of the popular photo-sharing application Instagram, told me during an interview. "They're the people who, if they're dealing with a bug in the photo posting flow on an iOS app ... have the instinct to spend the 20 minutes to wire things up so that they can press a button and get to the exact state they want in the flow every time."

The next time you find yourself repeatedly going through the same motions when you're fixing a bug or iterating on a feature, pause. Take a moment to think through whether you might be able to tighten that testing loop. It could save you time in the long run.

Master Your Programming Environment

Regardless of the types of software we build throughout our careers, many of the basic tools that we need to use on a daily basis remain the same. We spend countless hours working in text editors, integrated development environments (IDEs), web browsers, and mobile devices. We use version control and the command line. Moreover, certain basic skills are required for the craft of programming, including code navigation, code search, documentation lookup, code formatting, and many others. Given how much time we spend in our programming environments, the more efficient we can become, the more effective we will be as engineers.

I once worked with an engineer at Google who moused through the folder hierarchy of Mac's Finder every time he wanted to navigate to the code in another file. Say it took 12 seconds to find the file, and say he switched files 60 times per day. That's 12 minutes he spent navigating between files every day. If he had learned some text editor keyboard shortcuts that let him navigate to a file in 2 seconds instead of 12, then over the course of one day, he would have saved 10 minutes. That translates to 40 hours, or an entire work week, each year.

There are numerous other examples of simple, common tasks that can take a wide range of times for different people to complete. These include:

- Tracking changes in version control
- Compiling or building code
- Running a unit test or program
- Reloading a web page on a development server with new changes
- Testing out the behavior of an expression
- Looking up the documentation for a certain function
- Jumping to a function definition
- Reformatting code or data in text editor
- Finding the callers of a function
- Rearranging desktop windows
- Navigating to a specific place within a file

Fine-tuning the efficiency of simple actions and saving a second here or there may not seem worth it at first glance. It requires an upfront investment, and you'll very likely be slower the first few times you try out a new and unfamiliar workflow. But consider that you'll repeat those actions at least tens of thousands of times during your career: minor improvements easily compound over time. Not looking at the keyboard when you first learned to touch type might have slowed you down initially, but the massive, long-term productivity gains made the investment worthwhile. Similarly, no one masters these other skills overnight. Mastery is a process, not an event, and as you get more comfortable, the time savings will start to build. The key is to be mindful of which of your common, everyday actions slow you down, and then figure out how to perform those actions more efficiently. Fortunately, decades of software engineers have preceded us; chances are, others have already built the tools we need to accelerate our most common workflows. Often, all we need to do is to invest our time to learn them well.

Here are some ways you can get started on mastering your programming fundamentals:

- **Get proficient with your favorite text editor or IDE.** There are countless debates over which is the best text editor: Emacs, Vim, TextMate, Sublime, or something else. What's most important for you is mastering the tool that you use for the most purposes. Run a Google search on productivity tips for your programming environment. Ask your more effective friends and co-workers if they'd mind you watching them for a bit while they're coding. Figure out the workflows for efficient file navigation, search and replace, auto-completion, and other common tasks for manipulating text and files. Learn and practice them.

- **Learn at least one productive, high-level programming language.** Scripting languages work wonders in comparison to compiled languages when you need to get something done quickly. Empirically, languages like C, C++, and Java tend to be 2–3x more verbose in terms of lines of code than higher-level languages like Python and Ruby; moreover, the higher-level languages come with more powerful, built-in primitives, including list comprehensions, functional arguments, and destructuring assignment. [22] Once you factor in the additional time needed to recover from mistakes or bugs, the absolute time differences start to compound. Each minute spent writing boilerplate code for a less productive language is a minute not spent tackling the meatier aspects of a problem.
- **Get familiar with UNIX (or Windows) shell commands.** Being able to manipulate and process data with basic UNIX tools instead of writing a Python or Java program can reduce the time to complete a task from minutes down to seconds. Learn basic commands like `grep`, `sort`, `uniq`, `wc`, `awk`, `sed`, `xargs`, and `find`, all of which can be piped together to execute arbitrarily powerful transformations. Read through helpful documentation in the `man` pages for a command if you're not sure what it does. Pick up or bookmark some useful one-liners. [23]
- **Prefer the keyboard over the mouse.** Seasoned programmers train themselves to navigate within files, launch applications, and even browse the web using their keyboards as much as possible, rather than a mouse or trackpad. This is because moving our hands back and forth from the keyboard to the mouse takes time, and, given how often we do it, provides a considerable opportunity for optimization. Many applications offer keyboard shortcuts

for common tasks, and most text editors and IDEs provide ways to bind custom key sequences to special actions for this purpose.

- **Automate your manual workflows.** Developing the skills to automate takes time, whether they be using shell scripts, browser extensions, or something else. But the cost of mastering these skills gets smaller the more often you do it and the better you get at it. As a rule of thumb, once I've manually performed a task three or more times, I start thinking about whether it would be worthwhile to automate it. For example, anyone working on web development has gone through the flow of editing the HTML or CSS for a web page, switching to the web browser, and reloading the page to see the changes. Wouldn't it be much more efficient to set up a tool that automatically re-renders the web page in real-time when you save your changes? [24] [25]
- **Test out ideas on an interactive interpreter.** In many traditional languages like C, C++, and Java, testing the behavior of even a small expression requires you to compile a program and run it. Languages like Python, Ruby, and JavaScript, however, have interpreters available allowing you to evaluate and test out expressions. Using them to build confidence that your program behaves as expected will provide a significant boost in iteration speed.
- **Make it fast and easy to run just the unit tests associated with your current changes.** Use testing tools that run only the subset of tests affected by your code. Even better, integrate the tool with your text editor or IDE so that you can invoke them with a few keystrokes. In general, the faster that you can run your tests, both in terms of how long it takes to invoke the tests and how long they take to run, the more you'll use tests as a normal part of your development—and the more time you'll save.

Given how much time we spend within our programming environments, mastering the basic tools that we use multiple times per day is a high-leverage investment. It lets us shift our limited time from the mechanics of programming to more important problems.

Don't Ignore Your Non-Engineering Bottlenecks

The best strategy for optimizing your iteration speed is the same as for optimizing the performance of any system: identify the biggest bottlenecks, and figure out how to eliminate them. What makes this difficult is that while tools, debugging workflows, and programming environments might be the areas most directly under your control as an engineer, sometimes they're not the only bottlenecks slowing you down.

Non-engineering constraints may also hinder your iteration speed. Customer support might be slow at collecting the details for a bug report. The company might have service-level agreements that guarantee their customers certain levels of uptime, and those constraints might limit how frequently you can release new software. Or your organization might have particular processes that you need to follow. Effective engineers identify and tackle the biggest bottlenecks, even if those bottlenecks don't involve writing code or fall within their comfort zone. They proactively try to fix processes inside their sphere of influence, and they do their best to work around areas outside of their control.

One common type of bottleneck is dependency on other people. A product manager might be slow at gathering the customer requirements that you need; a designer might not be providing the Photoshop mocks for a key workflow; another engineering team might not have delivered a promised feature, thus blocking your own development. While it's possible that laziness or incompetence is at play, oftentimes the cause is a misalignment of priorities rather than negative intention. Your frontend team might be slated to deliver a user-facing feature this quarter that depends on a piece of critical functionality from a backend team; but the backend team might have put it at the bottom of its priority list, under a slew of other projects dealing with scaling and reliability. This misalignment of priorities makes it difficult for you to succeed. The sooner you acknowledge that you need to personally address this bottleneck, the more likely you'll be able to either adapt your goals or establish consensus on the functionality's priority.

Communication is critical for making progress on people-related bottlenecks. Ask for updates and commitments from team members at meetings or daily stand-ups. Periodically check in with that product manager to make sure what you need hasn't gotten dropped. Follow up with written communication (email or meeting notes) on key action items and dates that were decided in-person. Projects fail from under-communicating, not over-communicating. Even if resource constraints preclude the dependency that you want from being delivered any sooner, clarifying priorities and expectations enables you to plan ahead and work through alternatives. You might decide, for example, to handle the project dependency yourself; even though it will take additional time to learn how to do it, it will enable you to launch your feature sooner. This is a hard decision to make unless you've communicated regularly with the other party.

Another common type of bottleneck is obtaining approval from a key decision maker, typically an executive at the company. While I was at Google, for example, any user interface (UI) change to search results needed to be approved in a weekly UI review meeting with then-VP Marissa Mayer. There was a limited supply of review slots in those weekly meetings, coupled with high demand, and sometimes a change required multiple reviews.

Given that bottlenecks like these generally fall outside of an engineer's control, oftentimes the best that we can do is to work around them. Focus on securing buy-in as soon as possible. Mayer held occasional office hours, [26] and the teams who got things done were the ones who took advantage of those informal meetings to solicit early and frequent feedback. Don't wait until after you've invested massive amounts of engineering time to seek final project approval. Instead, prioritize building prototypes, collecting early data, conducting user studies, or whatever else is necessary to get preliminary project approval. Explicitly ask the decision makers what they care about the most, so that you can make sure to get those details right. If meeting with the decision makers isn't possible, talk with the product managers, designers, or other leaders who have worked closely with them and who might be able to provide insight into their thought processes. I've heard countless stories of engineers ready to launch their work, only to get last-minute feedback from key decision-makers that they needed to make significant changes—changes which would undo weeks of engineering effort. Don't let that be you. Don't defer approvals until the end. We'll revisit this theme of early feedback in more depth in Chapter 6.

A third type of bottleneck is the review processes that accompany any project launch, whether they be verification by the quality assurance team, a scalability or reliability review by the performance team, or an audit by the security team. It's easy to get so focused on getting a feature to work that you defer these reviews to the last minute—only to realize that the team that needs to sign off on your work hadn't been aware of your launch plans and won't be available until two weeks from now. Plan ahead. Expend slightly more effort in coordination; it could make a significant dent in your iteration speed. Get the ball rolling on the requirements in your launch checklist, and don't wait until the last minute to schedule necessary reviews. Again, communication is key to ensure that review processes don't become bottlenecks.

At larger companies, fixing the bottlenecks might be out of your circle of influence, and the best you can do is work around them. At smaller startups, you often can directly address the bottlenecks themselves. When I started working on the user growth team at Quora, for example, we had to get design approval for most of our live traffic experiments. Approval meetings were a bottleneck. But over time, we eliminated that bottleneck by building up mutual trust; the founders knew that our team would use our best judgment and solicit feedback on the experiments that might be controversial. Not having to explicitly secure approval for every single experiment meant that our team could iterate at a much faster pace and try out many more ideas.

Given the different forms that your bottlenecks can take, Donald Knuth's oft-cited mantra, "premature optimization is the root of all evil," is a good heuristic to use. Building continuous deployment for search interface changes at Google, for example, wouldn't have made much of an impact in iteration speed, given that the weekly UI review was a much bigger bottleneck. Time would have been better spent figuring out how to speed up the approval process.

Find out where the biggest bottlenecks in your iteration cycle are, whether they're in the engineering tools, cross-team dependencies, approvals from decision-makers, or organizational processes. Then, work to optimize them.

Key Takeaways

- **The faster you can iterate, the more you can learn.** Conversely, when you move too slowly trying to avoid mistakes, you lose opportunities.
- **Invest in tooling.** Faster compile times, faster deployment cycles, and faster turnaround times for development all provide time-saving benefits that compound the more you use them.
- **Optimize your debugging workflow.** Don't underestimate how much time gets spent validating that your code works. Invest enough time to shorten those workflows.
- **Master the fundamentals of your craft.** Get comfortable and efficient with the development environment that you use on a daily basis. This will pay off dividends throughout your career.
- **Take a holistic view of your iteration loop.** Don't ignore any organizational and team-related bottlenecks that may be within your circle of influence.

5

Measure What You Want to Improve

Soon after I joined Google's Search Quality team, I began work with a team of engineers focused on increasing user happiness. Every time a user entered a query into Google's search box, sophisticated algorithms sifted through billions of possible web pages, images, and videos. The algorithms evaluated over 200 signals—ones like PageRank, anchor text matches, website freshness, proximity of keyword matches, query synonyms, or geographic location [1]—and returned the top 10 results in a few hundred milliseconds. [2] But how did we know that users were finding what they were looking for, and that they were happy when they left their search? Our intuition may have suggested that one user interface was better than another or that one particular combination of weights for signals was optimal. But without a reliable way of measuring user happiness, it would have been hard to determine whether a given change to the search results page actually resulted in forward progress.

One way to assess user happiness is to directly ask users about their experiences. Dan Russell, a tech lead responsible for search quality and user happiness at Google, has done exactly that in his field studies. He interviews people to understand what makes them tick and why they query for what they do. [3] In his talks, Russell explains that user happiness is correlated to "that sense of delight" you get in successful searches, like when you type the query `weather` and the results include a cartoon result of the week's forecast, or when the query `28 euro to usd` automatically converts the currency for you. [4] While increasing user delight is a valuable and laudable notion, delight is difficult to quantify; it's not something that can be collected and monitored as an operational guide for day-to-day decisions. It's much better to use a metric based on the behavior of Google's 100+ million monthly active users. [5]

Google logs a treasure trove's worth of data when people search—what gets clicked on, how people refine their queries, when they click through to the next page of results [6] [7]—and perhaps the most obvious metric to guide search quality would be result clicks. But click-through rate as a metric has its shortcomings. A user might click on a result with a seemingly reasonable snippet only to land on a low-quality web page that doesn't satisfy her intent. And she might even have to pogostick and bounce through results for multiple queries before finding what she's looking for (or perhaps even abandoning her attempt). Clearly, click-through rate, while important, is insufficient.

For over a decade, Google guarded what key metrics it used to guide search quality experiments. But in his 2011 book *In the Plex*, Steven Levy finally shed some light on the subject: he revealed that Google's best indication of user happiness is the "long click." This occurs when someone clicks a search result and doesn't return to the search page, or stays on the result page for a long time. A long click means that Google has successfully displayed a result that the user has been searching for. On the other hand, a "short click"—occurring when someone follows a link only to return immediately to the results page to try another one—indicates unhappiness with the result. Unhappy users also tend to change their queries or go to the next page of search results.

One set of results leads to happier users than another if it has a higher percentage of long clicks. [8] That metric, the long click-through rate, turns out to be a surprisingly versatile metric.

One team, for example, worked on a multi-year effort to produce a name detection system. Early on, Amit Singhal, the head of Google's ranking team, had observed that the query `audrey fino` would return heaps of Italian pages for the actress Audrey Hepburn (fino means fine in Italian), but none for the attorney Audrey Fino based in Malta. Given that 8% of Google's queries were names, the example revealed a huge problem. To help train the classifier, they licensed the White Pages with its millions of names. But even volumes of name data couldn't answer the question of whether someone searching for `houston baker` was looking for a Texan bread baker or someone with that name. To do that, they also needed to use millions of long clicks and short clicks to determine which results matched the user's intent and which didn't. Through this mechanism, Singhal's team successfully taught the name classifier that the user's intent depended on whether he was searching from Texas. [9]

Similarly, when engineer David Bailey first worked on universal search to enable a single query to search all of Google's corpora—images, videos, news, locations, products, etc.—he faced the difficult problem of how to weigh the relative importance of different result types. Someone searching for `cute puppies` might want to see images and videos; someone searching for `us china relations` might want news results; and someone searching for `palo alto restaurants` might want reviews and maps. Deciding which result type to rank higher was akin to comparing apples and oranges. The solution again came partly in the form of analyzing long click data to decode the intent of a query. Have users who searched for `cute puppies` historically clicked and spent time on more images or more web results? From long clicks and other signals, Bailey's team was able to accurately combine results from different corpora with sensible and data-driven rankings. [10] Today, we take for granted Google's ability to search over everything, but that wasn't the case for more than ten years after the company was founded.

My experience at Google demonstrated the power of a well-chosen metric and its ability to tackle a wide range of problems. Google runs thousands of live traffic search experiments per year, [11] and their reliance on metrics played a key role in ensuring search quality and building their market share.

In this chapter, we'll look at why metrics are important tools for effective engineers, to not only measure progress but also to drive it. We'll see how choosing which key metrics to use—and not use!—can completely change what work gets prioritized. We'll walk through the importance of instrumenting our systems to increase our understanding of what's happening. We'll go over how internalizing some useful numbers can help shortcut many decisions. And lastly, we'll close by discussing why we need to be skeptical of data integrity and how we can defend ourselves against bad data.

Use Metrics to Drive Progress

Measuring progress and performance might seem to fall within your manager's purview, but it's actually a powerful tool for assessing your own effectiveness and prioritizing your work. As Peter Drucker points out in *The Effective Executive*, "If you can't measure it, you can't improve it." [12] In product development, it's not uncommon for a manager to conceive of some new feature, for engineers to build and ship it, and for the team to celebrate—all without implementing any mechanism to measure whether the feature actually improved the product experience.

Good metrics accomplish a number of goals. First, they help you focus on the right things. They confirm that your product changes—and all the effort you've put into them—actually achieve your objectives. How do you know whether the fancy new widget that you've added to your product improved user engagement? Or whether a speed optimization fixed the performance bottleneck? Or whether a new recommendations algorithm produced better suggestions? The only way to be consistently confident when answering questions like these is to define a metric associated with your goal—whether that metric is weekly active rate, response time, click-through rate, or something else—and then measure the change's impact. Without those measurements, we're only able to proceed based on intuition; and we have few avenues for understanding whether our intuition is correct.

Second, when visualized over time, good metrics help guard against future regressions. Engineers know the value of writing a regression test while fixing bugs: it confirms that a patch actually fixes a bug and detects if the bug resurfaces in the future. Good metrics play a similar role, but on a system-wide scale. Say your signup rate drops. In your investigation, you might find that a recent JavaScript library change caused a bug in Internet Explorer, a browser that you don't test frequently. Or if the application latency spikes, that might tell you that a newly-added feature is putting too much load on the database.

Without a dashboard of signup rates, application latency, and other useful metrics, it would be hard to identify many of these regressions.

Third, good metrics can drive forward progress. At Box, a company that builds collaboration software for the enterprise market, the engineers care deeply about their application's latency. A dedicated performance team worked hard over three months to shave seconds off of their main page. However, the other application teams added those seconds right back when they launched new features, making the page no faster than before. In a conversation I had with Sam Schillace, Box's VP of Engineering, he explained a technique called *performance ratcheting* that they now use to address this problem and apply downward pressure on performance metrics. In mechanics, a ratchet is a device that allows a wheel with many teeth along its edge to rotate in one direction while preventing motion in the opposite direction. At Box, they use metrics to set a threshold that they call a performance ratchet. Any new change that would push latency or other key indicators past the ratchet can't get deployed until it's optimized, or until some other feature is improved by a counterbalancing amount. Moreover, every time the performance team makes a system-level improvement, they lower the ratchet further. The practice ensures that performance trends in the right direction.

Fourth, a good metric lets you measure your effectiveness over time and compare the leverage of what you're doing against other activities you could be doing instead. If historically you've been able to improve a performance metric or a user engagement metric by 1% per week, that number can be used as a target for establishing future goals. The metric also can become a way to prioritize ideas on the roadmap; you can compare a task's estimated impact for its expected time investment against your historical rate. A task that could improve metrics by more than 1% with a week's worth of effort would be higher-leverage; a task with lower estimated impact would get deprioritized.

Quantifying goals with a metric isn't always easy. An individual bug fix, for example, might be visible in the product but not make much of a dent in core metrics. But consistent bug fixing could be reflected somewhere, whether it be in reduced customer complaints, higher user ratings in an app store, or higher product quality. Even these seemingly subjective notions can still be quantified over time via user surveys. Moreover, just because it's hard to measure a goal doesn't mean that it's not worthwhile to do so. We'll often be faced with tricky situations where intuitively something seems valuable, but it is hard to quantify or takes too much effort to measure.

Even still, given the benefits of good metrics, it's worth asking yourself:

- Is there some way to measure the progress of what I'm doing?
- If a task I'm working on doesn't move a core metric, is it worth doing? Or is there a missing key metric?

So how do you actually pick good metrics? We'll look at that next.

Pick the Right Metric to Incentivize the Behavior You Want

Selecting what you measure is as important as measuring itself. As engineers, we often set metrics and goals for our teams, or we work to improve the metrics set for us. We tend to be good at solving problems and optimizing a metric once it's been set. However, it's crucial to remember that the *choice* of which metric to measure dramatically impacts and influences the type of work that we do. The right metric functions as a North Star, aligning team efforts toward a common goal; the wrong metric leads to efforts that might be ineffective or even counterproductive.

Consider a few examples of how tracking different metrics can affect team behavior:

- **Hours worked per week vs. productivity per week.** During my first five years at startups, I've gone through a few crunch periods where engineering managers pushed for 70-hour work weeks in the hopes of shipping a product faster. Not once have I come out of the experience thinking that it was the right decision for the team. The marginal productivity of each additional work hour drops precipitously once you reach anywhere near this number. Average productivity per hour goes down, errors and bug rates increase, burnout and turnover—with their own difficult-to-measure costs—intensify, and overtime is typically followed by an equal period of "undertime" as employees try to catch up with their lives. [13] Ultimately, attempting to increase output by increasing hours worked per week is unsustainable. It is much more reasonable to align your metric with productivity per week, where productivity in your focus area is measured by factors like product quality, site speed, or user growth.

- **Click-through rates vs. long click-through rates.** When working on ranking for search or recommendations, a common approach is to use click-through rates to measure results quality. However, as previously discussed, optimizing for click-through rate can be problematic when "short clicks" (where users follow a superficially relevant link only to bounce back to the search page to try another one) skew the results. Although short clicks appear to improve the click-through rate metric, they actually indicate that the page was irrelevant; this is why Google measures "long clicks" instead. Only "when someone [goes] to a search result, ideally the top one, and [does] not return," Steven Levy writes in his book *In the Plex*, does it mean that "Google has successfully fulfilled the query." [14]
- **Average response times vs. 95th or 99th percentile response times.** Numerous studies by Google, Yahoo, Amazon, and Facebook show that the speed of website response times matters to users. [15] [16] [17] [18] But how should you measure speed? Focusing on the average response time leads to a very different set of priorities than focusing on the highest 95th or 99th percentile of response times. To decrease the average, you'll focus more on general infrastructure improvements that can shave off milliseconds from all requests. The average is the right metric to use if your goal is to reduce server costs by cutting down aggregate computation time. To decrease the 95th or 99th percentile, however, you'll need to hunt down the worst-case behaviors in your system. In this case, it's important to focus on the slowest responses because they tend to reflect the experiences of your power users—users who have the most data and the most activity and who tend to be more computationally expensive to support.
- **Bugs fixed vs. bugs outstanding.** A friend who used to work on Adobe quality assurance shared a story about how his team would reward developers for bugs fixed. Unfortunately, this only incentivized the developers to

be less rigorous about testing when building new features: they were giving themselves the opportunity to fix easy bugs later and rack up points. Tracking the number of outstanding bugs instead of bugs fixed would have de-incentivized this behavior.

- **Registered users vs. weekly growth rate of registered users.** When growing a product's user base, it's tempting to track gross numbers of total registered users and be content with seeing those metrics move up and to the right. Unfortunately, those numbers don't indicate whether you're sustainably increasing growth. A good press article might spark a one-time bump to growth numbers but not have much long-term impact. On the other hand, measuring growth in terms of your weekly growth rate (for example, the ratio of new registered users in a week over total registered users), shows whether growth is slowing down.
- **Weekly active users vs. weekly active rate by age of cohort.** When tracking user engagement, the number of weekly active users doesn't provide a complete picture. In fact, that number might increase temporarily even if product changes are actually reducing engagement over time. Users could be signing up as a result of prior momentum, before there's time for the long-term effects of the changes to be reflected in the gross numbers. And they might be more likely to churn and abandon the product after signing up than before. An alternative and more accurate metric would be the weekly active rate by age of cohort. In other words, measure the fraction of users who are still weekly actives the *n*th week after signing up, and track how that number changes over time. This metric provides more actionable insight into how product changes have affected the engagement of newer cohorts of users as compared to older ones.

These examples illustrate that there can be more than one way to measure progress toward any given goal. In addition, the magnitude of the goal for a metric also matters. For example, if your goal is to reduce website latency but you don't have a specific target, you may be satisfied with small, incremental improvements. But if your goal is to drastically reduce latency to below 400ms for a website that currently takes multiple seconds to render, it may necessitate cutting features, re-architecting the system, or rewriting a bottleneck to a faster language. It no longer makes sense to tackle small wins if you have a more aggressive goal. The metric you choose influences your decisions and behavior.

What you *don't* measure is important as well. In *Delivering Happiness*, Zappos CEO Tony Hsieh shares a story of how he built a culture of great customer service by making a key decision about what not to measure. Most call centers assess the performance of customer service representatives using their "average handle time." This measures the average number of minutes it takes an employee to handle a customer call. Reducing this metric saves costs because employees handle more phone calls per day—but this was something that Hsieh didn't actually want to optimize for. "This [metric] translates into reps worrying about how quickly they can get a customer off the phone, which in our eyes is not delivering great customer service," Hsieh explains. "At Zappos, we don't measure call times (our longest phone call was almost six hours long!) … We just care about whether the rep goes above and beyond for every customer." [19] This decision enabled Zappos to distinguish itself in customer service. As a result, the company grew from zero revenues in 1999 to over $1 billion in annual revenue by the time that it was acquired by Amazon in 2009.

Picking the right metric applies to your personal goals as well as your professional ones. I knew writing this book would be a long and challenging project, so I established the habit of writing every day. Early on, I set a goal of writing for at least three hours per day, and I kept track of my progress. What I noticed after a few weeks, however, was that I would spend much of those three hours re-reading and re-writing to perfect my sentences. In fact, some days after editing, I actually would end up with fewer words than I had started out with initially. Great writers like Stephen King and Mark Twain underscore the importance of revision, but I knew that I was rewriting too much too early, and that I would be better off drafting more chapters. And so, I changed my metric. Rather than focusing on writing three hours per day, I focused on writing 1,000 words per day. Some days, that took me two hours; other days, it took four or five. The new metric incentivized me to focus on drafting new content rather than focusing on sentence quality—something I could revisit at a later time. That simple change was all I needed to significantly increase my writing pace.

The more complex the product and the goal, the more options there are for what to measure and not to measure, and the more flexibility there is to guide where effort gets spent and what output gets produced. When deciding which metrics to use, choose ones that 1) *maximize impact*, 2) are *actionable*, and 3) are *responsive* yet *robust*.

Look for a metric that, when optimized, *maximizes impact* for the team. Jim Collins, the author of *Good to Great*, argues that what differentiates great companies from good companies is that they align all employees along a single, core metric that he calls the *economic denominator*. The economic denominator answers the question: "If you could pick one and only one ratio—profit per *x* ...—to systematically increase over time, what *x* would have the greatest and most sustainable impact on your economic engine?" [20] In the context of engineering, the core metric should be the one that, when systematically increased over time, leads you and the rest of your team to make the greatest and most sustainable impact. Having a single, unifying metric—whether it's products sold, rentals booked, content generated, or something else—enables you to compare the output of disparate projects and helps your team decide how to handle externalities. For example, should a performance team cut a product feature to improve page load times? That decision might be a yes if they're just optimizing a site speed metric, but it will be more nuanced (and more likely aligned with the company's desired impact) if they're optimizing a higher-level product metric.

An *actionable* metric is one whose movements can be causally explained by the team's efforts. In contrast, *vanity* metrics, as Eric Ries explains in *The Lean Startup*, track gross numbers like page views per month, total registered users, or total paying customers. Increases in vanity metrics may imply forward product progress, but they don't necessarily reflect the actual quality of the team's work. For example, page views might continue to increase (at least initially) after a mediocre product change, due to prior press coverage or growth in organic search traffic from the momentum of past launches. [21] Actionable metrics, on the other hand, include things like signup conversion rate, or the percentage of registered users that are active weekly over time. Through A/B testing (a topic we'll discuss in Chapter 6), we can trace the movement of actionable metrics directly back to product changes on the signup page or to feature launches.

A *responsive* metric updates quickly enough to give feedback about whether a given change was positive or negative, so that your team can learn where to apply future efforts. It is a leading indicator of how your team is currently doing. A metric that measures active users in the past week is more responsive than one that tracks active users in the past month, since the latter requires a month after any change to fully capture the effects. However, a metric also needs to be *robust* enough that external factors outside of the team's control don't lead to significant noise. Trying to track performance improvements with per-minute response time metrics would be difficult because of their high variance. However, tracking the response times averaged over an hour or a day would make the metric more robust to noise and allow trends to be detected more easily. Responsiveness needs to be balanced with robustness.

Because the choice of metric can have such a significant impact on behavior, it's a powerful leverage point. Dedicate the time to pick the right metric, whether it's just for yourself or for your team.

Instrument Everything to Understand What's Going On

When establishing our goals, it's important to choose carefully what core metrics to measure (or not measure) and optimize. When it comes to day-to-day operations, however, you should be less discriminatory: measure and instrument as much as possible. Although these two principles may seem contradictory, they actually complement each other. The first describes a high-level, big-picture activity, whereas the second is about gaining insight into what's going on with systems that we've built.

The goal of airline pilots is to fly their passengers from point A to point B, as measured by distance to their destination; but they do not fly blind—they have sets of instruments to understand and monitor the state of their aircraft. The altimeter measures pressure differences to show the plane's altitude above sea level. The attitude indicator shows the aircraft's relation to the horizon and whether the wings are level. The vertical speed indicator measures the rate of climb or fall. [22] These and the many hundreds of other cockpit instruments empower pilots to understand the complexity of the plane and cross-check its health. [23]

If we're not mindful, we will fly blind when we're building software—and we will pay the cost. Jack Dorsey, co-founder of Twitter and founder and CEO of the mobile payments company Square, reiterated this in a Stanford entrepreneurship lecture. He told us that one of the most valuable lessons he learned at Twitter was the importance of instrumenting everything. "For the first two years of Twitter's life, we were flying blind," Dorsey explained. "We had no idea what was going on with the network. We had no idea what was going on with the system, with how people were using it … We were going down all the time because of it, because we could not see what was happening." Twitter users were becoming accustomed to seeing the "Fail Whale" graphic—a whale held up by a flock of birds—since the site was overloaded so frequently. Only after Twitter engineers started monitoring and instrumenting their systems were they able to identify problems and build the much more reliable service that over 240 million people now use every month.

When we don't have visibility into our software, all we can do is guess at what's wrong. That's a main reason why the 2013 HealthCare.gov launch was such an abysmal failure. The website was a central feature of the United States' Affordable Care Act (a.k.a. Obamacare), and government contractors had spent nearly $292 million building a site plagued with technical issues. [24] Estimates suggest that only 1% of the 3.7 million people who tried to register in the first week were actually successful; the rest hit error messages, timeouts, or login issues and couldn't load the site. [25] "There's no sugarcoating," President Obama admitted. "The website has been too slow, people have been getting stuck during the application process, and I think it's fair to say that nobody's more frustrated by that than I am." [26] Even worse, as one journalist reported, the contracted engineers attempted to fix the site "much as you or I might reboot or otherwise play with a laptop to see if some shot in the dark fixes a snafu." [27] They were flying blind and guessing at fixes because they had no instruments.

A team of Silicon Valley veterans finally flew into Washington to help fix the site. The first thing they did was to instrument key parts of the system and build a dashboard, one that would surface how many people were using the site, the response times, and where traffic was going. Once they had some visibility into what was happening, they were able to add caching to bring down load times from 8 seconds down to 2, fix bugs to reduce error rates down from an egregious 6% to 0.5%, and scale the site up so that it could support over 83k simultaneous users. [27] Six weeks after the trauma team arrived and added monitoring, the site was finally in a reasonable working condition. Because of their efforts, over 8 million Americans were able to sign up for private health insurance. [28]

The stories from Twitter and Obamacare illustrate that when it comes to diagnosing problems, instrumentation is critical. Suppose there's a spike in the number of user login errors. Was a new bug was introduced? Did the authentication backend hit a network glitch? Was a malicious user programmatically guessing passwords? Was it something else entirely? To effectively answer these questions, we need to know when the errors started, the time of the latest code deployment, the network traffic of the authentication service, the maximum number of authentication attempts per account over various time windows, and possibly more pieces of information. Without these metrics, we're left guessing—and we might end up wasting effort addressing non-problematic areas.

Or suppose our web application suddenly fails to load in production. Did a traffic spike from Reddit overload our servers? Did our Memcached caching layer or MySQL database layer run out of space or start throwing errors? Did a team accidentally deploy a broken module? Dashboards with tables of top referrers, performance graphs for the data stores, and error graphs for the application all can help narrow down the list of possible hypotheses.

In a similar way, effectively optimizing a core metric requires systematically measuring a slew of other supporting metrics. To optimize overall signup rate, you need to start measuring signup rates by referral type (whether the user came from Facebook, Twitter, search, direct navigation, email campaigns, etc.), landing page, and many other dimensions. To optimize a web application's response time, you need to decompose the metric and measure time spent in the database layer, the caching layer, server-side rendering logic, data transfer over the network, and client-side rendering code. To optimize search quality, you need to start measuring click-through rates, the number of results, the searches per session, the time to first result click, and more. The supporting metrics explain the story behind the core metric.

Adopting a mindset of instrumentation means ensuring we have a set of dashboards that surface key health metrics and that enable us to drill down to the relevant data. However, many of the questions we want to answer tend to be exploratory, since we often don't know everything that we want to measure ahead of time. Therefore, we need to build flexible tools and abstractions that make it easy to track additional metrics.

Etsy, a company that sells handmade crafts online, does this exceptionally well. The engineering team instruments their web application according to their philosophy of "measure anything, measure everything." [29] They release code and application configurations over 25 times per day, and they move quickly by investing time in gathering metrics for their servers, application behavior, network performance, and the countless other inputs that drive their platform. To do this effectively, they use a system called Graphite that supports flexible, real-time graphing, [30] and a library called StatsD for aggregating metrics. [31] A single line of code lets them define a new counter or timer on the fly, track statistics every time the code is executed, and automatically generate a time series graph that can be transformed and composed with any number of other metrics. They measure everything including "numbers of new registrations, shopping carts, items sold, image uploaded, forum posts, and application errors." [32] By graphically correlating these metrics with the times of code deployments, they're able to quickly spot when a certain deployment goes awry.

Successful technology companies build the equivalent of a pilot's flight instruments, making it easy for engineers to measure, monitor, and visualize system behavior. The more quickly that teams can identify the root cause of certain behaviors, the more rapidly they can address issues and make progress. At Google, site reliability engineers use a monitoring system called Borgmon to collect, aggregate, and graph metrics and to send alerts when it detects anomalies. [33] Twitter built a distributed platform called Observability to collect, store, and present a volume of 170 million individual metrics per minute. [34] LinkedIn developed a graphing and analytics system called inGraphs that lets engineers view site dashboards, compare metrics over time, and set up threshold-based alerts, all with a few lines of configuration. [35]

You don't have to be a large engineering team operating at scale to start instrumenting your systems. Open-source tools like Graphite, StatsD, InfluxDB, Ganglia, Nagios, and Munin make it easy to monitor systems in near real-time. Teams who want a managed, enterprise solution have options like New Relic or AppDynamics that can quickly provide code-level performance visibility into many standard platforms. Given how much insight instrumentation can provide, how can you afford not to prioritize it?

Internalize Useful Numbers

The company Percona provides MySQL-related consulting services. [36] If you want to optimize the performance of your MySQL database, Percona consultants can audit everything from your configuration, operating system, and hardware to your architecture and table design, and, within a day or two, assess how well your database is performing. [37] They can quickly determine whether any queries are running slower than normal and how much faster they could get; whether there are too many connections; how much more runway a single master database has before data needs to be partitioned across multiple machines; and what type of performance improvement might result if you switched from hard disk drives to solid-state ones. Their expertise is in part due to their familiarity with MySQL internals. However, even more significant is their collective experience of working with the MySQL installations of thousands of customers.

"We've generally seen just about everything people throw at databases," explains Percona consultant Baron Schwartz. "Tagging, friends, queues, click tracking, search, paginated displays—we've seen these and dozens of other common patterns done a hundred different ways." [38] As a result, they've internalized useful numbers that they can use to benchmark a particular system's performance. They might not know exactly how much better your system might behave with a certain change, but they can compare your performance with expected numbers and let you know what's going well and what has ample room for improvement. In contrast, someone less knowledgeable would need to test various MySQL configurations or architectures and measure what difference (if any) the changes made. This, of course, would take significantly more time. The knowledge of useful numbers provides a valuable shortcut for knowing where to invest effort to maximize gains.

We've seen that measuring the goals you want to achieve and instrumenting the systems that you want to understand are high-leverage activities. They both take some upfront work, but their long-term payoffs are high. Oftentimes, however, you don't need accurate numbers to make effective decisions; you just need ones that are in the right ballpark. Ensuring you have access to a few useful numbers to approximate your progress and benchmark your performance is a high-leverage investment: they provide the benefits of metrics at a much lower cost.

The numbers that matter to you will vary based on your focus area and your product. When it comes to building software systems, for example, Jeff Dean—a long-time Googler who has been instrumental in building many of the company's core abstractions like Protocol Buffers, MapReduce, and BigTable, as well as key systems like search, indexing, advertising, and language translation [39]—has shared a list of 13 numbers that every engineer ought to know. [40] [41] These numbers are illustrated in Table 1.

Access Type	Latency
L1 cache reference	0.5 ns
Branch mispredict	5 ns
L2 cache reference	7 ns
Mutex lock/unlock	100 ns
Main memory reference	100 ns
Compress 1K bytes with Snappy	10,000 ns = 10 μs
Send 2K bytes over 1 Gbps network	20,000 ns = 20 μs
Read 1 MB sequentially from memory	250,000 ns = 250 μs
Round trip within same datacenter	500,000 ns = 500 μs
Disk seek	10,000,000 ns = 10 ms
Read 1 MB sequentially from network	10,000,000 ns = 10 ms
Read 1 MB sequentially from disk	30,000,000 ns = 30 ms
Send packet CA → Netherlands → CA	150,000,000 ns = 150 ms

Table 1: Common latency numbers.

These numbers tell us the latencies associated with common operations and let us compare their relative orders of magnitude. For example, accessing 1MB worth of data from memory is 120x faster than accessing the same data from disk, and 40x faster than reading it over a 1 Gbps network. Also, a cheap compression algorithm like Snappy that can compress data by, say, a factor of 2, can halve your network traffic while adding only 50% more latency. [42]

Knowing useful numbers like these enables you, with a few back-of-the-envelope calculations, to quickly estimate the performance properties of a design without actually having to build it. Suppose you're building a data storage system, a messaging system, or some other application with persistent storage where performance is important. In these systems, writes need to be persisted to disk, but data is often cached in memory to improve read performance. What kind of read and write throughput can we expect? You might reason that:

- Your writes will go to disk, and since each disk seek takes 10 ms, you can do at most 100 writes per second.
- Your reads hit the in-memory cache, and since it takes 250 μs to read 1MB from memory, you can read 4GB per second.
- If your in-memory objects are no more than 1MB in size, you can read at least 4,000 objects per second from memory.

That means that in this standard design, you can handle reads roughly 40x faster than you can handle writes. Writes tend to be the bottleneck for many systems, and if that's the case for your system, then designing the system to scale the writes might mean parallelizing them across more machines or batching multiple writes to disk.

Internalizing useful numbers can also help you spot anomalies in data measurements. For example, suppose you're an engineer building web applications on top of a standard software stack like Ruby on Rails. Numbers that you care about might include the time it takes to fetch a database row, perform an aggregation query, join two database tables, or look up data from the caching layer. If your development web server is taking a slow 400ms to load a simple, static page, that might suggest that all the static assets—your images, CSS, and JavaScript—are being served from disk and not from cache. If a dynamic page is taking too long to load and you find that the time spent in the database is over a second, perhaps some code in your application's model is doing an expensive table join that you didn't expect. These are, of course, just possible hypotheses, but it's easy to formulate them quickly when you have ready access to baseline numbers regarding normal performance.

Lastly, knowledge of useful numbers can clarify both the areas and scope for improvement. Suppose you're an engineer responsible for improving user engagement for a social product. If the product sends out email campaigns to users, knowing your industry's average open and click-through rates can be very illuminating. The email marketing service MailChimp, for example, has published delivery data from hundreds of millions emails and computed open and click-through rates by industry. Emails to social networks or online communities get roughly 22% open rates and 3.9% click-through rates. These numbers can give you a sense of whether your own emails are doing poorly, satisfactorily, or extremely well. [43] If your emails perform poorly, then investments to improve them can potentially be high-leverage and have huge payoffs. Similarly, knowing typical conversion rates for landing pages, the acceptance rates for invite emails, and the types of daily, weekly, and monthly active rates seen by similar products can highlight other underinvested areas.

Taken all together, these numbers help you to build more intuition about where to direct effort to maximize your leverage. They allow you to do the mental math and back-of-the-envelope calculations necessary to quickly reason about decisions. Other numbers that might be useful to internalize or at least have readily at hand include:

- the number of registered users, weekly active users, and monthly users
- the number of requests per second
- the amount and total capacity of data stored
- the amount of data written and accessed daily
- the number of servers needed to support a given service
- the throughput of different services or endpoints
- the growth rate of traffic
- the average page load time
- the distribution of traffic across different parts of a product
- the distribution of traffic across web browsers, mobile devices, and operating system versions

The small amount of upfront work it takes to accumulate all this information gives you valuable rules of thumb that you can apply in the future. To obtain performance-related numbers, you can write small benchmarks to gather data you need. For example, write a small program that profiles the common operations you do on your key building blocks and subsystems. Other numbers may require more research, like talking with teams (possibly at other companies) that have worked in similar focus areas, digging through your own historical data, or measuring parts of the data yourself.

When you find yourself wondering which of several designs might be more performant, whether a number is in the right ballpark, how much better a feature could be doing, or whether a metric is behaving normally, pause for a moment. Think about whether these are recurring questions and whether some useful numbers or benchmarks might be helpful for answering them. If so, spend some time gathering and internalizing that data.

Be Skeptical about Data Integrity

Using data to support your arguments is powerful. The right metric can slice through office politics, philosophical biases, and product arguments, quickly resolving discussions. Unfortunately, the wrong metric can do the same thing—with disastrous results. And that means we have to be careful how we use data.

Sam Schillace, who ran engineering for Google Apps before his role at Box, warned, "One of my counter-intuitive lessons from Google is that all data can be abused ... People interpret data the way they want to interpret it." Sometimes, we pick easy-to-measure or slightly irrelevant metrics, and use them to tell a false narrative about what's happening. Other times, we confuse correlation with causality. We might see users spending more time on a newly redesigned feature and optimistically attribute it to increased engagement—when in reality, they are struggling to understand a confusing interface. Or perhaps we've made a change to improve search results and celebrate when we see that ad click-through rates are increasing—but users actually are clicking on ads because the search quality dropped. Or maybe we see a sustained spike in page views and celebrate the organic growth—but a large fraction of the new requests had really just come from a single user who had deployed a bot to automatically scrape product data.

When I asked Schillace how to protect ourselves against data abuse, he argued that our best defense is skepticism. Schillace, who was trained as a mathematician, tries to run the numbers whenever he's analyzing data. He explains, "Bad math students—they get to the end of the problem, and they're just done. Good math students get to the end of the problem, look at their answer, and say, 'Does that roughly make sense?'" When it comes to metrics, compare the numbers with your intuition to see if they align. Try to arrive at the same data from a different direction and see if the metrics still make sense. If a metric implies some other property, try to measure the other property to make sure the conclusions are consistent. The useful numbers described in the previous section come in handy for many of these sanity checks.

Other times, data can simply be flat-out wrong or misinterpreted, leading us to derive the wrong conclusions. Engineers learn quickly that writing unit tests can help ensure code correctness; in contrast, the learning curve for carefully validating data correctness tends to be much higher. In a common scenario, a team launches a product or an experiment and logs user interactions to collect different metrics. The data initially appears acceptable (or the team doesn't even bother to check), and the team focuses their attention elsewhere. A week or two later, when they start to analyze the data, they realize that it had been logged incorrectly or that some critical behavior isn't tracked. By the time they get around to fix the logging, weeks of iteration time have been wasted—all because they didn't proactively invest in data accuracy.

Untrustworthy data that gets incorporated into decision-making processes provides negative leverage. It may lead teams to make the wrong decision or waste cognitive cycles second-guessing themselves. Unfortunately, it's all too common for engineers to underinvest in data integrity, for a few reasons:

1. Since engineers often work against tight deadlines, metrics—whose importance only shows up after launch—can get deprioritized.
2. When building a new product or feature, it's much easier to test and validate their interactions than to verify whether some seemingly plausible metric (like page views) is actually accurate.
3. Engineers reason that because their metrics-related code was well unit-tested, the metrics themselves also should be accurate, even though there could be system-level errors or incorrect assumptions.

The net result is that metrics-related code tends to be less robust than code for other features. Errors can get introduced anywhere in the data collection or processing pipeline. It's easy to forget to measure a particular code path if there are multiple entry points. Data can get dropped when sent over the network, leading to inaccurate ground truth data. When data from multiple sources get merged, not paying attention to how different teams interpreted the definitions, units, or standards for what ought to have been logged can introduce inconsistencies. Bugs crop up in data processing and transformation pipelines. Data visualization is hard to unit test, so errors can often appear in a dashboard. As we can see, there are a myriad of reasons why it's hard to tell from visual inspection whether a metric that claims 1,024 views or a conversion rate of 3.1% is accurate.

Given the importance of metrics, investing the effort to ensure that your data is accurate is high-leverage. Here are some strategies that you can use to increase confidence in your data integrity:

- **Log data liberally, in case it turns out to be useful later on.** Eric Colson, former VP of Data Science and Engineering at Netflix, explained that Netflix throws reams of semi-structured logs into a scalable data store called Cassandra, and decides later on whether that data might be useful for analysis.[44]
- **Build tools to iterate on data accuracy sooner.** Real-time analytics address this issue, as do tools that visualize collected data during development. When I worked on the experiment and analytics frameworks at Quora, we built tools to easily inspect what was being logged by each interaction.[45] This paid off huge dividends.
- **Write end-to-end integration tests to validate your entire analytics pipeline.** These tests may be time-consuming to write. Ultimately, however, they will help increase confidence in your data integrity and also protect against future changes that might introduce inaccuracies.
- **Examine collected data sooner.** Even if you need to wait weeks or months to have enough data for a meaningful analysis, check the data sooner to ensure that a sufficient amount was logged correctly. Treat data measurement and analysis as parts of the product development workflow rather than as activities to be bolted on afterwards.

- **Cross-validate data accuracy by computing the same metric in multiple ways.** This is a great way to sanity check that the number is in the right ballpark.
- **When a number does look off, dig in to it early.** Understand what's going on. Figure out whether the discrepancy is due to a bug, a misinterpretation, or something else.

Make sure your data is reliable. The only thing worse than having no data is the illusion of having the right data.

Key Takeaways

- **Measure your progress.** It's hard to improve what you don't measure. How would you know what types of effort are well spent?
- **Carefully choose your top-level metric.** Different metrics incentivize different behaviors. Figure out which behaviors you want.
- **Instrument your system.** The higher your system's complexity, the more you need instrumentation to ensure that you're not flying blind. The easier it is to instrument more metrics, the more often you'll do it.
- **Know your numbers.** Memorize or have easy access to numbers that can benchmark your progress or help with back-of-the-envelope calculations.
- **Prioritize data integrity.** Having bad data is worse than having no data, because you'll make the wrong decisions thinking that you're right.

6

Validate Your Ideas Early and Often

Joshua Levy had barely slept for days. He and his 20-person team had just unveiled Cuil (pronounced "cool"), the stealth search engine highly anticipated as a potential Google-killer. [1] With over 120 billion pages in its web index, Cuil claimed to have crawled an index that was three times the size of Google's, on infrastructure that was only a tenth of the cost. [2] [3] And on July 28, 2008, millions of users finally got to try out what Levy and his team had been cooking up for the past few years. [4] But rather than popping open champagne bottles, the Director of Engineering was scrambling to fight fires and keep everything running under a brutal onslaught of traffic.

The crawling, indexing, and serving infrastructure running across over a thousand machines was aflame under the heavy load. [5] And because Cuil had built out its own computing hardware in an era before Amazon Web Services had popularized cloud computing, the engineering team didn't have many extra machines with idle capacity. Users were typing in distinct queries like their own names, and the diversity of searches was overwhelming the in-memory cache of common query results and slowing down the search engine. [6] Shards of the index were crashing and leaving gaping holes in the search results, and massive computations over petabytes of data were hitting hard-to-track bugs. It was very hard to keep things stable, let alone do fixes or upgrades. "It felt like being in a car knowing you're going off a cliff, and thinking, 'Well, maybe if we hit on the gas, we can make it across,'" Levy recounts.

To top all it off, it was clear that users weren't happy with the service. An editor from PC Magazine called Cuil "buggy," "slow," and "pathetic." [7] CNet characterized its search results as "incomplete, weird, and missing." [8] Time Magazine called it "lackluster," [9] and the Huffington Post called it "stupid." [10] Users criticized the poor quality of the search results and complained about how the search engine lacked rudimentary features like spelling correction. Most damningly, they pointed out that for the majority of queries, Cuil returned fewer results than Google, despite its larger index. The launch was a public relations disaster.

Ultimately, Cuil was a failed experiment—one that cost over $33 million in venture capital and decades of engineering person-years. "It definitely was a frustrating and humbling experience to work on something so hard and then see it all come to naught," reflected Levy. Levy had joined Cuil as an early engineer and bought into the founders' game-changing vision of building a better Google. "The company had a very solid set of engineers," he told me, and two of the founders even came with decorated pedigrees from Google's own search team. So what went wrong? How could Cuil have missed such obvious shortcomings in a product that so many tech bloggers wrote about?

When I asked Levy what key lessons he learned from this experience, the one that stood out was the importance of validating the product sooner. Because Cuil had wanted to make a big splash at launch and feared leaking details to the press, they hadn't hired any alpha testers to play around with the product. Prior to launch, there was no external feedback to point out that the search quality wasn't there, that the search engine wasn't returning enough results, and that users didn't care about the size of the index if it didn't actually lead to higher quality results. Cuil didn't even have anyone working full-time on spam, whereas Google had a whole team of engineers fighting web spam and an entire organization focused on search quality. Not validating their product early led Cuil to overinvest efforts in cost-efficient indexing and to underinvest in quality. This was a harsh lesson learned.

When Levy left Cuil to be the second hire at his next startup, BloomReach, he took that lesson with him. BloomReach builds a marketing platform to help e-commerce sites optimize their search traffic and maximize their online revenue. There were many unknowns about what the product would look like and what would and wouldn't work. Rather than repeat Cuil's fatal mistake of spending years building a product that nobody wanted, Levy and his team took a drastically different approach. They built a very minimal but functional system and released it to their beta customers within four months. Those customers shared thoughts on what they liked and didn't like and what they cared about, and that feedback helped the team prioritize what to build next.

Optimizing for feedback as soon as possible—in other words, understanding what customers actually want and then iterating on that feedback—has been critical for BloomReach's growth. The company now employs over 135 people, and counts top brands like Nieman Marcus and Crate & Barrel in its portfolio of customers. On average, it helps online brands generate 80% more non-branded search traffic, significantly increasing their revenue. [11] [12] "Don't delay … Get feedback. Figure out what's working," Levy, who eventually became the head of operations at BloomReach, told me. "That's by far better than trying to … build something and then trust that you got everything right—because you can't get everything right."

In Chapter 4, we learned that investing in iteration speed helps us get more things done. In this chapter, we'll learn how validating our ideas both early and often helps us get the *right* things done. We'll discuss the importance of finding low-effort and iterative ways to validate that we're on the right track and to reduce wasted effort. We'll learn how to use A/B testing to continuously validate our product changes with quantitative data, and we'll see how much impact that kind of testing can have. We'll examine a common anti-pattern—the one-person team—that sometimes hinders our ability to get feedback, and we'll address ways of dealing with that situation. Finally, we'll see how the theme of building feedback and validation loops applies to every decision we make.

Find Low-Effort Ways to Validate Your Work

During my junior year at MIT, three friends and I participated in the MASLab robotics competition. We had to build a one-foot-tall self-driving robot that could navigate around a field and gather red balls. [13] The first skill we taught our robot was how to drive forward toward a target. Simple enough, we thought. Our initial program scanned for a red ball with the robot's camera, turned the robot toward the target, and sent power to the motors until the robot reached its destination. Unfortunately, minor variations in the motor speed of the front and rear axles, differences in the tread of the tires, and slight bumps on the field surface all caused our simple-minded robot to drift off at an angle. The longer the path, the more these little errors compounded, and the less likely the robot was to reach the ball. We quickly realized that a more reliable approach was for the robot to move forward just a little bit, then re-check the camera and re-adjust the motors for errors in orientation, and repeat until it reached the target.

Our little robot's process for forward motion is not that different from how we should be moving forward in our work. Iterative approaches lead to fewer costly errors and give us opportunities between each iteration to collect data and correct our course. The shorter each iteration cycle, the more quickly we can learn from our mistakes. Conversely, the longer the iteration cycle, the more likely it is that incorrect assumptions and errors will compound. These cause us to veer off course and waste our time and effort. This is a key reason why the investments in iteration speed (discussed in Chapter 4) are so critical.

Oftentimes when we build products and set goals, we embark on paths that aren't clear-cut. We may have a general idea of where we're going but don't know the best way to get there. Or we may lack sufficient data to make an informed decision. The sooner that we gain a better understanding of a risky issue that impedes our progress, the earlier we can either address it to increase our chances of success, or change course to a more promising avenue. Zach Brock, an engineering manager at Square, frequently advises his team, "What's the scariest part of this project? That's the part with the most unknowns and the most risk. Do that part first." [14] Demystifying the riskiest areas first lets you proactively update your plan and avoid nasty surprises that might invalidate your efforts later. We'll revisit this theme of reducing risk early when we discuss how to improve our project estimation skills in Chapter 7.

When working on projects, in particular large ones, we should continually ask ourselves: *Can I expend a small fraction of the total effort to collect some data and validate that what I'm doing will work?* We often hesitate to add even 10% extra overhead because we're in a hurry to get things done or because we're overly confident about our implementation plans. It's true that this 10% might not end up contributing any useful insight or reusable work. On the other hand, it could save us the remaining 90% of wasted effort if it surfaces a large flaw in our plans.

Startup entrepreneurs and engineers think through these questions often, particularly when they're building what's called a "minimum viable product" (MVP). Eric Ries, author of *The Lean Startup,* defines the MVP as "that version of a new product which allows a team to collect the maximum amount of validated learning about customers with the least effort." [15] If you think that definition resembles our definition of leverage, you'd be spot on. When building an MVP, you want to focus on high-leverage activities that can validate hypotheses about your users as much as possible, using as little effort as possible, to maximize the chances that the product will succeed.

Sometimes, building an MVP requires being creative. When Drew Houston first started building Dropbox, an easy-to-use file-sharing tool, there were already countless other file-sharing applications on the market. Houston believed that users would prefer the seamless user experience his product could provide—but how could he validate this belief? His solution was to make a short 4-minute video as his MVP. [16] [17] Houston demoed a limited version of his product, showing files synchronizing seamlessly across a Mac, a Windows PC, and the web. Overnight, Dropbox's beta mailing list grew from 5k to 75k users, and Houston knew he was on to something. Dropbox used the MVP to build confidence and validate its premise, without having to invest too much work. As of February 2014, Dropbox has over 200 million users and is valued at $10 billion, [18] and it still continues to grow.

We might not all be working on startup products, but the principle of validating our work with small efforts holds true for many engineering projects. Suppose you're considering migrating from one software architecture to another. Perhaps your product is hitting the scalability limits of a MySQL database, and you're considering switching to a newer NoSQL architecture that claims to be more scalable. Or perhaps you're rewriting a service from one language to another with the goal of simplifying code maintenance, improving performance, or increasing your iteration speed. The migration would require a significant amount of effort, so how can you increase your confidence that completing it won't be a waste of time and that it will actually help achieve your goals?

One way to validate your idea would be to spend 10% of your effort building a small, informative prototype. Depending on your project goals, you can use your prototype for anything from measuring performance on a representative workload, to comparing the code footprint of the module you rewrote against the original module, to assessing the ease of adding new features. The cost of building a quick prototype doesn't amount to much in the scheme of the larger project, but the data that it produces can save you a significant amount of pain and effort if it surfaces problems early, or convinces you that the larger migration wouldn't be worthwhile.

Or suppose that you're redesigning the user interface of your product to make it speedier and more user-friendly. How can you increase confidence that your UI will boost user metrics without investing all the effort associated with a full redesign? 42Floors, a company that builds a search engine for office space rentals and commercial real estate listings, ran into this problem.[19] When users searched for office space on their product, they were shown all available listings via a Google Maps interface. Unfortunately, if there were many results, it could take upwards of 12 seconds to load them all. In their first attempt at a fix, 42Floors engineers spent three months building a faster view of office listings with big photos, infinite scrolling, and a mini-map. They expected the conversion rate of visitors who would request office tours to go up. However, none of their metrics moved even a little bit after they deployed the project.

The team had other ideas for what they could do, but no one wanted to invest so much effort into another redesign and have it fail. How could they validate those ideas in less time? The team came up with a clever solution: they decided to fake their redesign. They designed 8 Photoshop mockups, contracted a team to convert them to HTML, and ran a Google AdWords campaign that sent some users who searched for "new york office space" to these fake pages. The pages were pre-populated with static data and looked real to first-time visitors. Then, they measured what fraction of visitors requested tours. With a fraction of the effort they had invested in the first redesign, the team was able to use the conversion rates to validate 8 potential redesigns. They implemented the winning variation, shipped it to production, and finally got the conversion wins that they had been looking for.

The strategy of faking the full implementation of an idea to validate whether it will work is extremely powerful. At one point, Asana, a company that builds collaboration and task management software, was considering whether to implement a new Google Signup button on its home page. Its goal was to increase signups. Rather than building the entire signup flow, they validated the idea by adding a fake signup button: when visitors clicked the button, a pop-up message appeared, reading, "Thanks for your interest—the feature is coming soon." Asana engineers measured the click-through rates over a few days, and only built out the full flow after the data confirmed that it would help with signups. [20]

The list of scenarios in which small validations can save you time goes on and on. Maybe you have an idea for a scoring algorithm that you believe will improve ranking for a news feed. Rather than spending weeks building a production-quality system and running it over all the data, you can assess the new scoring metric on a small subset of data. You might have a brilliant product design idea; rather than building it in code, you can hack together a paper prototype or low-fidelity mock to show your teammates or participants in user studies. Or say you're asked if you'd be able to ship a new feature on an aggressive 10-week schedule. You can sketch out a timeline, validate whether you're on track after a week, and incorporate that data into your evaluation of whether the original schedule is even feasible. Or maybe you're contemplating tackling a gnarly bug. Before investing time into fixing it, you can use data from logs to validate whether the bug actually is affecting a sufficient numbers of users to justify spending your resources.

All these examples share a common takeaway lesson: Invest a small amount of work to gather data to validate your project assumptions and goals. In the long run, you'll save yourself a lot of wasted effort.

Continuously Validate Product Changes with A/B Testing

In June 2012, President Barack Obama's re-election campaign desperately needed more money. Obama's digital team decided to email his donor mailing list and explain that unless his supporters rallied together and raised support, Obama was at risk of being outspent by his opponent Mitt Romney. The email's proposed subject line, "Deadline: Join Michelle and me," was perfectly reasonable. But then the team began brainstorming other potential lines, ranging from "Change" to "Do this for Michelle" to "If you believe in what we're doing," to better catch donor attention. [21]

Ultimately, the email sent to 4.4 million subscribers' inboxes had an entirely different subject line: "I will be outspent." This line was deliberately engineered. The team had tested 17 sample subjects on small sets of subscribers and found that this particular wording would raise about 6x as much as some other subject lines—over $2 million more. And in fact, that single campaign email raised an astounding $2.6 million dollars. That's a huge payoff for tweaking a few words of copy.

Obama's campaign email test is a prime example of how using data to validate your ideas, even ones that seem perfectly reasonable, can be extremely high-leverage. More importantly, the email wasn't just a one-off test. It was part of a systematic process that the team established so that they could validate and optimize every single email campaign with real data and not just their intuition. They found the tests to be so effective that they hired an engineering team to build tools for measuring and improving email effectiveness, and a staff of 20 writers whose sole job was to brainstorm and draft email variations. [22]

In 2012, the team sent over 400 national fundraising emails and tested 10,000 different variations of subject lines, email copy, donation amounts, formatting, highlighting, font size, and buttons. [23] Each email from the Obama campaign was tested on as many as 18 smaller groups, and the best variations often raised 5 to 7x as many donations as the worst one. [24] Over the course of 20 months, the heavily-tested fundraising emails raised the majority of the Obama campaign's $690 million via online donations, well worth the investment of the team's time. [25] [26]

The concept of testing ideas with data doesn't just apply to emails; it applies to product development as well. Even a well-tested, cleanly designed, and scalable software product doesn't deliver much value if users don't engage with it or customers don't buy it. One problem that typically arises with product changes is that the team observes a shift in metrics (you *have* picked the right metric for your goal, right?) but can't be confident how much of the lift (or drop) can be attributed to the product launch. Was any of the movement due to traffic fluctuations from the day of the week, press coverage, ongoing product changes, performance issues, outstanding bugs, or anything else on the laundry list of factors? A powerful tool to isolate these effects and validate whether something is working is an experiment called an A/B test.

In an A/B test, a random subset of users sees a change or a new feature; everyone else in the control group doesn't. An A/B testing framework typically assigns users to buckets based on their browser cookie, user ID, or a random number, and the bucket determines the product variant that they see. Assuming there's no bias in bucket assignment, each bucket gets affected by traffic fluctuations in the same way. Therefore, by comparing metrics across the experimental and control groups, any statistically significant differences can then be attributed solely to differences in the change's variant. A/B tests provide a scientific way of measuring the effects of the change while controlling for other variations, letting us assess the product's impact if it's launched to all users.

An A/B test doesn't just help you decide which variation to launch. Even if you were absolutely convinced that a certain change would improve metrics, an A/B test tells you *how much* better that variation actually is. Quantifying that improvement informs whether it makes sense to keep investing in the same area. For instance, a large product investment that only yields a 1% lift in retention rates means that you'd likely find more leverage elsewhere, whereas you might decide to double down on the same area had it yielded a 10% improvement. You won't know which situation you're in unless you measure your impact.

A/B tests also encourage an iterative approach to product development, in which teams validate their theories and iterate toward changes that work. The metrics-driven culture at Etsy, the online marketplace for handmade crafts that we discussed in Chapter 5, prompted them to build their own A/B testing framework. This enabled them to continuously experiment with their product and measure the effects of those experiments. Marc Hedlund, Etsy's former Senior VP of Product Development and Engineering, told me the story of when his team redesigned the product listing page for a seller's item. This particular page displays a large photo of the product, product details, seller information, and a button to add the item to the shopping cart. Listing pages for the handmade and vintage products in Etsy's marketplace get nearly 15 million views per day and are often a visitor's first impression. [27] Before the redesign, nearly 22% of visitors entered the site through the listing page, usually by clicking on a Google search result, but 53% of them would bounce and leave immediately. [28] As part of the redesign, Etsy engineers wanted to reduce bounce rates, clarify to shoppers that they were purchasing from independent designers, makers, and curators, and make it easier for customers to shop and check out quickly.

This is where Etsy took a non-traditional approach. Many other engineering and product teams design and fully build out a product or feature before launching them to users. They might then discover, after months of work, that what they built didn't actually move core metrics as much as they had hoped. The Etsy listing page team approached their redesign much more incrementally. They would articulate a hypothesis, construct an A/B test to validate the hypothesis, and then iterate based on what they learned. For example, they hypothesized that "showing a visitor more marketplace items would decrease bounce rate," ran an experiment to show images of similar products at the top of the listing page, and analyzed whether the metrics supported or rejected the hypothesis (in fact, it reduced bounce rate by nearly 10%). Based on that experiment, the team learned that they should incorporate images of more marketplace products into their final design.

Like the team that worked on Obama's emails, the engineers at Etsy repeatedly tested different hypotheses using a feedback loop until they had a data-informed intuition of what would and would not work in the final design. "They did this redesign, and it took like eight months or so. And it was very rigorously driven by [A/B] testing," Hedlund explained. "It came out, and it had just ridiculously good numbers—far and away the single best project that we shipped in terms of performance. And it was quantifiable. We knew what the effect was going be." In 2013, Etsy topped $1 billion in sales. [29] Its experiment-driven culture played a large role in that growth.

Similarly, one of the highest-leverage investments that we made at Quora was constructing our in-house A/B testing framework. We built a simple abstraction for defining experiments, wrote tools to help us verify the different variants during development, enabled push-button deployments of tests, and automated the collection of real-time analytics—all of which helped to optimize our iteration loop for getting new ideas in front of live traffic. [30] The framework enabled us to run hundreds of user experiments. It also allowed us to measure the effects of changes resulting from a new signup flow, new interface features, and behind-the-scenes ranking adjustments. Without our A/B testing framework, we would've been guessing at what would improve our product rather than approaching the question scientifically.

Building your own A/B testing framework might seem daunting. Fortunately, there are many existing tools that you can use to test your product hypotheses. Free or open source A/B testing frameworks include Etsy's feature-flagging API, [31] Vanity, [32] Genetify, [33] and Google Content Experiments. [34] If you want more tooling and support, you can pay a monthly fee for software like Optimizely, [35] Apptimize, [36] Unbounce, [37] and Visual Website Optimizer. [38] Given how much you can learn through A/B testing, it's well worth the investment.

When deciding what to A/B test, time is your limiting resource. Hone into differences that are high-leverage and practically significant, the ones that actually matter for your particular scale. Google can afford to run tests on tiny details. For example, they analyzed which of 41 shades of blue they should use for a search result link, and picking the right shade netted the search company an additional $200M in ad revenue per year. [39] Google, of course, has enough traffic to achieve statistical significance in a reasonable amount of time; and, more to the point, even an ostensibly minute 0.01% improvement in revenue represents $3.1M to a company with an annual revenue of $31B. [40] For most other companies, however, such a test would be prohibitively expensive in terms of time and traffic; the gains, even if we could detect them, would not be meaningful. Initially, it's tricky to determine what's practically significant, but as you run more experiments, you'll be able to prioritize better and determine which tests might give large payoffs.

Performed correctly, A/B testing enables us to validate our product ideas and transform an otherwise-baffling black box of user behavior data into understandable and actionable knowledge. It enables us to iteratively validate our product changes, and it assures us that our time and effort are well-spent and that we're achieving our goals. Even when the luxury of quantitative data through A/B testing isn't available, however, we can still validate our ideas through qualitative feedback. We'll spend the remaining two sections discussing how.

Beware the One-Person Team

Given the importance of validating early and often, a common anti-pattern to watch out for is the one-person team. An iconic Silicon Valley story features the engineer who designs and builds an ambitious system all on his own. Expecting to launch his project soon, he sends a large code review to a teammate—only to learn about a major design flaw he'd missed, and to be informed that he should have built his system in a completely different way.

One summer, while I was interning at Google, I built a search feature for Orkut (one of Google's early social networking sites). I worked diligently on the project, tweaking the indexing, ranking, and filtering of user profiles in search results. I sanity-checked my initial design with other engineers, but because I got more and more pieces working every day and didn't have much experience with code reviews, I figured I didn't really need to show my actual code around. The last week of my internship, I packaged my summer's work into a multi-thousand-line code review. Google classifies code commits based on the number of lines of code changed. Sitting in my mentor's inbox was an email labeled: "Edmond sent you a ginormous code review."

Over lunch, I casually mentioned my code bomb to some other interns. I was feeling rather smug about what I'd accomplished that summer, but they were horrified. "You what?!? What if your mentor found a glaring design issue? Will your mentor even have time to review everything? Would you even have time to fix all the issues if he *did* find something? What if he doesn't let you check in your ginormous code commit?" My heart sank. Would my entire summer's work be wasted? I spent my last week at Google worrying about how events would unfold.

Fortunately, my mentor was accommodating and offered to handle any issues that surfaced after my internship. I was able to commit my code, and the feature launched within a few months of me leaving. But too much was left up to chance, and my whole project could have been scrapped. In hindsight, it's clear that if I had just committed my code more iteratively and in chunks, my work wouldn't have existed in isolation for so long and I would have eliminated a large amount of risk. My mentor would have had a much easier time reviewing my code, and I would have received valuable feedback along the way that I could have applied to future code. In the end, I got lucky: I learned a lesson about solo projects early in my career and with little cost.

There are many situations where you have to work on a project by yourself. Sometimes, in an attempt to get rid of the communication overhead, managers or technical leads staff single-person projects. Other times, teams split themselves up into one-person subteams so they can tackle smaller tasks independently and make coordination easier. Some organizations emphasize in their promotion processes that an engineer has to demonstrate ownership in a project; that can incentivize engineers to work on their own in the hopes of maximizing their chances for promotion. Some engineers simply prefer to work more independently.

While there isn't anything inherently wrong with working on a one-person project, it does introduce additional risks that, if not addressed, can reduce your chance of success. First and foremost, it adds friction to the process of getting feedback—and you need feedback to help validate that what you're doing will work. It's hard to get good feedback on a code review, for instance, unless the reviewer works on your team and shares your project context. If you're not mindful of setting up a feedback loop, it can be tempting to defer getting feedback on something until you think it's nearly perfect. And if you don't find out until the end that you've gone in the wrong direction, you'll waste a lot of effort.

There are other risks of one-person projects as well. The lows of a project are more demoralizing when you're working alone. Sand traps that you struggle to get out of, monotonous work that you need to grind through, and bugs that seem to defy all understanding become less draining and more bearable when there's someone there to share your pain. A single stall can grind the project to a halt, causing deadlines to slip (we'll see how to address this in Chapter 7). I've been in that situation, and I've seen it happen to other engineers as well. When there's at least one additional person on the project, however, the team can still maintain overall momentum and preserve morale even if someone gets stuck.

Similarly, the highs can be less motivating when you're working alone. Celebrating an achievement with teammates is a great way to boost morale. If you work alone, who's going to give you a high-five when you finally fix that frustrating data corruption bug? In addition, knowing that your teammates are depending on you increases your sense of accountability. The desire to help your team succeed can override the dips in motivation that everyone occasionally feels.

Even if you find yourself working a one-person project, don't despair. These risks are surmountable. Steve Wozniak invented the Apple I and Apple II computers, designing the hardware and the software by himself at home and later in Steve Jobs's garage. How were his inventions transformed from hobbyist toys for the Homebrew Computer Club into pillars of the personal computer revolution? One key factor for Wozniak was that Jobs provided him with a counterbalance and a feedback loop to validate his ideas. Although Wozniak was an introvert and ostensibly doing his own thing, he did not isolate himself and work in a vacuum—and spurred on by Jobs' vision and ambition, the two men eventually created Apple.[41]

Like Wozniak, we can also set up the necessary feedback channels to increase the chances of our projects succeeding. Here are some strategies:

- **Be open and receptive to feedback.** If you adopt a defensive mindset about your work, it will be difficult for you to listen to feedback—and people will be less willing to offer it in the future. Instead, optimize for learning. View feedback and criticism not as personal attacks but as opportunities for improvement.
- **Commit code early and often.** Large code changes are hard to review, take longer to get feedback, and are a big waste of time and work if it turns out that there's a design flaw. Focus on making iterative progress, and use those iterative commits as forcing functions for soliciting feedback. Don't be the person who sends out the ginormous code review.
- **Request code reviews from thorough critics.** There is a large variance in the rigor with which different engineers review code. If you're in a hurry to ship something, you might be tempted to send your code review to the engineer who skims and approves. But if you're optimizing for quality or if you want to make sure your approach works, you'll find much more leverage asking for a code review from someone who gives thoughtful criticism. It's better to get harsh feedback from a teammate early on than to get it from users later when something doesn't work.
- **Ask to bounce ideas off your teammates.** The most direct path to getting feedback is to request it. Ask a teammate who's lounging around the water cooler if you might have a few minutes of her time to talk through some ideas on a whiteboard. Research shows that explaining an idea to another person is one of the best ways of learning it yourself;[42] moreover, your explanation might reveal holes in your own understanding. Most people want to be helpful and appreciate a quick break to grapple with a different and possibly interesting problem. That said, if you want to keep the feedback channel open in the future, be respectful of your co-workers' time. Prepare beforehand. Make sure that you can articulate the problem that you're try-

ing to solve and the approaches that you've already tried. After the discussion, reciprocate with an offer to be a sounding board for their ideas.

- **Design the interface or API of a new system first.** After your interface is designed, prototype what the client code would look like if your feature were built. Creating a concrete picture of the interactions will surface poor assumptions or missing requirements, saving you time in the long run.
- **Send out a design document before devoting your energy to your code.** While it might seem like it adds extra overhead, this is an example of investing 10% of your effort to validate the other 90% of work that you plan to do. The document doesn't have to be particularly formal—it could just be a detailed email—but it should be comprehensive enough for your reader to understand what you're trying to do and be able to ask clarifying questions.
- **If possible, structure ongoing projects so that there is some shared context with your teammates.** Rather than working on a separate project in parallel with your teammates, consider working together on the same project and tackling the other project together afterwards. Or, consider working in the same focus area as your teammates. This creates a shared context that, in turn, reduces the friction in discussions and code reviews. Serializing team projects to increase collaboration rather than doing them independently and in parallel can provide learning benefits as well: each project takes a shorter amount of calendar time to complete, so within a given timeframe, you can be exposed to a larger diversity of project areas.
- **Solicit buy-in for controversial features before investing too much time.** This might mean floating the idea in conversations and building a prototype to help convince relevant stakeholders. Sometimes, engineers misconstrue or dismiss this type of selling and marketing as office politics, but it's a fairly logical decision from the viewpoint of leverage. If a conversation to get feedback only takes a few hours but an implementation takes weeks, the shorter path to earlier feedback is extremely valuable. Failing to get buy-in from those who understand the domain might mean you're on the wrong path. However, even if you think they're wrong, the conversations will at least surface the issues that others care about and that you should address if you decide to proceed.

The goal of all these strategies is to overcome the friction of collecting feedback when you're working alone so that you can validate your ideas earlier and more often. They're particularly important if you're working on a one-person project, where the default behavior, unless you're proactive, is to work in isolation. But the same strategies can be equally valuable even when you're working on a team. Brian Fitzpatrick and Ben Collins-Sussman, two Googlers who started the Chicago engineering office, capture the mentality well when they write in *Team Geek*, "[S]oftware development is a team sport." [43] Even if you prefer to work independently, you'll be more effective if you conceptualize your work as a team activity and build in feedback loops.

Build Feedback Loops for Your Decisions

Whether you're working on large implementation efforts, developing products, or working on teams, it's important to build feedback loops to validate your ideas. But even more broadly, the principle of validation generalizes to any decision you make.

Sometimes, validation is difficult. There might not be many data points, or there may only be qualitative data available. Which programming language should you use to write a new service? What should the abstraction or the interface look like? Is the design simple enough for what you're trying to do? Is it worth the engineering effort to invest in more scaling right now?

Moreover, the more senior of an engineer you become (and particularly if you enter into management), the tougher and the more nebulous your decisions become. How should you coordinate your team's work? Can your team afford to pause (or not pause) feature development to reduce technical debt? Should performance reviews and feedback be given anonymously, directly, or in an open setting? How should you arrange compensation structure to improve recruiting and retention?

When I interviewed Nimrod Hoofien, a Director of Engineering at Facebook, he said that creating a feedback loop is necessary for all aspects of a job. "It applies to recruiting. It applies to team design. It applies to how you build your culture. It applies to your compensation structure," Hoofien explained.

"Any decision you make ... should have a feedback loop for it. Otherwise, you're just ... guessing."

Previously, when Hoofien was the Senior VP of Engineering at Ooyala, he experimented with various aspects of building effective engineering teams, and built feedback loops to learn from those experiments. For example, when figuring out the optimal number of team members to maximize effectiveness, Hoofien varied the size of the team and looked for obvious dysfunctions. "The most common [dysfunction] is that the team starts behaving like two teams," observed Hoofien, "and these two groups will only work [on tasks] on their side of the board." Another experiment was tightly tying bonuses to engineering-wide metrics like reliability. It launched to an overwhelming positively sentiment because the bonus equation was clear-cut, but then was rolled back after a quarter because engineers became upset that they didn't have enough control over the metrics.

Hoofien has run similar experiments when researching fundamental questions in effective team structure at Ooyala: should tech leads also be managers (yes); should positions like site reliability engineers, designers, and product managers be embedded in development teams (yes for product managers); and under which situations should teams adopt methodologies like Scrum (it varied). Hoofien deployed many of these experiments for a few weeks and then gathered data—sometimes by just talking to people—to understand what worked and what didn't. Other ideas, however, like a radical proposal for doubling the salary of the best engineers to create a superstar team, were run as thought experiments. Hoofien gathered the engineering tech leads and discussed possible consequences (they predicted that non-top performers would quit in droves and that it would take too long to find great people to replace them).

The principle of validation shows us that many of our work decisions, which we might take for granted or adopt blindly from other people, in fact are testable hypotheses. How to discover what works best varies based on the situation and the people involved, and Hoofien's learnings on team setup might vary from your own. But regardless of whether we engineers are writing code, creating a product, or managing teams, the methodology of how to make decisions remains the same. And at its core, the willingness to run experiments demonstrates the scientific method at work.

Validation means formulating a hypothesis about what might work, designing an experiment to test it, understanding what good and bad outcomes look like, running the experiment, and learning from the results. You may not be able to test an idea as rigorously as you could with an A/B test and ample amounts of traffic, but you can still transform what otherwise would be guesswork into informed decision-making. Given the right mindset—a willingness to test your ideas—there's little that you can't validate by building feedback loops.

Key Takeaways

- **Approach a problem iteratively to reduce wasted effort.** Each iteration provides opportunities to validate new ideas. Iterate quickly to learn quickly.
- **Reduce the risk of large implementations by using small validations.** Invest a little extra effort to figure out if the rest of your plan is worth doing.
- **Use A/B testing to continuously validate your product hypotheses.** By incrementally developing a product and identifying what does and doesn't work, you increase the probability that your efforts are aligned with what users actually want.
- **When working on a solo project, find ways of soliciting regular feedback.** It may be easy and comfortable to keep working in a silo, but you run the huge risk of overlooking something that, if spotted early, could save you lots of wasted effort.
- **Adopt a willingness to validate your decisions.** Rather than making an important decision and moving on, set up feedback loops that enable you to collect data and assess your work's value and effectiveness.

7

Improve Your Project Estimation Skills

In August 2008, two months after I had joined Ooyala, the engineering team embarked on a mission to completely rewrite our Flash-based video player. Ooyala, an online video startup, helped customers like TV Guide, the Association of Tennis Professionals, Armani, and TechCrunch manage and serve the thousands of videos on their websites. We offered a content management system, video transcoding services, and a player that customers embedded on their web pages to deliver videos to their viewers.

Our top-tier customers cared about video performance: they wanted a player that would load faster, quickly adjust a viewer's video quality based on available network bandwidth, and support additional custom integrations. We wanted to make our customers happy. But because a large amount of technical debt had accumulated in the player codebase in the 18 months since the company had been founded, developing new features was slow and error-prone. There were no automated tests to ensure that changes wouldn't cause regressions. We knew we wouldn't be able to ship these and future customer requirements quickly enough without a more reliable foundation. And so we decided to rewrite the player to make it more modular and performant, and to build a cleaner and better-tested codebase.

During one of our weekly meetings, the CTO and the product manager unveiled the rewrite plan and schedule to the 8-person engineering team. Gantt charts broke down the work assignments, showed how long different tasks would take, and mapped out the dependencies between various parts. We were slated to work in parallel on the video playback, analytics, ads, user interface, and other modules, and then to spend a week at the end integrating everything together. A team of 3 senior engineers estimated it would take 4 months for the entire team to complete the project, right in time for the Christmas holidays. New feature development would pause for the next four months, and account managers had been instructed to push back on customer requests during that time.

It was an ambitious project, and I was looking forward to it. I was impressed by how much the team had accomplished in the past year and a half. However, the sprint to build a product quickly had left the codebase in a tattered state. I was used to building on top of Google's well-tested codebase that allowed quick feature development, and I viewed Ooyala's rewrite as an opportunity to bring us closer toward that state. I raised an eyebrow when I noticed the schedule overlaps and the aggressive assignment of the same engineer to two projects at once. But since we couldn't afford to delay new feature development for much longer than 4 months, I brushed off the worry and hoped that we'd finish some pieces earlier than expected.

A few hiccups surfaced along the way that, with more experience, I would have recognized as red flags. We wanted to make the analytics module more extensible by encoding analytics data in Thrift, a new protocol that Facebook had open sourced, but we had only dedicated a few days to this endeavor. And because Thrift didn't support ActionScript, the programming language for Flash, I had to write a C++ compiler extension for Thrift to auto-generate the ActionScript code we needed; that in itself took over a week. We wanted to integrate some new third-party ad modules into the new player, but they turned out to be buggy; one, under some fairly normal conditions, even caused the video player to screech painfully. While building the video playback module, a teammate discovered that one of Adobe's core, low-level interfaces that we wanted to use for better performance didn't reliably report whether the video was buffering or playing. We had to painstakingly develop heuristics to understand what was happening.

As we approached the December deadline, we knew we were falling behind. We plowed ahead anyway, mentioning to the release manager that, if we weren't careful, our launch might be pushed back into January. Even then, I don't think anyone on the team had an inkling of how much we would actually slip.

The new player—ironically named "Swift"—fully shipped 5 months later in May 2009, nearly 9 months after the project initially started. [1] Our journey—while formative and eye-opening—was anything but swift. Had we known that the project would have taken 9 months instead of 4, we would've thoroughly explored other alternatives like scoping down the project, doing a more incremental rewrite, or cutting back on other customer obligations. Instead, I worried with every passing month whether our small startup would survive the late schedule. We were in the middle of the 2009 recession; customers had tight budgets and venture capitalists were loathe to fund. Fortunately, our company stayed afloat, and the launch opened up many other business opportunities. Today, Ooyala delivers over 1 billion videos to nearly 200 million unique viewers across the globe every month. [2]

I've since learned, both from my own experiences and from discussions with other engineers, that the Ooyala story isn't all that out of the ordinary. Windows Vista slipped behind by over 3 years. [3] [4] Netscape 5.0 slipped by 2 years, and the browser saw its market share plummet from 80% to 20%. [5] [6] The game Daikatana, aggressively slated to launch in 7 months, slipped multiple times; it didn't launch until two and half years past the original delivery date, went millions of dollars overbudget, and led to the demise of the company. In 2009, after studying over 50,000 software projects, the Standish Group concluded that 44% of projects are delivered late, overbudget, or missing requirements; 24% fail to complete; and the average slipped project overruns its time budget by 79%. [7]

Project estimation is one of the hardest skills that an effective engineer needs to learn. But it's crucial to master: businesses need accurate estimates to make long-term plans for their products. They need to know when resources might free up to work on upcoming features or when they can promise feature requests to customers. And even when we don't have pressure to ship against a deadline, how long we think a project will take affects our decisions of what to work on.

We'll always operate under imperfect information. Therefore, successful project planning requires increasing the accuracy of our project estimates and increasing our ability to adapt to changing requirements. These two goals are particularly important for larger projects. Short projects don't tend to slip too much in absolute terms. A project estimated to take a few hours might slip to a few days, and one estimated for a few days might slip by a week or two. We sometimes don't even notice these little blips. But then there are the multi-week and multi-month projects that slip by months, or sometimes even years. These become the war stories.

In this chapter, we'll arm you with the tools to take charge of your own project plans and push back against unrealistic schedules. We'll look at ways of decomposing project estimates to increase accuracy. We'll walk through how we can do a better job of budgeting for the unknown. We'll talk about how to clearly define a project's scope and establish measurable milestones, and then we'll cover how to reduce risk as early as possible so that we can adapt sooner. And finally, we'll close with a discussion of why we need to be careful not to use overtime to sprint toward a deadline if we find ourselves falling behind: we may actually still be in the middle of a marathon.

Use Accurate Estimates to Drive Project Planning

"How long do you think it will take to finish this project?" We're often asked this question on software projects, and our estimates, even if they're inaccurate, feed into other business decisions. Poor estimates can be costly, so how do we do better?

Steve McConnell, in his book *Software Estimation*, lays out a working definition of a good estimate. "A good estimate," he writes, "is an estimate that provides a clear enough view of the project reality to allow the project leadership to make good decisions about how to control the project to hit its targets." [8] His definition distinguishes the notion of an *estimate*, which reflects our best guess about how long or how much work a project will take, from a *target*, which captures a desired business goal. Engineers create estimates, and managers and business leaders specify targets. How to effectively handle gaps between the estimates and targets is the focus of this chapter.

Project schedules often slip because we allow the target to alter the estimate. Business leaders set a particular deadline for a project—say 3 months out. Engineers estimate that the feature requirements will take 4 months to build. After a heated discussion about how the deadline is immovable, perhaps because the sales team has already promised the project to a customer, engineers then massage their estimates to shoehorn the necessary work into an unrealistic 3-month project plan. Reality sinks in when the deadline approaches, and the team must then readjust their prior commitments.

A more productive approach is to use the estimates to inform project planning, rather than the other way around. Given that it's not possible to deliver all features by the target date, is it more important to hold the date constant and deliver what *is* possible, or to hold the feature set constant and push back the date until all the features can be delivered? Understanding your business priorities fosters more productive conversations, letting you devise a better project plan. Doing so requires accurate estimates.

So how do we produce accurate estimates that provide us the flexibility we need? Here are some concrete strategies:

- **Decompose the project into granular tasks.** When estimating a large project, decompose it into small tasks and estimate each one of them. If a task will take more than two days, decompose it further. A long estimate is a hiding place for nasty surprises. Treat it as a warning that you haven't thought through the task thoroughly enough to understand what's involved. The more granular a task's breakdown, the less likely that an unconsidered subtask will sneak up later.
- **Estimate based on how long tasks will take, not on how long you or someone else wants them to take.** It's natural for managers to adopt some version of Parkinson's law, which argues that "work expands so as to fill the time available for its completion."[9] Managers challenge estimates, pushing

for tasks to be completed sooner. If you've made your estimates granular, however, you can defend them more easily. One compromise that I've seen is to use the estimates to set a public goal and the manager's demands to set an internal stretch goal.

- **Think of estimates as probability distributions, not best-case scenarios.** Tom DeMarco, in his book *Controlling Software Projects,* writes that we often treat an estimate as "the most optimistic prediction that has a non-zero probability of coming true." Estimation becomes a game of "what's the earliest date by which you can't prove you won't be finished?" [10] Because we operate with imperfect information, we instead should consider our estimates as probability distributions over a range of outcomes, spanning the best-case and worst-case scenarios. Instead of telling a product manager or other stakeholder that we'll finish a feature in 6 weeks, we might instead tell them, "There's a 50% likelihood that we can deliver the feature 4 weeks from now, and a 90% chance that we can deliver it within 8 weeks."
- **Let the person doing the actual task make the estimate.** People have different skill sets and levels of familiarity with the codebase. Therefore, what takes you one hour to complete might take someone else three hours. As much as possible, have the person who will work on a task do the actual estimation. Part of what made the estimates for Ooyala's player rewrite project unrealistic is that a small set of people estimated the work for the entire team. Divvying up the estimation work also enables more team members to practice estimation skills and builds team-wide visibility into how different members over- or underestimate their work (most people underestimate). When I now need to set project goals, I schedule sessions with my team where we dedicate time to estimate work.
- **Beware of anchoring bias.** Dan Ariely, a Duke professor who studies behavioral economics, conducted an experiment where he asked students to write down the last two digits of their social security number and then estimate the price of a bottle of wine. Students with higher social security number digits estimated significantly higher prices for the wine, sometimes more than twice as high. The arbitrary numbers had subconsciously anchored and affected their estimates. [11] A similar effect often happens in

software projects where a manager might casually guess at the amount of work (again, usually an underestimate) required for a project or ask you for a quick ballpark estimate. Avoid committing to an initial number before actually outlining the tasks involved, as a low estimate can set an initial anchor that makes it hard to establish a more accurate estimate later on.

- **Use multiple approaches to estimate the same task.** This can help increase confidence that your approach is sound. For example, suppose you're building a new feature. You can 1) decompose the project into granular tasks, estimate each individual task, and create a bottom-up estimate; 2) gather historical data on how long it took to build something similar; and 3) count the number of subsystems you have to build and estimate the average time required for each one.
- **Beware the mythical man-month.** In engineering, project durations typically get measured in terms of person-hours, person-days, person-weeks, or person-months—i.e. the number of hours, days, weeks, or months of work that it takes an average engineer to complete a project. Unfortunately, this type of accounting leads to the myth that people and time are interchangeable. But just because one woman can give birth to a baby in nine months doesn't mean that nine women can give birth to a baby in one month. As Frederick Brooks explains in *The Mythical Man-Month*, as additional members join, the communication overhead from meetings, emails, one-on-ones, discussions, etc., grows quadratically with the size of the team. [12] [13] Moreover, new team members require time to ramp up on a project before they're productive, so don't assume that adding more people will shorten a project timeline.
- **Validate estimates against historical data.** Joel Spolsky, the co-founder of Stack Exchange, argues for using data-driven estimates backed by historical evidence. [14] If you know that historically, you've tended to underestimate by 20%, then you'll know that it's worthwhile to scale up your overall estimate by 25%. Or, you might argue that because you increased the growth rate of users or revenue by 25% last quarter, you might expect to do something similar this quarter.

- **Use timeboxing to constrain tasks that can grow in scope.** You can always spend more time researching which database technology or which JavaScript library to use for a new feature, but there will be diminishing returns on the time invested and growing costs on the schedule. Plan instead to allocate a fixed amount of time, or a *time box*, to open-ended activities. Rather than estimating that the research will likely take three days, commit to making the best possible decision you can, given the available data after three days.
- **Allow others to challenge estimates.** Because estimation is hard, we have a tendency to cut corners or eyeball numbers. By reviewing estimates at a team meeting, we can increase accuracy and buy-in at the cost of some additional overhead. Others may have knowledge or experience that can help highlight poor or incomplete estimates.

In Chapter 6, we learned that iteratively validating our ideas can lead us to better engineering outcomes. In the same way, iteratively revising our estimates can lead us to better project outcomes. Estimates contain more uncertainty at the beginning of a project, but the variance decreases as we flesh out the details. Use incoming data to revise existing estimates and, in turn, the project plan; otherwise, it will remain based on stale information.

Measuring the actual time it takes to perform a task and comparing it against the estimated time helps reduce the error bounds both when we're revising past estimates or making future ones. Over time, the evidence teaches us whether we tend to underestimate or overestimate, or if we're usually on target. From that data, we may, for instance, adopt a rule of thumb of multiplying our engineering estimates by a factor of 2 to capture unestimated tasks. As discussed in Chapter 5, we should measure what we want to improve, which in this case, is our project estimation skills. When schedules slip for small tasks, pause to consider whether future tasks will be affected as well.

A little measurement can go a long way. For one project where a team had to port a Python application to Scala, I set up a simple spreadsheet for team members to track how many hours they estimated a task would take and how long it actually took. Most team members initially underestimated, often by a factor of two. Within a week or two, the visibility enabled people to get a more accurate sense of how many lines of code they could migrate in a week. This paid off later when it helped them make more accurate estimates of timeframes for future milestones.

Discovering that certain tasks take much longer than expected lets us know sooner if we're falling behind. This, in turn, allows us to adjust the schedule or cut lower-priority features sooner. Those adjustments aren't possible if we're not aware how behind we are.

Budget for the Unknown

Many software projects miss their deadlines for multiple reasons, and it's usually not due to a lack of hard work. The engineering team at Ooyala certainly didn't lack talent or motivation. It was just as strong—if not stronger—than the typical team I worked with at Google. Most people pulled 70–80-hour weeks for months, and many of us, trying to finish the project, coded away even as we visited family over the holidays.

But try as we might, we just could not deliver the player rewrite on time. We had underestimated the timeframes for individual tasks, and that mistake alone might have been salvageable. What caused the schedule to slip excessively were all the unknown projects and issues that we hadn't estimated or accounted for at all. These included:

- Developing a unit testing harness for our new codebase, and writing our own mocking and assertion libraries for testing. These were tasks that we wanted to start doing as a best practice, but they hadn't been included in the original estimates.
- Realizing that a set of style guidelines could improve long-term code quality and that we should develop those guidelines before writing so much code.
- Getting interrupted by a few high-priority customer deals, each of which pulled a few engineers off the team for a week or two.

- Debugging video corruption issues that would crash Adobe's player if a user jumped to video frames in certain, difficult-to-reproduce ways on Internet Explorer.
- Firefighting scalability problems in the product as our customers' video libraries grew larger and we needed to process more analytics data per day.
- Losing an early engineer to another company mid-project, necessitating a large amount of knowledge transfer and work redistribution.
- Resuming new product development after 4 months, since the organization couldn't afford to postpone it further.
- Rewriting user interface components from scratch instead of using the third-party rendering libraries we had previously used, to meet the goal of reducing the size of the player's binary.
- Migrating our Subversion repository to Git to improve our development speed.

Each of these would have been surmountable in isolation. But the compounded effects of each event wreaked havoc with our schedule.

In his book *The Mythical Man-Month*, Frederick Brooks explains that my particular project experience actually reflects a general pattern in slipped software projects. He writes, "When one hears of disastrous schedule slippage in a project, he imagines that a series of major calamities must have befallen it. Usually, however, the disaster is due to termites, not tornadoes." [15] Little decisions and unknowns caused the Ooyala schedule to slip slowly, one day at a time.

We can better deal with unknowns by acknowledging that the longer a project is, the more likely that an unexpected problem will arise. The first step in dealing with this is to separate estimated work time from calendar time. Deadlines often catch us by surprise because we conflate statements like "this project will take one month of engineering work to complete" with "this project will be completed in one calendar month." Our estimates more naturally revolve around the time required to complete work, but managers, customers, and marketers think in terms of delivery dates. The problem is that a month of estimated work takes longer than one calendar month to complete.

As engineers, our jobs typically require us to fix outstanding bugs, conduct interviews, attend team meetings, hold one-on-ones with our managers, participate in pager duty rotations, train new engineers who join the team, respond to email, and tackle many other recurring duties. Once you factor in these details, an 8-hour workday doesn't actually provide 8 hours of working time on a project.

One-off interruptions happen as well. Engineering organizations may schedule bug fixing days, hackathons, off-sites, or performance reviews. Operations teams may schedule mandatory downtime of core developer services for upgrades, maintenance, or data migrations. The sales team may urgently need some custom work to be done to close a deal. Unexpected outages or high-priority security bugs may need to be fixed. A sudden drop in a key business metric may require investigation. Team members may fall sick, get called for jury duty, or head out on vacation. In any given week, the probability that any one of these interruptions happens may be predictable or low. But the larger and longer a project, the more likely that some subset of these factors will affect some members of the team and throw off the schedule in a significant way.

The effect of these interruptions is further compounded when schedules slip. Suppose that after missing a deadline, a team estimates that there is still one more month of work remaining. That month is likely to expand for the exact same reasons as before. Moreover, there may be a buildup of demand for engineering time immediately after the original delivery date. Teammates may have scheduled their vacations for a week after the original deadline. If the project was slated to finish before some holiday, the holiday delays the delivery date even further. Tasks that have been postponed until the project was finished may be deemed undelayable for any longer. Because our team at Ooyala had deferred new feature development for 4 months, when that time budget expired, we suddenly found ourselves hurrying to both complete the player rewrite *and* address the requests that customers had been patiently waiting for. The net result was that our development speed slowed down even more after we missed the original delivery date.

When setting schedules, build in buffer time for the unexpected interruptions. Some combination of them will occur with reasonable probability during long projects. Be explicit about how much time per day each member of the team will realistically spend on a given project. For example, Jack Heart, an engineering manager at Asana, explained that the team maps each ideal engineering day to 2 workdays to account for daily interruptions. [16]

If someone is staffed on large projects, be clear that a certain schedule is contingent on that person spending a certain amount of time each week on the project. Factor in competing time investments, and leave buffer room for unknowns. Alex Allain, who leads the internal platforms and libraries teams at Dropbox, sometimes lays out the week-by-week project schedule in a spreadsheet, annotates it with who's working on what each week, and blocks off the holidays and vacations. [17] The lightweight exercise provides a quick sanity check.

Explicitly track the time spent on tasks not initially part of the project plan, in order to build awareness. By doing so, you can reduce the chance that these distractions will catch your project plan by surprise.

Define Specific Project Goals and Measurable Milestones

While we were rewriting the analytics module in Ooyala's video player, we knew that we would eventually switch to a more extensible logging format. So why rebuild the module on top of the old format, given that it would soon be replaced? It would be less work in the long run to make the change up front, or so the argument went. Unfortunately, a series of well-intentioned decisions like this one created costly delays for our project. What frequently causes a project to slip is a fuzzy understanding of what constitutes success—in Ooyala's case, reducing total work vs. shipping a working product earlier—which, in turn, makes it difficult to make effective tradeoffs and assess whether a project is actually on track.

Define specific goals for a project based on the problem you're working to solve, and then use milestones to measure progress on those goals. Tamar Bercovici used these techniques to successfully manage one of her large infrastructure projects at Box, the cloud storage company. In late 2012, Bercovici's team faced a critical scaling challenge. For the previous 7 years, their entire application database had resided on a single MySQL database instance, and the simple arrangement had sufficed. But now, database traffic had grown to nearly 1.7 billion queries per day, and even though the team had replicated the database to other servers, most of the traffic still needed to go through a single, primary master database. Key tables that stored folders and files had grown to tens and hundreds of millions of rows, respectively; they were increasingly difficult to manage and update. The team anticipated aggressive customer growth, and they knew that they would outgrow their architecture's capacity in a few months. [18]

After researching potential scaling options, Bercovici and her team kicked off a project to shard the massive folder and file tables. The goal was to horizontally partition the two tables so that they could store the partitions, or *shards*, on different databases. When the web application needed to access any data, it would first check a lookup table to see which shard contained the data, and then query the appropriate database storing that shard. Under a sharded architecture, they could accommodate future growth simply by splitting the data into more shards, moving them to additional database machines, and updating the lookup table. The tricky part was doing it without any downtime.

The project was time-sensitive and involved modifying large swaths of their 800K-line codebase. Every code path that queried one of the two tables needed to be modified and tested. Bercovici described it as "a project where you're going to be touching everything … [and] literally changing the way that the basic data components are fetched." It was also a risky project. It had the potential to grow in scope and slip behind schedule, much like Ooyala's player rewrite, and failing to complete the transition before their data and traffic exceeded capacity could spell disaster for Box.

Bercovici used a key strategy for reducing risk: she articulated a clear goal for her project based on a clear problem. The problem was that Box would soon be unable to support its growing traffic on a single database. Her goal was to migrate to a sharded architecture as soon as possible without any downtime.

The simple exercise of setting a project goal produces two concrete benefits. First, a well-defined goal provides an important filter for separating the must-haves from the nice-to-haves in the task list. It helps defend against feature creep when someone inevitably asks, "Wouldn't it be great to take this opportunity to also do X? We've always wanted to do that!" In fact, during Box's architecture migration, Bercovici initially pushed for rewriting the data access layer so that engineers couldn't pass in arbitrary SQL snippets to filter results. Arbitrary filtering made sharding more complicated because they had to parse the SQL snippets to determine whether they touched the file and folder tables; plus, removing it would also provide other benefits like easier performance optimizations in the future. But when they considered their goal, the engineers agreed that the rewrite would make the project a lot longer, and they could work around it in other ways. "[B]eing very, very explicit about what exactly … we were trying to solve helped us to determine what was in scope and what was out of scope," Bercovici emphasized.

The more specific the goal, the more it can help us discriminate between features. Some examples of specific project goals are:

- To reduce the 95th percentile of user latency for the home page to under 500 milliseconds.
- To launch a new search feature that lets users filter their results by content type.
- To port a service from Ruby to C++ to improve performance.
- To redesign a web application to request configuration parameters from the server.
- To build offline support for a mobile application so that content is accessible even when there is no cell connection.
- To A/B test the product checkout flow to increase sales per customer.
- To develop a new analytics report that segments key metrics by country.

The second benefit of defining specific project goals is that it builds clarity and alignment across key stakeholders. "[I]t's very, very important to understand what the goal is, what your constraints are, and to call out the assumptions that you're making," Bercovici explained. "[M]ake sure that you build alignment on that … with any other stakeholders you might have in your project." Skipping this step makes it easy to over-optimize for what you believe to be the main concerns—only to have a manager ask, right as you're about to ship, "What about these key X, Y, and Z features that you didn't address?"

Building alignment also helps team members be more accountable for local tradeoffs that might hurt global goals. In the middle of a long project, it's easy for someone to disappear down a rabbit hole for a week, rewriting some code library or building a partially-related feature. From the perspective of each individual engineer, taking a small detour won't slow the schedule down that much, and tasks like cleaning up the codebase may even reduce work in the long-term. Many of the benefits from local engineering tradeoffs, however, don't materialize until after the project finishes, whereas increasing the total work inside a project's time window introduces delays. The costs of these delays depend on the project, and building alignment helps ensure that team members internalize those costs and make consistent tradeoffs. Otherwise, what ensues is a classic tragedy of the commons, [19] where each individual tradeoff is rational but translates into an unacceptable delay in the aggregate. A well-defined scope makes it easier for team members to check on each other and ask, "Does what you're doing contribute to the main goal?"

In retrospect, defining a more specific goal than "Rewrite Ooyala's player in 4 months" would have been an effective way of shortening the project's timeline. For example, we could have chosen as our goal, "As soon as possible, build a drop-in replacement for the video player that supports dynamically loadable modules, is unit tested, and can later be extended to support additional ad integrations, analytics reports, and video controls." Doing so would have enabled us to build alignment around the required tasks and the ones that could be deferred and incrementally added later.

Even more effective than defining specific goals is outlining measurable milestones to achieve them. This is the second complementary strategy that Bercovici's team used to reduce risk. When asked about the status of a certain task or project, our answer is frequently, "Almost done," or "90% code complete," partly again because we're poor at estimating our status and how much work is left. A concrete milestone, with a specified set of features X, Y, and Z and preferably accompanied by a target completion date, keeps us honest and lets us more accurately measure whether we're on track or far behind.

For the sharding project, the milestones included:

1. Refactor the code so that file and folder queries can be sharded, e.g., by converting single-database MySQL joins into application-level joins that can work across multiple databases.
2. Logically shard the application so that it goes through the motions of looking up a shard's location but still accesses data from a single database.
3. Move a single shard to another database.
4. Completely shard all file and folder data for all accounts.

"Each milestone was a very clear point where we had introduced some value that we didn't have before," Bercovici explained. In other words, the milestones were measurable; either the system met the criteria and behaved as promised or it didn't. The measurable quality enabled her team to scrutinize every single task and ask, "Is this task a prerequisite for this milestone?" This lens allowed them to aggressively prioritize the right things to work on.

If scoping a project with specific goals is like laying down the racetrack to the finish line, outlining measurable milestones is like putting down the mile markers so that we can periodically check that we're still on pace to finish. Milestones act as checkpoints for evaluating the progress of a project and as channels for communicating the team's progress to the rest of the organization. If we've fallen behind, a milestone provides an opportunity to revise our plan, either by extending the deadline or by cutting tasks.

Months later, Bercovici and her team at Box had successfully migrated to a sharded architecture, and grew to support billions of files across tens of shards. [20] Bugs certainly were introduced along the way—including one where the application would show duplicate folders as a shard was being copied from one database to another—but the team managed to avoid an overly long and drawn-out project by sticking to their goals and milestones.

We can benefit from the same techniques. Define specific goals to reduce risk and efficiently allocate time, and outline milestones to track progress. This allows us to build alignment around what tasks can be deferred and decreases the chance that a project inadvertently grows in scope.

Reduce Risk Early

As engineers, we like to build things. Seeing things work and getting things done fire off endorphins in our brains and get us excited in a way that planning and attending meetings do not. This tendency can bias us toward making visible progress on the easier parts of a project that we understand well. We then convince ourselves that we're right on track, because the cost of riskier areas hasn't yet materialized. Unfortunately, this only provides a false sense of security.

Effectively executing on a project means minimizing the risk that a deadline might slip and surfacing unexpected issues as early as possible. Others may depend on the initial projected timeline, and the later they discover the slippage, the higher the cost of failure. Therefore, if a problem turns out to be harder than expected, it's better to find out and adjust the target date sooner rather than later.

Tackling the riskiest areas first helps us identify any estimation errors associated with them. The techniques to validate our ideas early and often (outlined in Chapter 6) also can defuse the risks associated with projects. If we're switching to a new technology, building a small-scale end-to-end prototype can surface many issues that might arise. If we're adopting new backend infrastructure, gaining an early systematic understanding of its performance and failure characteristics can provide insight into what's needed to make it robust. If we're considering a new design to improve application performance, benchmarking core pieces of code can increase confidence that it meets performance goals. The goal from the beginning should be to maximize learning and minimize risk, so that we can adjust our project plan if necessary.

In addition to the specific risks associated with a project, a risk common to all large projects comes during system integration, which almost always takes longer than planned. Unexpected interactions between subsystems, differing expectations of how components behave under edge cases, and previously unconsidered design problems all surface their nasty heads when we put different pieces of software together. Code complexity grows as a function of the number of *interactions* between lines of code more than the actual number of lines, so we get surprised when subsystems interact in complex ways. Moreover, it's extremely hard to decompose integration into granular tasks during the early estimation phases of a project, when you're not sure what the end state will look like. For example, in one project, we realized only at integration time that a number of comments with to-dos were still scattered throughout the codebase. The time to finish the punted tasks wasn't included in the budget for integration testing, so teams had to scramble to meet the deadline.

How can we reduce integration risk? One effective strategy is to build end-to-end scaffolding and do system testing earlier. Stub out incomplete functions and modules, and assemble an end-to-end system as soon as possible, even if it's only partly functional. Front-loading the integration work provides a number of benefits. First, it forces you to think more about the necessary glue between different pieces and how they interact, which can help refine the integration estimates and reduce project risk. Second, if something breaks the end-to-end system during development, you can identify and fix it along the way, while dealing with much less code complexity, rather than scrambling to tackle it at the end. Third, it amortizes the cost of integration throughout the development process, which helps build a stronger awareness of how much integration work is actually left.

Our initial project estimates will exhibit high variance because we're operating under uncertainty and imperfect information. As we gain more information and revise our estimates, the variance narrows. By shifting the work that can take highly variable amounts of time to earlier in the process, we reduce risk and give ourselves more time and information to make effective project plans.

Approach Rewrite Projects with Extreme Caution

A very common characteristic of software engineers is our desire to rewrite something from scratch. Perhaps the original codebase is littered with technical debt or covered with monkey patches accumulated over time, and we think, *Wouldn't it be nice to redesign it and make it cleaner?* Or perhaps the original design was too simple and lacked features—*Wouldn't it be great if we could do X and Y?*

Unfortunately, rewrite projects are also some of the riskiest projects. My Ooyala story gives one example of how the timeline for a rewrite project can spiral out of control and put a business in jeopardy. When I asked Sam Schillace, who ran Gmail and Google Apps for four years, about the costliest mistake he's seen engineers make, his response was, "Trying to rewrite stuff from scratch—that's the cardinal sin."

Rewrite projects are particularly troublesome for a few reasons:

- They share the same project planning and estimation difficulties as other software projects.
- Because we tend to be familiar with the original version, we typically underestimate rewrite projects more drastically than we would an undertaking in a new area.
- It is easy and tempting to bundle additional improvements into a rewrite. Why not refactor the code to reduce some technical debt, use a more performant algorithm, or redesign this subsystem while we're rewriting the code?
- When a rewrite is ongoing, any new features or improvements must either be added to the rewritten version (in which case they won't launch until the rewrite completes) or they must be duplicated across the existing version and the new version (in order to get the feature or improvement out sooner). The cost of either option grows with the timeline of the project.

Frederick Brooks coined the term "second-system effect" to describe the difficulties involved in rewrites. When we build something for the first time, we don't know what we're doing, and we tend to proceed with caution. We punt on improvements and try to keep things simple. But the second system, Brooks warns, is "the most dangerous system a man ever designs … The general tendency is to overdesign the second system, using all the ideas and frills that were cautiously sidetracked on the first one." We see opportunities for improvement, and in tackling them, we increase the project's complexity. Second systems are particularly susceptible to schedule delays as a result of over-confidence.

Engineers who successfully rewrite systems tend to do so by converting a large rewrite project into a series of smaller projects. They rewrite a software system incrementally, in more controlled phases. They adopt the mindset that Martin Fowler advocates in *Refactoring:* engineers should use a series of incremental, behavior-preserving transformations to refactor code. "By doing them in small steps you reduce the risk of introducing errors," Fowler advises. "You also avoid having the system broken while you are carrying out the restructuring—which allows you to gradually refactor a system over an extended period of time." [21]

Rewriting a system incrementally is a high-leverage activity. It provides additional flexibility at each step to shift to other work that might be higher-leverage, whether it's because the project is taking longer than expected or because something unexpected comes up. Using an incremental approach may increase the overall amount of work, but the dramatically reduced risk is often worth it. After the player rewrite, Phil Crosby, a fellow tech lead at Ooyala, led a project to migrate a large Flash-based content management system over to HTML5 to increase future iteration speed. Attempting a full rewrite all at once, however, carried a large risk: if the schedule slipped, new feature development would have to happen in both Flash and HTML5 until the rewrite launched. Instead, Crosby's team took a different approach. They invested some time up front building infrastructure to support a hybrid version of the application, one that allowed them to embed HTML5 components within the Flash application. This allowed them to incrementally port and launch HTML5 components one at a time, while also opening the doors for new features to be written solely in HTML5. The approach took more work overall, but it increased the team's flexibility and also significantly reduced the time pressure of the project.

Harry Zhang took a similar approach when rewriting the software that powers the API at Lob. Zhang's team builds an API for companies to print and mail documents and products. Their codebase had become messy and difficult to work with, and they decided to rewrite their API services in Node.js. Rather than doing it all at once, they built a proxy server that would selectively route traffic for different API endpoints between the old and new API servers. As long as they preserved the interface, they could incrementally deploy their servers to handle new endpoints and also switch back if they encountered errors or issues. The incremental approach gave them significantly more leeway to complete the rewrite while addressing ongoing customers issues.

Sometimes, doing an incremental rewrite might not be possible—perhaps there's no way to simultaneously deploy the old and new versions to different slices of traffic. The next best approach is to break the rewrite down into separate, targeted phases. Schillace's startup Upstartle had built an online documents product called Writely that went viral and grew to half a million users before it was acquired by Google (and subsequently became Google Docs). His four-person team had written Writely in C#, but Google didn't support the language in its data centers. Thousands of users continued to sign up every day, and the team was expending too much energy patching up a codebase that they knew wouldn't scale.

Their first task, therefore, was to translate the original C# codebase into Java so that it could leverage Google's infrastructure. One of Schillace's co-founders argued that they ought to rewrite the parts of the codebase they didn't like at the same time. After all, why rewrite the codebase to Java only to have to immediately throw parts away? Schillace fought hard against that logic, saying, "We're not doing that because we'll get lost. Step one is translate to Java and get it stood back up on its feet again … [O]nce it's working again in Java, step two is … go refactor and rewrite stuff that's bugging you." In the end, he convinced the team to set a very clear goal for their rewrite: to take the shortest possible path toward getting the site up and running in Google's data centers. Even that alone was painfully hard. They had to learn and integrate 12 different internal Google technologies for the product's new infrastructure. They spent a week running the codebase through a series of regular expressions to convert large batches of code to Java and then painstakingly fixed up tens to hundreds of thousands of compile errors. But as a result of their disciplined two-step approach, their four-person team completed the rewrite in just 12 weeks, setting the record for the fastest team to port into Google infrastructure as an acquisition and paving the way for the growth of Google Docs. [22]

In hindsight, pursuing a similar two-phase approach with Ooyala's player rewrite is likely the single, most effective change that we could have made to maximize our chances of delivering a working product in time. Had we set our goal as deploying a new, modularized player with feature and performance parity as soon as possible, we would have aggressively deferred anything unnecessary (like migrating to Thrift for analytics, integrating with additional ad modules, designing a sleeker player skin, or improving performance beyond what was minimally viable). Subsequent improvements could then have been prioritized against other tasks on our roadmap and tackled incrementally, after the initial version had launched. That would have meant fewer 70–80 hour weeks, fewer features that we subsequently had to duplicate between the old and new players, and increased flexibility to respond to unexpected issues.

Convincing yourself and team members to do a phased rewrite can be difficult. It's discouraging to write code for earlier phases, knowing that you'll soon be throwing the intermediate code away. But it would be even more demoralizing to miss the target date by a wide margin, delay the launch of new features, or be forced to build urgent functionality twice. For large rewrite projects, an incremental or phased approach is a much safer bet. It avoids the risks—and associated costs—of slipping and offers valuable flexibility to address new issues that arise.

Don't Sprint in the Middle of a Marathon

I've been involved in two major, multi-month projects where an ambitious and well-intentioned engineering manager pushed the team to work overtime in a sprint to the end. Both teams consisted of talented and dedicated people trying to hit an aggressive deadline, convinced that a project slip would break the business. We increased working hours from 60 to roughly 70 hours per week. And in each case, after several months of sprinting, the project still wasn't finished. It turned out that we weren't actually in the home stretch of a marathon. We had started sprinting somewhere in the middle, and our efforts weren't sustainable.

Despite our best efforts, we'll still sometimes find ourselves in projects with slipping deadlines. How we deal with these situations is as important as making accurate estimates in the first place. Suppose with two months remaining until a deadline, a manager realizes that the project is two weeks behind schedule. She probably thinks something along these lines: The team needs to put in 25% more hours—working 50 hours per week instead of 40—for the next two months, in order to hit the deadline. Unfortunately, the actual math is not that simple. There are a number of reasons why working more hours doesn't necessarily mean hitting the launch date:

- **Hourly productivity decreases with additional hours worked.** Over a century of research shows that long hours actually can decrease productivity.[23] Employers in the 1890s achieved higher total output per worker when they experimented with 8-hour work days.[24] In 1909, Sidney Chapman found that productivity during overtime declines rapidly; fatigued workers start making mistakes, and the short-term increase in output comes at the expense of subsequent days' output.[25] Henry Ford instituted a 40-hour work week in 1922 because years of experiments showed him that it increased total worker output.[26][27] The decrease in marginal productivity during overtime hours means that a team won't increase output by 25% by working 25% more hours. A boost in total weekly output may, in fact, not materialize at all. A 1980 study found that in situations "[w]here a work schedule of 60 or more hours per week is continued longer than about two months, the cumulative effect of decreased productivity will cause a delay in the completion date beyond that which could have been realized … on a 40-hour week."[28]
- **You're probably more behind schedule than you think.** The fact that your schedule has slipped means that the work in previous months was underestimated. This, in turn, likely means that the entire project was underestimated, including the remaining two months. Moreover, we tend to be much better at estimating the beginnings of projects, where we're working on concrete development tasks that we understand. In contrast, estimating the ends of projects is more difficult; teams often underestimate how long integration takes, and each unexpected issue can throw schedules off by a week or more.

- **Additional hours can burn out team members.** Those extra overtime hours come from somewhere—people are sacrificing time that would otherwise be spent with friends or family, exercising, resting, or sleeping. That recovery time is being traded for stressful work hours, with the attendant (if hard-to-quantify) risk of burning out. In their book *Peopleware*, Tom DeMarco and Timothy Lister document a phenomenon they call "undertime." They have found that overtime is "almost always followed by an equal period of compensatory undertime while the workers catch up with their lives." [29] Furthermore, they add, "the positive potential of working extra hours is far exaggerated, and that its negative impact … can be substantial: error, burnout, [and] accelerated turnover." [30]
- **Working extra hours can hurt team dynamics.** Not everyone on the team will have the flexibility to pitch in the extra hours. Perhaps one team member has children at home whom he has to take care of. Maybe someone else has a 2-week trip planned in the upcoming months, or she has to commute a long distance and can't work as many hours. Whereas once the team jelled together and everyone worked fairly and equally, now those who work more hours have to carry the weight of those who can't or don't. The result can be bitterness or resentment between members of a formerly-happy team.
- **Communication overhead increases as the deadline looms.** A frenzy of activity often accompanies the days or weeks leading up to the launch date. The team holds more meetings and shares more frequent status updates to ensure everyone's working on the right things. The additional coordination requirements mean that people have less time to devote to the remaining work.
- **The sprint toward the deadline incentivizes technical debt.** When a team works overtime to hit a deadline, it's almost unavoidable that they'll cut corners to hit milestones. After the project finishes, they're left with a pile of technical debt that they have to pay off. Maybe they'll make a note to revisit the hacks after the project is over, but they'll have to prioritize code cleanup against the next critical project that comes up.

Overtime, therefore, is not a panacea for poor project planning, and it comes with high long-term risks and costs. Unless there is a realistic plan for actually hitting the launch date by working extra hours, the best strategy in the long run is either to redefine the launch to encompass what the team can deliver by the target date, or to postpone the deadline to something more realistic.

Having said this, at times you'll still be in situations where you think a small dose of overtime is necessary to hit a key deadline. Perhaps everyone in the organization has been expecting the launch for a while. Perhaps the project is so critical that your manager believes the business will fail if it gets delayed. Or perhaps you fear what would happen if your team misses the deadline. And so sometimes, despite the long-term costs, you make the decision that it is necessary. In this case, secure buy-in from everyone on the team. Increase the probability that overtime will actually accomplish your goals by:

- **Making sure everyone understands the primary causes for why the timeline has slipped thus far.** Is momentum slowing down because people are slacking off, or have parts of the project turned out to be more complex and time-consuming than expected? Are you sure those same problems will not persist going forward?
- **Developing a realistic and revised version of the project plan and timeline.** Explain how and why working more hours will actually mean hitting the launch date. Define measurable milestones to detect whether the new and revised project plan falls behind.
- **Being ready to abandon the sprint if you slip even further from the revised timeline.** Accept that you might have sprinted in the middle of a marathon and that the finish line is farther away than you thought. Cut your losses. It's unlikely that working even harder will fix things.

Don't rely on the possibility of overtime as a crutch for not making a contingency plan. When you're backed into a corner and have no other options, you're more likely to panic and scramble as the deadline looms closer. An effective engineer knows to plan ahead.

Project estimation and project planning are extremely difficult to get right, and many engineers (myself included) have learned this the hard way. The only way to get better is by practicing these concepts, especially on smaller projects where the cost of poor estimations is lower. The larger the project, the higher the risks, and the more leverage that good project planning and estimation skills will have on your success.

Key Takeaways

- **Incorporate estimates into the project plan.** These estimates should be used as an input to decide whether delivering a set of features by a certain date is feasible. If it is not, they should lead to a conversation about whether to change the feature set or the delivery date. Don't let a desired target dictate the estimates.
- **Allow buffer room for the unknown in the schedule.** Take into account competing work obligations, holidays, illnesses, etc. The longer a project, the higher the probability that some of these will occur.
- **Define measurable milestones.** Clear milestones can alert you as to whether you're on track or falling behind. Use them as opportunities to revise your estimates.
- **Do the riskiest tasks first.** Reduce variance in your estimates and risk in your project by exploring the unknown early on. Don't give yourself the illusion of progress by focusing first on what's easy to do.
- **Know the limits of overtime.** Many teams burn out because they start sprinting before they're even close to the finish line. Don't sprint just because you're behind and don't know what else to do. Work overtime only if you're confident that it will enable you to finish on time.

Part 3: Build Long-Term Value

8

Balance Quality with Pragmatism

GOOGLE HAS EXCEPTIONALLY HIGH CODING STANDARDS. PROGRAMMING style guides dictate conventions for C++, Java, Python, JavaScript, and other languages used within the company. They spell out mundane details like whitespace and variable naming, and they dictate which language features and programming idioms are allowed within Google's codebase. [1] Before any code change can be checked in, another engineer must review it and verify that the change adheres to style conventions, has adequate unit test coverage, and meets Google's high standards. [2]

Google even requires engineers to formally pass a readability review for each programming language that they use at the company. Engineers must submit a code sample to an internal committee and demonstrate that they have read and internalized all the documented style guidelines. Without the committee's stamp of approval, another engineer who has passed the review must approve each and every code change.

This high bar for code quality has enabled an organization of over 45,000 employees distributed across offices in over 60 countries to scale incredibly effectively. [3] [4] Google had the fourth highest market capitalization of any publicly traded company in the world at the end of 2013, further validating that its approach to scaling engineering can build a massively successful business. [5] Its code remains comparatively easy to both read and maintain, especially relative to many other organizations. The code quality also self-propagates; new engineers model their own code based on the excellent code that they see, creating a positive feedback loop. When I joined Google's Search Quality Team right out of college, I picked up best practices for programming and software engineering much faster than I could have at many other places.

But this upside comes with a cost. Since every code change, regardless of whether it's designed for 100 users or 10 million, is held to the same standard, the overhead associated with experimental code is extremely high. If an experiment fails—and, by definition, most do—much of the effort spent in writing high quality, performant, and scalable code gets wasted. As a result, it's harder to nimbly prototype and validate new products within the organization. Many impatient engineers, longing to build new products more quickly, end up leaving for startups or smaller companies that trade off some of Google's stringent code and product requirements for higher iteration speed.

The engineering practices that work for Google would be overkill at a startup or a small company. Requiring new engineers to read and pass a readability review would add unnecessary overhead to getting things done. Imposing strict coding standards on prototypes or experiments that might get thrown away would stifle new ideas. Writing tests and thoroughly reviewing prototype code might make sense, but blanket requirements don't. It's possible to over-invest in quality, to the point where there are diminishing returns for time spent.

Ultimately, software quality boils down to a matter of tradeoffs, and there's no one universal rule for how to do things. In fact, Bobby Johnson, a former Director of Engineering at Facebook, claims that "[Thinking in terms of] right and wrong … isn't a very accurate or useful framework for viewing the world … Instead of right and wrong, I prefer to look at things in terms of works and doesn't work. It brings more clarity and is more effective for making decisions."[6] Rigidly adhering to a notion of building something "the right way" can paralyze discussions about tradeoffs and other viable options. Pragmatism—thinking in terms of what does and doesn't work for achieving our goals—is a more effective lens through which to reason about quality.

High software quality enables organizations to scale and increases the rate at which engineers can produce value, and underinvesting in quality can hamper your ability to move quickly. On the other hand, it's also possible to be overly dogmatic about code reviews, standardization, and test coverage—to the point where the processes provide diminishing returns on quality and actually reduce your effectiveness. "[Y]ou must move quickly to build quality software (if you don't, you can't react properly when things—or your understanding of things—change ...)," writes early Facebook engineer Evan Priestley. "[A]nd you must build quality software to move quickly (if you don't, ... you lose more time dealing with it than you ever gained by building it poorly ...)." [7] Where is time better spent? On increasing unit test coverage or prototyping more product ideas? On reviewing code or writing more code? Given the benefits of high code quality, finding a pragmatic balance for yourself and for your team can be extremely high-leverage.

In this chapter, we'll examine several strategies for building a high-quality codebase and consider the tradeoffs involved: the pros, the cons, and the pragmatic approaches for implementing them. We'll cover both the benefits and the costs of code reviews, and we'll lay out some ways that teams can review code without unduly compromising iteration speed. We'll look at how building the right abstraction can manage complexity and amplify engineering output—and how generalizing code too soon can slow us down. We'll show how extensive and automated testing makes fast iteration speed possible, and why some tests have higher leverage than others. And lastly, we'll discuss when it makes sense to accumulate technical debt and when we should repay it.

Establish a Sustainable Code Review Process

Engineering teams differ in their attitudes toward code reviews. Code reviews are so ingrained in some team cultures that engineers can't imagine working in an environment without them. At Google, for instance, software checks prevent engineers from committing code into the repository without a code review, and every commit needs to be reviewed by at least one other person.

To these engineers, the benefits of code reviews are obvious. They include:

- **Catching bugs or design shortcomings early.** It takes less time and energy to address problems earlier in the development process; it costs significantly more after they've been deployed to production. A 2008 study of software quality across 12,500 projects from 650 companies found that a pass of design and code reviews remove, on average, 85% of remaining bugs. [8]
- **Increasing accountability for code changes.** You're much less likely to add a quick and dirty monkey patch to the code and leave the mess for another person to fix if you know that someone else on your team will be reviewing your code.
- **Positive modeling of how to write good code.** Code reviews provide an avenue for sharing best practices, and engineers can learn from their own code reviews as well as from others'. Moreover, engineers pattern-match based on the code that they see. Seeing better code means writing better code.
- **Sharing working knowledge of the codebase.** When someone reviews your code, this ensures that at least one other person is familiar with your work and can address high-priority bugs or other issues in your absence.
- **Increasing long-term agility.** Higher-quality code is easier to understand, quicker to modify, and less susceptible to bugs. These all translate directly into faster iteration speed for the engineering team.

Although they usually acknowledge that code reviews can improve quality, engineers who *don't* do them often cite their concern about their impact on iteration speed. They argue that the time and effort associated with code reviews is better spent on other aspects of product development. For example, Dropbox, a file sharing service founded in 2007, didn't formally require code reviews for its first four years. [9] Despite that, the company was able to build a strong engineering team and a compelling product with tens of million of users, before they had to institute code reviews to help scale code quality. [10] [11]

Fundamentally, there's a tradeoff between the additional quality that code reviews can provide and the short-term productivity win from spending that time to add value in other ways. Teams that don't do code reviews may experience increasing pressure to do them as they grow. Newly hired engineers may reason incorrectly about code, pattern-match from bad code, or start re-solving similar problems in different ways, all because they don't have access to the senior engineers' institutionalized knowledge.

Given these tradeoffs, does it make sense to do code reviews? Successfully navigating this question requires a key insight: deciding on code reviews doesn't need to be a binary choice, where all code is either reviewed or not reviewed. Rather, think of code reviews as being on a continuum. They can be structured in different ways to reduce their overhead while still maintaining their benefits.

At one extreme, there's Google, which requires all code changes to be reviewed. [12] At the other end of the spectrum, smaller teams employ much nimbler code review processes. In the early days of Instagram, engineers often did over-the-shoulder code reviews where one person would walk through another's code on a shared monitor. [13] Square and Twitter often use pair programming in place of code reviews. [14] [15] When we introduced code reviews at Ooyala, we started off with comments over email cc'ed to the team and only reviewed the trickier pieces of core functionality; to move more quickly, we also reviewed code *post-commit*, after it had already been pushed to the master branch.

At Quora, we only required reviews of model and controller code for business logic; view code that rendered the web interface to users didn't need to be reviewed. We reviewed most code after it was pushed to production; we didn't want to slow down iteration speed, but at the same time, we wanted to ensure that we were investing in a high-quality codebase for the future. Code that touched hairy infrastructure internals tended to be riskier, so we frequently reviewed those types of changes before they were committed. The more recent the employee, the more valuable reviews are for bringing their code quality and style up to the team's standard, and so we would also review new hires' code sooner and with more attention. These examples illustrate that code review processes can be tuned to reduce friction while still retaining the benefits.

In addition, code review tools have improved dramatically in the past few years, significantly reducing overhead. When I first started working at Google, engineers sent reviews over email, manually referencing line numbers in their comments. Reviews at other companies meant teams sitting in conference rooms reading code on projectors. Today, code review tools like GitHub and Phabricator provide lightweight web interfaces. When engineers mention a teammate's name in a commit message, facilities like git hooks can automatically send a code review request to that person. Reviewers can make inline comments right in a web interface, easily seeing what changed since the last round of feedback. Lint checkers can automatically identify deviations from style guidelines, boosting consistency. [16] [17] These tools all help reduce code review friction and focus engineering time on what matters: getting valuable feedback to the implementer.

Experiment to find the right balance of code reviews that works for you and your team. In the early days of Ooyala, our team operated without code reviews. But because lower quality code interfered with product development, we eventually introduced reviews as a way to increase quality. Later, some teammates even built an open source code review tool called Barkeep to further streamline the process. [18]

Manage Complexity through Abstraction

At Google, I could write a simple C++ MapReduce program to compute the frequency of every single word across the billions of web pages in its search index—with just half an hour of effort. The MapReduce programming framework allowed engineers without any expertise in distributed processing, networking, or building fault-tolerant systems to easily define parallelized computations over a large, distributed cluster of machines. I could use MapReduce to orchestrate thousands of machines in Google's data centers to do my bidding. Other engineers used it for web indexing, ranking, machine learning, graph computations, data analysis, large database joins, and many other complex tasks. [19]

In contrast, my experience prototyping a distributed database for my Master's thesis at MIT back in 2005 was much more painful. I spent weeks writing thousands of lines of code to define distributed query trees, collect and organize computational output, start and stop services on machines, define my own communication protocol, set up a data serialization format, and gracefully recover from failures. The net result of all this work: I could run a query on my distributed database ... of 4 machines. [20] Admittedly, this was not quite at Google's scale.

If every engineer at Google had to spend weeks like I did to assemble all the plumbing needed for distributed computations, it would take much longer and significantly more code to get things done. Instead, MapReduce abstracted away the complexity and let engineers focus on what they actually cared about: the application logic. Most engineers using the MapReduce abstraction didn't have to know about the abstraction's internals, and small teams could easily parallelize computations over massive amounts of data without specialized knowledge. Within 4 years of its internal release within Google, engineers had written over 10,000 unique MapReduce applications [21]—a testament that the right abstraction makes a huge difference. Later abstractions, like Sawzall, even made it possible to write simple scripts that could be compiled into MapReduce programs, requiring tenfold less code than equivalent C++ programs. [22] Google's MapReduce inspired the popular open-source Hadoop MapReduce framework, which has enabled other companies to reap the same benefits.

MapReduce illustrates how the right abstraction can dramatically amplify an engineer's output. In his book *Software Abstractions*, MIT Professor Daniel Jackson explains just how important it is to choose the right abstractions. "Pick the right ones, and programming will flow naturally from design; modules will have small and simple interfaces; and new functionality will more likely fit in without extensive reorganization," Jackson writes. "Pick the wrong ones, and programming will be a series of nasty surprises: interfaces will become baroque and clumsy as they are forced to accommodate unanticipated interactions, and even the simplest of changes will be hard to make." [23]

Jackson's short quote touches on how the right abstraction increases engineering productivity:

- **It reduces the complexity of the original problem into easier-to-understand primitives.** Rather than having to reason about reliability and fault tolerance, engineers using MapReduce deal with two much simpler concepts: a Map function to transform inputs from one form to another, and a Reduce function to combine intermediate data and produce output. Many complex problems can be expressed using a sequence of Map and Reduce transformations.

- **It reduces future application maintenance and makes it easier to apply future improvements.** My simple MapReduce program to count words was no more than 20 lines of custom code. The thousands of lines of plumbing code that I needed to write for my distributed database at MIT were unnecessary at Google because MapReduce already provided all the plumbing—in other words, these were thousands of lines of code that didn't have to be written, maintained, or modified later.
- **It solves the hard problems once and enables the solutions to be used multiple times.** A simple application of the Don't Repeat Yourself (DRY) principle, [24] a good abstraction consolidates all of the shared and oftentimes-complex details into one place. The hard problems are tackled and solved once, and the solution pays off with every additional use.

Similar to the time-saving tools we studied in Chapter 4, the right abstraction can increase engineering productivity by an order of magnitude. Strong engineering teams invest heavily in these abstractions. In addition to MapReduce, Google built Protocol Buffers to encode structured data in an extensible way, [25] Sawzall to simplify distributed logs processing, [22] BigTable to store and manage petabytes of structured data, [26] and many other programs to increase productivity. Facebook built Thrift to support cross-language service development, [27] Hive to support relational queries over semi-structured data, [28] and Tao to simplify graph queries on top of a MySQL database. [29] At Quora, we created abstractions like WebNode and LiveNode that made it easy to add real-time updates to any feature we built in our web framework. [30] In many cases, these tools reduce the time to build new features from weeks or months down to hours or days.

But like many other aspects of code quality, building an abstraction for a problem comes with tradeoffs. Building a generalized solution takes more time than building one specific to a given problem. To break even, the time saved by the abstraction for future engineers needs to outweigh the time invested. That's more likely to happen with software the team relies heavily on—such as logging or user authentication libraries—than with peripheral parts of the codebase, so focus more energy on making the core abstractions great.

Even with core abstractions, however, it's possible to overinvest in them up front. Asana, a startup that builds a task and project management tool, spent nearly the entire first year of its existence developing Luna, a new framework for building web applications. The team even developed their own accompanying programming language called Lunascript. [31] Jack Heart, an engineering manager at Asana, explained the team's early reasoning, "The opinion of Asana is that the power of the abstraction granted by Lunascript is so great that, eventually, it will have been faster to write Lunascript and then write a webapp on the scale of Asana than to write a webapp on the scale of Asana without writing Lunascript." [32] The engineering investment brought with it a massive opportunity cost: the team didn't have a product to publicly demo until two years after the company's inception. Ultimately, the team had to abandon their ambitious goals with the Lunascript compiler (though they were still able to reuse parts of the framework) and revert back to using JavaScript. There were too many unsolved research-level problems for generating performant code and insufficient tool support for the language, and both detracted the team's time and energy away from actually building the product.

Just as overinvesting in an abstraction can be costly, so too can building a poor abstraction. When we're looking for the right tool for the job and we find it easier to build something from scratch rather than incorporate an existing abstraction intended for our use case, that's a signal that the abstraction might be ill-designed. Create an abstraction too early, before you have a firm handle on the general problem you're solving, and the resulting design can be overfitted to the available use cases. Other engineers (or even you) might haphazardly bolt on modifications, tip-toe around the shortcomings of the abstraction, or avoid the abstraction entirely because it's too hard to use. Bad abstractions aren't just wasted effort; they're also liabilities that slow down future development.

So what makes an abstraction good? Years ago, I attended a lecture by Joshua Bloch, the architect behind many of Java's core libraries and, at the time, a principal software engineer at Google. He talked about "How to Design a Good API and Why it Matters," discussing the characteristics of good software interfaces, and showing how those same properties apply to good abstractions as well. [33] Good abstractions should be: [34]

- easy to learn
- easy to use even without documentation
- hard to misuse
- sufficiently powerful to satisfy requirements
- easy to extend
- appropriate to the audience

Moreover, good abstractions disentwine complex concepts into simpler ones. Rich Hickey, the author of the programming language Clojure, explains in his talk "Simple Made Easy" that simple things take on one role, fulfill one task, accomplish one objective, or deal with one concept. [35] Simple abstractions avoid interweaving multiple concepts, so that you can reason about them independently rather than being forced to consider them together. Techniques such as avoiding mutable state, using functional rather than imperative programming, preferring composition over inheritance, and expressing data manipulations declaratively rather than imperatively are just a few examples of how to reduce incidental complexity when building software.

Designing good abstractions take work. Study other people's abstractions to learn how to build good ones yourself. Because the adoption of an abstraction scales with its ease of use and its payoffs, an abstraction's usage and popularity provides a reasonable proxy for its quality. Here are some ideas to get you started:

- Find popular abstractions in your codebase at work or from repositories on GitHub. Read through their documentation, dig through their source code, and try extending them.
- Look through the open source projects at technology companies like Google, Facebook, LinkedIn, and Twitter. Learn why abstractions like Pro-

tocol Buffers, Thrift, Hive, and MapReduce have been indispensable to their growth.
- Study the interfaces of popular APIs developed by Parse, Stripe, Dropbox, Facebook, and Amazon Web Services, and figure out what makes it so easy for developers to build on top of their platforms. Also reflect on APIs that you or the rest of community don't like, and understand what you don't like about them.

Automate Testing

Unit test coverage and some degree of integration test coverage provide a scalable way of managing a growing codebase with a large team without constantly breaking the build or the product. In the absence of rigorous automated testing, the time required to thoroughly do manual testing can become prohibitive. Many bugs get detected through production usage and external bug reports. Each major feature release and each refactor of existing code become a risk, resulting in a spike to the error rate that gradually recovers as bugs get reported and fixed. This leads to software error rates like the solid line in the graph shown in Figure 1: [36]

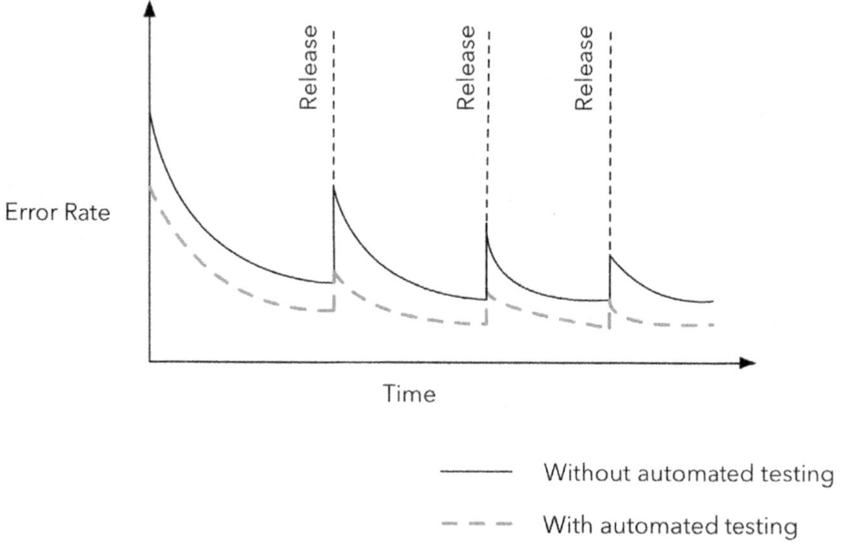

Figure 1: Error rates over time, with and without automated testing.

A suite of extensive and automated tests can smooth out the spikes and reduce overall error rates by validating the quality of new code and by safeguarding changes of old code against regressions. This leads to the improved dotted line in the graph. In fact, before modifying a piece of untested code, first add missing tests to ensure that your changes don't cause regressions. Similarly, when fixing a bug, first add a test that the bug breaks. This way, when you get the test to pass, you're more confident that you've actually addressed the bug.

Automated testing doesn't just reduce bugs; it provides other benefits as well. The most immediate payoff comes from decreasing repetitive work that we'd otherwise need to do by hand. Rather than manually triggering variations from different code branches, we can programmatically—and quickly—run through large numbers of branches to verify correctness. Moreover, the more closely the tests mirror actual conditions in a production environment and the easier it is for engineers to run those tests, the more likely it is that engineers will incorporate testing into their development workflow to automate checks. This, in turn, leads engineers to be much more accountable for the quality of their own work.

Tests also allow engineers to make changes, especially large refactorings, with significantly higher confidence. When I perform multi-thousand-line refactors to improve code quality or to implement a new abstraction, I'm extremely grateful for the protection afforded by unit tests. This protection is particularly important when the person or team modifying the code didn't write the original code (a common scenario) and isn't aware of all the edge cases. Automated tests mitigate against a culture in which people are fearful of modifying and improving a piece of code just because it might break. They make it easier to do future code transformations.

When code does break, automated tests help to efficiently identify who's accountable. Without an automated test failure, a problem takes longer to be discovered and often gets misrouted to whoever owns the feature that broke rather than whoever authored the change. Alex Allain, an engineering manager at Dropbox, recalls a time when certain user flows for business customers mysteriously stopped working. Multiple teams, including his, had to scramble and investigate what went wrong before they finally traced it back to a seemingly harmless change from the data team. An engineer had tweaked how object caching worked in the database layer and inadvertently modified the behavior of the internal database API—and Allain's team had depended on the old behavior. Had his team written an automated test that exercised the API dependencies (or had the data engineer written tests to catch the discrepancy between the old and new APIs), the right person might have been looking at the bug from the start, saving his team the wasted effort.

Finally, tests offer executable documentation of what cases the original author considered and how to invoke the code. Average familiarity with a codebase decreases as both the code and the team grow, making it difficult to make future modifications without sufficient tests. And, just like documentation, writing tests is done more easily by the original authors when their code is fresh in their minds, rather than by those who try to modify it months or years later.

Just because automated testing is beneficial, however, doesn't mean that building automated tests for everything is always a good idea. 100% code coverage is difficult to achieve. Some code is harder to test automatically than others. Moreover, unless you're working on mission-critical or safety-critical pieces of software, dogmatically requiring test coverage for all code is unlikely to be the best use of your time. The extent to which you should automate testing again boils down to a matter of tradeoffs. Small unit tests tend to be easy to write, and while each one might only provide a small benefit, a large library of them quickly builds confidence in code correctness. Integration tests are harder to write and maintain, but creating just a few is a high-leverage investment.

Despite its benefits, it can be difficult to foster a culture of automated testing. There may be organizational inertia: people may believe writing unit tests will reduce their iteration speed. Perhaps historically, parts of the code have been untested because tests were hard to write. Or it may not be clear whether the code currently being written actually will get shipped to production—and people have little incentive to write tests for a product that may not even ship.

This is the dilemma that Kartik Ayyar found himself in when he was leading the development of Cityville, a social online game at Zynga. [37] In Cityville, players grow a virtual city from a small development into a bustling metropolis by building houses, laying out roads, and running businesses. The game skyrocketed to over 61 million monthly users within 50 days of its launch; at one point, it had the highest number of monthly active users of any Facebook application. [38] Ayyar joined the Cityville team as an individual contributor when it was still a handful of engineers, but he soon became the engineering director of the 50-person team.

Before Cityville became a hit, Ayyar told me, many of the gameplay iterations didn't make it into the launched product. This made it difficult to justify investing in testing. "How much do we invest in testing if you're actually throwing away so much of this gameplay?" he had asked himself. Moreover, even after the game had launched, the need to continuously ship new content to sustain its growth trumped other needs. Content creation, in the form of adding new types of buildings, was the top priority. Teams of artists, product managers, and engineers collaborated to aggressively release new content almost three times a day. There was little time left over to build automated tests, and the value they could provide was unclear.

Moreover, achieving high test coverage was extremely daunting. The constructor for a class that represented an item in the game's city map contained around 3,000 lines of code, and a single city building might have 50–100 lines of textual configuration specifying the look-and-feel and the dependencies of the building. Testing that many permutations was intimidating.

The inflection point came when a simple unit test visibly started to save them time. Because the dependencies for a building were so complex, deployments often ran into problems: engineers would accidentally drop dependencies when they merged in feature code for a release. One engineer finally wrote a basic automated test for a city building, ensuring that an image asset referenced by a building's configuration was actually in the codebase and not deleted mistakenly during a code merge. That simple test started catching a lot of bugs in Cityville's deployments, paying for itself many times over in terms of time saved. When the time savings became obvious, people looked for other strategic tests to help them iterate faster. "Well, we're checking this image, so why can't we check other parts of the configuration file?" Kartik explained. "Once people really started running those unit tests and [integrated them] into the build, they really started seeing how much time it saved."

Writing the first test is often the hardest. An effective way to initiate the habit of testing, particularly when working with a large codebase with few automated tests, is to focus on high-leverage tests—ones that can save you a disproportionate amount of time relative to how long they take to write. Once you have a few good tests, testing patterns, and libraries in place, the effort required to write future tests drops. That tips the balance in favor of writing more tests, creating a virtuous feedback cycle and saving more development time. Start with the most valuable tests, and go from there.

Repay Technical Debt

Sometimes, we build things in a way that makes sense in the short-term but that can be costly in the long-term. We work around design guidelines because it's faster and easier than following them. We punt on writing test cases for a new feature because there's too much work to finish before the deadline. We copy, paste, and tweak small chunks of existing code instead of refactoring it to support our use cases. Each of these tradeoffs, whether they're made from laziness or out of a conscious decision to ship sooner, can increase the amount of *technical debt* in our codebase.

Technical debt refers to all the deferred work that's necessary to improve the health and quality of the codebase and that would slow us down if left unaddressed. Ward Cunningham, the inventor of the wiki, coined the term in a 1992 conference paper: "Shipping first time code is like going into debt. A little debt speeds development so long as it is paid back promptly with a rewrite … The danger occurs when the debt is not repaid. Every minute spent on not-quite-right code counts as interest on that debt."[39] Just like financial debt, failure to repay the principal on our technical debt means that increasing amounts of time and energy get devoted to repaying the accumulating interest rather than to building value.

Past some point, too much debt impedes our ability to make progress. Debt-ridden code is hard to understand and even harder to modify, slowing down iteration speed. It's easier to inadvertently introduce bugs, which further compounds the time needed to successfully make changes. As a result, engineers actively avoid debt-ridden code, even if work in that area might be high-leverage. Many decide to write roundabout solutions simply to dodge the painful area.

Technical debt doesn't just accumulate when we make quick and dirty workarounds. Whenever we write software without fully understanding the problem space, our first version will likely end up being less cleanly designed than we'd like. Over time, we develop new insights into better ways of doing things. Since our initial understanding of problems always will be incomplete, incurring a little debt is unavoidable; it's just part of getting things done.

The key to being a more effective engineer is to incur technical debt when it's necessary to get things done for a deadline, but to pay off that debt periodically. As Martin Fowler, author of the book *Refactoring*, points out, "The all too common problem is that development organizations let their debt get out of control and spend most of their future development effort paying crippling interest payments."[40] Different organizations use various strategies to manage technical debt. Asana, a startup that builds an online productivity tool, schedules a Polish and Grease Week at the end of every quarter to pay off any UI and internal tools debt that they might have accumulated. Quora devotes a day after every week-long hackathon to do cleanup work. Some companies explicitly schedule rewrite projects (with their attendant risks) when their technical debt gets too high, evidenced by slow development speed visibly taxing the team's ability to execute. Google holds Fixit days like Docs Fixit, Customer Happiness Fixit, or Internationalization Fixit—where engineers are encouraged to tackle specific themes—as a lightweight mechanism to pay off technical debt. [41] LinkedIn, for example, paused feature development for two whole months after the company went public. They used the downtime to fix a broken process—engineers were taking a month to deploy new features—and then resumed development at a much faster rate. [42]

At many other companies, however, it's up to individual engineers to schedule and prioritize repayment of technical debt against other work. It might even be up to you to argue for and justify the time spent. Unfortunately, technical debt often is hard to quantify. The less confident you are about how long a rewrite will take or how much time it will save, the better off you are starting small and approaching the problem incrementally. This reduces the risk of your fix becoming too complex, and it gives you opportunities to prove to yourself and others that the technical debt is worth repaying. I once organized a Code Purge Day where a group of teammates and I deleted code that was no longer being used from the codebase. It was a small but focused effort with little risk of failure—plus, who doesn't like the feeling of getting rid of unused code? We purged about 3% of our application-level code, and it was easy to justify because it saved other engineers wasted time navigating around stale and irrelevant parts of the codebase.

Like the other tradeoffs we've talked about, not all technical debt is worth repaying. You only have a finite amount of time, and time spent paying off technical debt is time not spent building other sources of value. Moreover, interest payments on some technical code debt is higher than others. The more frequently a part of the codebase is read, invoked, and modified, the higher the interest payments for any technical debt in that code. Code that's peripheral to a product or that rarely gets read and modified doesn't affect overall development speed as much, even if it's laden with technical debt.

Rather than blindly repaying technical debt wherever they find it, effective engineers spend their finite time repaying the debt with the highest leverage—code in highly-trafficked parts of the codebase that takes the least time to fix up. These improvements generate the highest impact for your effort.

Key Takeaways

- **Establish a culture of reviewing code.** Code reviews facilitate positive modeling of good coding practices. Find the right balance between code reviews and tooling to trade off code quality and development speed.
- **Invest in good software abstractions to simplify difficult problems.** Good abstractions solve a hard problem once and for all, and significantly increase the productivity of those who use it. But if you try to build abstractions when you have incomplete information about use cases, you'll end up with something clunky and unusable.
- **Scale code quality with automated testing.** A suite of unit and integration tests can help alleviate the fear of modifying what might otherwise be brittle code. Focus on ones that save the most time first.
- **Manage your technical debt.** If you spend all your resources paying off interest on your debt, you won't have enough time left to work on new things. Focus on the debt that incurs the most interest.

9

Minimize Operational Burden

With one small tap, I applied the Nashville filter to my otherwise-mundane iPhone photo and transformed it into a stylistic and retro Polaroid shot. This was the magic of Instagram, a photo-sharing mobile app that promised people a "fast, beautiful, and fun way to share moments with friends and family" [1] and that turned millions of amateur photographers—myself included—into budding artists. I could follow friends, celebrities, and even professional photographers; their artwork would fill my Instagram feed, inspiring me to share more.

Instagram grew like magic as well. They launched to the public via Apple's App Store on October 6, 2010. [2] Within hours, Instagram's app had already been downloaded over 10,000 times, and usage exploded in the coming months. [3] A year and a half later, when Facebook acquired the company for over $1 billion, Instagram's user base had skyrocketed to 40 million. [4]

Few other mobile apps have grown at Instagram's pace. Scaling a product to support that much growth in such a short period of time would be extremely challenging for any team. What's surprising, however, is that when Instagram was acquired in April 2012, it had only 13 employees. Its ratio of users to employees was over 3 million to one—much higher than most other companies. [5] This was a testament to just how effective each member of that small team was.

How did Instagram's engineers manage such a feat? What high-leverage principles enabled them to support so many users, given their limited time and resources? I sat down with Mike Krieger, Instagram's co-founder and CTO, to find out.

During Instagram's early years, Krieger explained, its team consisted of no more than five engineers. That scarcity led to focus. They couldn't afford to engineer any solutions that would break frequently or require constant maintenance. Far and away, the most valuable lesson they learned was to minimize operational burden. Krieger operated like the chief of a small fire department: he knew that each additional feature and new system represented an extra house that the team needed to support—and possibly firefight. Development costs didn't stop accruing at launch time; in fact, they were just starting to accumulate.

Keeping a system up and running, scaling a feature to support more users, fixing the bugs that surface, transferring an ever-growing body of institutional knowledge to new engineers—all of these costs continue to tax a team's resources, even after a feature or system ships. When a team is small, minimizing that tax is critical.

Unfortunately, it is tough to fully internalize this cost. Even the smartest and most talented engineers can become enamored with the hottest new technologies and dream of ways of incorporating them into their next project. They'll try out a new system that's yet to find major adoption, a new language that few team members know, or some experimental piece of infrastructure, all without factoring in the future maintenance costs. These decisions impose an ongoing cost on their time and reduce their engineering efficiency.

This is why minimizing operational burden is so critical. The recurring costs of operating a system or product require time and energy that could be spent on higher-leverage activities. How much time do you spend each day or week on maintaining systems and fixing bugs, rather than on building new things? How often do you find yourself interrupted by operational and product issues and switching contexts to address them, rather than making progress on tasks that you've prioritized? Shaving time off of recurring costs frees you to focus on what matters most.

Whenever they could, the Instagram team picked proven and solid technologies instead of shiny or sexy new ones. "Every single, additional [technology] you add," Krieger cautions, "is guaranteed mathematically over time to go wrong, and at some point, you'll have consumed your entire team with operations." And so, whereas many other startup teams adopted trendy NoSQL data stores and then struggled to manage and operate them, the Instagram team stuck with tried and true options like PostgreSQL, Memcache, and Redis that were stable, easy to manage, and simple to understand.[6] [7] They avoided re-inventing the wheel and writing unnecessary custom software that they would have to maintain. These decisions made it significantly easier for the small team to operate and scale their popular app.

In this chapter, we'll examine strategies for minimizing operational burden. We'll analyze Instagram's core mantra—do the simple thing first—to learn why we should embrace operational simplicity. We'll show how building systems to fail fast makes them easier to maintain. We'll walk through the importance of relentlessly automating mechanical tasks. We'll talk about how making automation idempotent reduces recurring costs. And we'll close with why we should practice and develop our ability to recover quickly.

Embrace Operational Simplicity

Effective engineers focus on simplicity. Simple solutions impose a lower operational burden because they're easier to understand, maintain, and modify. At Instagram, simplicity was a key principle enabling the team to scale. "One of the core engineering tenets is to do the simple thing first," Krieger explained. "We apply that to product. We apply that to hiring. We apply it to engineering. We have posters that say it." In reviewing each other's designs, the team would ask, "Is this the simplest thing?" or, "Is the simplest thing to create an entirely new system for this one feature you're writing?" If the answer was no, then they reconsidered their approach.

As a product grows, software complexity tends to grow along with it. New features may require engineers to build new systems to support them. Increased traffic may require additional infrastructure to successfully scale the product and maintain its speed and quality. A newly-open-sourced piece of architecture or a new programming language may promise attractive benefits, luring engineers into trying them out on problems they're facing. Or, engineers may decide to build a new feature with a non-standard toolchain because it has slightly better performance characteristics or features than what other team members use. The additional complexity may be a necessary evil—but oftentimes, it's not.

When asked what he'd learned from designing the iPod, Steve Jobs responded, "When you first start off trying to solve a problem, the first solutions you come up with are very complex, and most people stop there. But if you keep going, and live with the problem and peel more layers of the onion off, you can oftentimes arrive at some very elegant and simple solutions. Most people just don't put in the time or energy to get there." [8]

Simplicity has been a value and characteristic of Instagram from the beginning. When Krieger and his co-founder, Kevin Systrom, first embarked on their venture, they were working on a location-based social networking application called Burbn. Tackling the same crowded space as other startups like Foursquare and Gowalla, Burbn would award points to its users for checking into locations, hanging out with friends, and posting pictures. Krieger and Systrom spent over a year building an iPhone app—and then decided that it was too complex. "We actually got an entire version of Burbn done as an iPhone app, but it felt cluttered, and overrun with features," writes Systrom. So the two of them shed all of Burbn's complexity and honed in on the one activity that users flocked to the most: sharing photos. "It was really difficult to decide to start from scratch, but we … basically cut everything in the Burbn app except for its photo, comment, and 'like' capabilities," Systrom continues. "What remained was Instagram." [9]

When engineering teams don't focus on doing the simple thing first, they either end up being less effective over time because their energy is spent on a high upkeep cost, or they reach a point where the operational burden gets so high that they're forced to simplify their architecture. In fact, the engineering team at Pinterest—the popular online pinboard where users collect and organize things from around the web—made this mistake in its early days. Over the course of two years, Pinterest grew rapidly from 0 to 10s of billions of page views per month. In a talk entitled "Scaling Pinterest," engineers Yashwanth Nelapati and Marty Weiner describe how the team initially introduced more and more complexity into their infrastructure to overcome the scaling problems they encountered. [10] At one point, their database and caching layers alone involved a mixture of seven different technologies: MySQL, Cassandra, Membase, Memcache, Redis, Elastic Search, and MongoDB. [11] This was much more complexity than their small engineering team (3 people at that time) could handle.

Having too complex of an architecture imposes a maintenance cost in a few ways:

- **Engineering expertise gets splintered across multiple systems.** Every system has its own unique set of properties and failure modes that must be discovered, understood, and mastered. The more systems there are, the longer this process takes.
- **Increased complexity introduces more potential single points of failure.** Too much surface area in the system architecture, coupled with too few engineering resources, means it's harder to ensure that at least two people can cover any given area. What happens when the only person familiar with a critical component gets sick or goes on vacation?
- **New engineers face a steeper learning curve when learning and understanding the new systems**. Ramp up time increases, since every engineer must internalize a larger body of knowledge to be productive. In comparison, an architecture with a smaller set of reusable abstractions and tools is easier to learn.
- **Effort towards improving abstractions, libraries, and tools gets diluted across the different systems.** As a result, no one system is as well-supported as it could be if engineering resources were pooled together and focused on a smaller set of building blocks.

When system complexity grows faster than the engineering team's ability to maintain the system, productivity and progress suffer. More and more time gets diverted towards maintenance and figuring out how things work; less time is spent finding new ways to build value.

Eventually, the Pinterest team realized that they needed to simplify their architecture to reduce their operational burden. They learned the hard way that a well-designed architecture supports additional growth by adding more of the same types of components, not by introducing more complex systems. By January 2012, they had substantially simplified their data and caching architecture to just MySQL, Memcache, Redis, and Solr. Since then, they've grown more than 4x by just scaling up the number of machines in each service rather than introducing any new services. [12]

Instagram and Pinterest demonstrate that the discipline to focus on simplicity provides high leverage. That lesson applies to a variety of scenarios:

- It's fine to experiment with a new programming language for a prototype or a toy project, but think hard before using it in a new production system. Do other team members have experience with the language? Is it easy to pick up? Will it be hard to hire engineers fluent in it?
- Proponents of new data stores promise that their systems solve the problems in battle-tested relational databases like MySQL and PostgreSQL. Before using these new storage systems in production, however, do your research. Find out if other teams have successfully used them for projects of a similar scope and whether they have actually been able to maintain and scale them with lower operational burden than more standard solutions.
- When tackling a new problem, consider whether repurposing an existing abstraction or tool would be simpler than developing a custom solution. People often say, "Use the right tool for the job"—but that can also increase the number of moving parts. Does the complexity of having more parts outweigh the benefits of simplicity through standardization?
- If you're processing large amounts of data, consider whether the data is actually large enough such that you need a distributed cluster, or whether a single, beefy machine will suffice. Clusters are harder to manage and debug than single machines.

Remember: do the simple thing first. Always ask, "What's the simplest solution that can get the job done while also reducing our future operational burden?" Revisit sources of complexity, and find opportunities to trim them away.

Build Systems to Fail Fast

Many engineers associate robustness and reliability with an absence of crashes. They spend their energy adding workarounds to automatically handle software errors so that their programs can continue to function. Workarounds may include setting misconfigured parameters to default values, adding catch-all exception handlers to deal with unexpected issues, and swallowing unexpected return values.

These techniques cause software to *fail slowly*. The software may continue to run after an error, but this is often in exchange for less decipherable bugs further down the road. Suppose we introduce logic into a web server so that if it reads in a misspelled configuration parameter for `max_database_connections`, it defaults the parameter to 5. The program might start and run as usual, but once deployed to production, we'll be searching everywhere trying to understand why database queries are slower than usual. Or suppose our application silently fails to save a user's state to a data structure or database, so that it can keep running for longer. Later on, when it doesn't read back the expected data, the program might be so far removed from the failure that it's difficult to pinpoint the root cause. Or suppose an analytics program that processes log files simply skips over all corrupted data that it encounters. It'll be able to continue generating reports, but days later, when customers complain that their numbers are inconsistent, we'll be scratching our heads and struggling to find the cause.

Slowly failing systems muddy the sources of code errors, making it difficult for us to discover what went wrong. As we discussed in Chapter 4, debugging is an integral part of software development. Inevitably, bugs will arise and software will be misconfigured, and we will need to spend time reproducing the issues and pinpointing the sources of errors. The more directly we can link the feedback to a source, the more quickly that we can reproduce the problem and address the issue.

A valuable technique for shortening that feedback loop is to make your software fail fast. Jim Shore explains the technique in his *IEEE Software* article "Fail Fast": "[In] a system that fails fast ..., when a problem occurs, it fails immediately and visibly. Failing fast is a nonintuitive technique: 'failing immediately and visibly' sounds like it would make your software more fragile, but it actually makes it more robust. Bugs are easier to find and fix, so fewer go into production."[13] By failing fast, we can more quickly and effectively surface and address issues.

Examples of failing fast include:

- Crashing at startup time when encountering configuration errors
- Validating software inputs, particularly if they won't be consumed until much later
- Bubbling up an error from an external service that you don't know how to handle, rather than swallowing it
- Throwing an exception as soon as possible when certain modifications to a data structure, like a collection, would render dependent data structures, like an iterator, unusable
- Throwing an exception if key data structures have been corrupted rather than propagating that corruption further within the system
- Asserting that key invariants hold before or after complex logic flows and attaching sufficiently descriptive failure messages
- Alerting engineers about any invalid or inconsistent program state as early as possible

The more complex the system, the more time that fail-fast techniques can save. My team once encountered a nasty data corruption bug on a web application: reads from the data store generally worked fine, but a few times a day, they would return completely unrelated data. Code would request one type of data and get back another, or it would ask for a single value and get back a list of objects of a completely different type. We suspected everything from data corruption in our application-level caching layers, to bugs in the open source caching services themselves, to threads overwriting each other's data. It took multiple team members over a week to resolve the problem.

It turned out that when a web request timed out, the application didn't properly reset the MySQL connection that was part of a shared connection pool. When the next unsuspecting web request came in and reused the same connection, its first query would get the response intended for the timed-out request. The erroneous response would propagate throughout the caching layer. Because the web application was under more intense load that week, the latent bug surfaced more frequently than usual. Failing fast by killing the connection on timeout or by asserting that a connection was clean at the start of a web request would have saved us many collective hours of grief.

Another time, I was working with Memcached, a high-performance and distributed in-memory caching system. Engineering teams at many web companies cache values retrieved from their databases in Memcached to improve read performance and reduce database load. Memcached essentially behaves like a big hash table; clients write key-value pairs and then later retrieve the data by key very quickly. Clients also can specify an expiration time on a key to expire stale data and manage the amount of memory consumed by it.

To reduce the load on our database, I decided to increase the expiration time (from 10 days to 40) for a key that cached the results of certain expensive database queries. After deploying the change to production, however, alerts on our database started firing; the load on the database spiked and was even higher than before. I quickly reverted the change, trying to understand how increasing the expiration time could have *increased* load. After much investigation, it turned out that a Memcached expiration time was expressed in seconds, but only up to 30 days. Any number larger than 30 days (2,592,000 seconds) was interpreted as a UNIX timestamp. Memcached had treated what I thought was 40 days as a timestamp from 1970, even though that made little sense. [14] As a result, values expired immediately after being set, as if they weren't being cached at all. If Memcached's interface had failed fast and returned a more sensible error rather than just using my invalid input (or if the interface had been more intuitive), the error would have easily been caught during development and would never have made it to production. In both of these cases, failing fast would have made errors more easily detectable, helping to reduce the frequency and duration of production issues.

Failing fast doesn't necessarily mean crashing your programs for users. You can take a hybrid approach: use fail-fast techniques to surface issues immediately and as close to the actual source of error as possible; and complement them with a global exception handler that reports the error to engineers while failing gracefully to the end user. For example, suppose you're working on a complex web application where the rendering engine produces hundreds of components on a page. Each component might fail fast if it encounters an error, but a global exception handler could catch the exception, log it, and then fail more gracefully for the user by not rendering that particular component. Or the global exception handler might show a notification requesting the user to reload the page. What's more, you can build automated pipelines to aggregate the logged errors and sort them by frequency in a dashboard, so that engineers can address them in order of importance. In contrast to a situation where components simply overlook the error and proceed as usual, failing fast allows you to capture the specific error.

Building systems to fail fast can be a very high-leverage activity. It helps reduce the time you spend maintaining and debugging software by surfacing problematic issues sooner and more directly.

Relentlessly Automate Mechanical Tasks

Launching new products and features is a big rush. However, every launch typically brings with it the dreaded—but necessary—responsibility of pager duty, a job that I've become intimately familiar with throughout my software engineering career. Somebody has to keep everything up and running. During pager duty rotation, on-call engineers take turns at being the first line of defense against any and all production issues. Being on-call means traveling with your laptop and a wireless data card so that no matter where you are, you can quickly hop online if you get an alert. It creates an unpredictable schedule: you might get called away at any moment, sometimes to address nerve-wracking and time-sensitive outages that legitimately require your attention, but other times to deal with trifling issues. It's particularly frustrating to get woken up at 3AM only to find out that you need to run a series of 5 commands that a machine could have done for you. And yet, it's surprisingly easy to forge ahead with other work the next day, particularly if there's deadline pressure, instead of creating a long-term fix.

Time is our most valuable resource. Pushing relentlessly toward automation to reduce avoidable situations like 3AM wake-up calls is one high-leverage way to free up our time and energy so we can focus on other activities. Applying a quick manual band-aid to address a problem might take less time than building a sustainable fix. But in the long run, automating solutions and scripting repetitive tasks reduce our operational burden, providing powerful ways to scale our impact.

When deciding whether to automate, the judgment call that an engineer must make is: *Will I save more time overall by manually doing a particular task or by paying the upfront cost of automating the process?* When the manual labor required is obviously high, the decision to automate seems simple enough. Unfortunately, situations are rarely that black and white. Engineers automate less frequently than they should, for a few reasons:

- **They don't have the time right now.** Upcoming deadlines and managerial pressure often prompt engineers to sacrifice the long-term benefits of automation for the short-term benefit of shipping a product sooner. Launching the product in a timely fashion may very well be important right now, but consistently deferring the decision to automate will eventually erode engineering productivity.
- **They suffer from the *tragedy of the commons*,** in which individuals act rationally according to their own self-interest but contrary to the group's best long-term interests. [15] When manual work is spread across multiple engineers and teams, it reduces the incentive of any individual engineer to spend the time to automate. This happens often with those weekly pager duty rotations, for example. As teams get bigger, each individual rotation occurs less frequently—and it's tempting to apply quick manual fixes that

last just long enough for you to punt the responsibility to the next on-call engineer.

- **They lack familiarity with automation tools.** Many types of automation rely on systems skills that non-systems engineers are not as familiar with. It takes time to learn how to quickly assemble command-line scripts, combine UNIX primitives, and hack together different services. Like most skills, however, automation gets easier with practice.
- **They underestimate the future frequency of the task.** Even when you think a manual task might only need to be completed once, requirements sometimes change and mistakes get made. It's fairly straightforward to update a script, but manually redoing the entire task over and over again is time-consuming.
- **They don't internalize the time savings over a long time horizon.** Saving 10 seconds per task might not seem like a big deal, even if it happens 10 times a day. But over the the course of year, that's almost an entire workday saved.

Every time you do something that a machine can do, ask yourself whether it's worthwhile to automate it. Don't let your willingness to work hard and grind through manual tasks cause you to throw hours at a problem, if what's really needed is a little cleverness. Activities where automation can help include:

- Validating that a piece of code, an interaction, or a system behaves as expected
- Extracting, transforming, and summarizing data
- Detecting spikes in the error rate
- Building and deploying software to new machines
- Capturing and restoring database snapshots
- Periodically running batch computations
- Restarting a web service
- Checking code to ensure it conforms to style guidelines
- Training a machine learning model
- Managing user accounts or user data
- Adding or removing a server to or from a group of services

The cost of automating (including learning how to automate) may initially be higher than the cost of doing the job manually. However, if the experience increases the efficiency with which you can automate in the future, that skill will compound and pay for itself as you use automation for more and more problems.

Do certain activities make more sense to automate than others? Bobby Johnson, a former Director of Engineering at Facebook who ran the infrastructure team, provided valuable insight into this question. Facebook runs one of the largest MySQL database installations in the world, with many thousands of servers across multiple data centers. Each Facebook user's profile is assigned to one of many thousands of partitions, called shards, and each database server contains multiple shards. If a server fails (and tens or hundreds might fail on a given day) or a shard gets too big, one or more shards need to be redistributed to another database server. [16]

Given the complexity of their MySQL configuration, one would imagine that Facebook must have built systems to automagically handle MySQL failovers and load balancing early on in their history. Not so, according to Johnson. "I was at a conference, and all these people were talking to me about these crazy things they had for magically failing over on MySQL and doing magical load balancing," Johnson explained. "We actually still just had a guy who did that." Engineers at companies managing just 20 servers were writing scripts that tried to get the system to automatically heal and correct itself when things went wrong. But at Facebook, an engineer was manually load balancing their massive database cluster.

That doesn't mean that automation wasn't important; it would have been impossible for one person to manage thousands of machines without automated tools. Johnson, however, distinguished between two types of automation: automating mechanics and automating decision-making. Automating the mechanics of a sequence of steps tends to be straightforward and testable. Automating the right decisions to make, particularly in the context of building systems that can heal and repair themselves when things go wrong, turns out to be much more challenging. "[T]he problem when you do build those systems is that they tend to run amok," Johnson added. "So many of the worst outages we ever had were because those things went crazy. They rarely get tested well, because by definition they run in unusual circumstances."

For example, consider a simple automated rule for a load balancer that handles a failed server by routing traffic destined to that server to others in the group. This policy works great when one server goes down, but what happens if half the servers fail? The policy routes all the traffic destined to those failed servers to the other half. And if the servers had gone down because of too much load, then the automation would end up taking down the entire cluster. That's a much worse situation than just dropping half of the requests to shed load.

And so, for a long time, to balance database shards at Facebook, an engineer ran a script to look for the most overloaded machines and then ran another script to move some shards off of those machines. The mechanics of moving a shard from one database server to another was heavily automated, but a human decided which of thousands of shards to move where. It would be many years before Facebook reached the point in their development where it was worthwhile to tackle the harder task of decision automation. They ultimately deployed a system called MySQL Pool Scanner to automatically rebalance shards.

Automation can produce diminishing returns as you move from automating mechanics to automating decision-making. Given your finite time, focus first on automating mechanics. Simplify a complicated chain of 12 commands into a single script that unambiguously does what you want. Only after you've picked all the low-hanging fruit should you try to address the much harder problem of automating smart decisions.

Make Batch Processes Idempotent

As you automate more operations, your time's leverage increases—but so does the probability that some of your automation will fail. Scripts executing a sequence of actions without human intervention (also known as *batch processes*) that you schedule to run periodically, will hit network timeouts or unexpected hiccups. Scripts processing large amounts of data, increasingly common as data analytics become key to more businesses, work most of the time, but they take a long time to retry or recover when they fail. If you're not careful, the time required to maintain your automation will climb. Therefore, minimizing that burden is a high-leverage activity.

One technique to make batch processes easier to maintain and more resilient to failure is to make them *idempotent*. An *idempotent* process produces the same results regardless of whether it's run once or multiple times. It therefore can be retried as often as necessary without unintended side effects. For example, imagine that you're processing the day's application logs to update the weekly database counts of different user actions. A non-idempotent approach might iterate over each log line and increment the appropriate counter. If the script ever crashed and needed to be re-run, however, you could inadvertently increment some counters twice and others once. A more robust, idempotent approach would keep track of the counts of each user action by day. It would read through the logs to compute the counters for the current day, and only after that's successful, would it derive the weekly totals by summing the daily counters for that week. Retrying a failed process in the idempotent approach simply overwrites the daily counters and re-derives the weekly count, so there's no double counting. A day's counters could similarly be derived from separate hourly counters if there's too much data.

When idempotence isn't possible, structuring a batch process so that it's at least *retryable* or *reentrant* can still help. A *retryable* or *reentrant* process is able to complete successfully after a previous interrupted call. A process that's not reentrant typically leaves side effects on some global state that prevents it from successfully completing on a retry. For instance, a failed process might still be holding onto a global lock or have emitted partial output; designing the process so that it knows how to handle these inconsistent states can reduce the amount of manual handholding required later. Make each process either fail entirely or succeed entirely.

Idempotence also offers another benefit that many effective engineers take advantage of: the ability to run infrequent processes at a more frequent rate than strictly necessary, to expose problems sooner. Suppose you have a script that runs once a month. Perhaps it generates a monthly analytics report, produces a new search index, or archives stale user data. Much can change in a month. Initially valid assumptions about the data size, codebase, or architecture may no longer be true. If these false assumptions break the script, this can cause a monthly scramble to figure out the cause, perhaps under extreme time pressure. One powerful technique made possible by a idempotent script is to convert infrequent workflows into more common ones by scheduling dry runs every day or week; this way, you get quicker feedback when something breaks. If a dry run fails in the middle of the month, there's still ample time to figure out what went wrong; moreover, the window of potential causes is much narrower. Rajiv Eranki, a former Dropbox engineer responsible for scaling infrastructure from 4K to 40M users, even suggests scheduling scripts intended only for manual invocation (like scripts to fix user state or to run diagnostics) to be run regularly to detect errors. [17]

Running batch processes more frequently also allows you to handle assorted glitches transparently. A system check that runs every 5 to 10 minutes might raise spurious alarms because a temporary network glitch causes it to fail, but running the check every 60 seconds and only raising an alarm on consecutive failures dramatically decreases the chances of false positives. Many temporary failures might resolve themselves within a minute, reducing the need for manual intervention.

Idempotence and reentrancy can reduce some of the complexity and recurring costs involved in maintaining automated and batch processes. They make automation cheaper, freeing you to work on other things.

Hone Your Ability to Respond and Recover Quickly

At Netflix, engineers did something counterintuitive: they built a system called Chaos Monkey that randomly kills services in its own infrastructure. [18] Rather than spending energy keeping services alive, they actively wreak havoc on their own system. It turns out that this strategy actually makes their infrastructure more robust and reduces the pain of pager duty. By configuring Chaos Monkey to kill services on weekdays during regular work hours, engineers can identify architectural weaknesses while they're in the office rather than having to deal with unexpected and untimely emergencies on the weekends or in the middle of the night. As they note on their blog, "The best defense against major unexpected failures is to fail often."[19] When Amazon Web Services, which Netflix depends on for its cloud services, suffered major outages, Netflix was able to escape with little service disruption—while other companies like Airbnb, Reddit, Foursquare, Hootsuite, and Quora suffered multiple hours of downtime.[20]

Netflix's approach illustrates a powerful strategy for reducing operational burden: developing the ability to recover quickly. Regardless of what we're working on, things will go wrong some of the time. If we're building a product that depends on the web, some downtime is inevitable. If we're building desktop software, some bugs will pass through undetected and get released to users. Even if we're doing something as fundamental as checking in code, we'll occasionally break the build or the test suite, no matter how careful we are. It's important to focus on uptime and quality, but as we go down the list of probable failure modes or known bugs, we will find that our time investments produce diminishing returns. No matter how careful we are, unexpected failures will always occur.

Therefore, how we handle failures plays a large role in our effectiveness. And at some point, it becomes higher leverage to focus our time and energy on our ability to recover quickly than on preventing failures in the first place. The better our tools and processes for recovering quickly from failures, and the more we practice using them, the higher our confidence and the lower our stress levels. This allows us to move forward much more quickly.

However, even though the cost of failure can be very high, we often don't devote enough resources to developing strategies that address failure scenarios. Simulating failures accurately is difficult, and because they happen infrequently, the payoff for handling them better seems lower than working on more pressing product issues. Recovery processes to handle server failures, database failovers, and other failure modes therefore tend to be inadequate at best. When we do need the processes, we bumble around trying to figure things out when stress levels are at their highest, leading to subpar performance.

One strategy for fixing this imbalance comes from Bill Walsh, former coach of the San Francisco 49ers. In *The Score Takes Care of Itself*, Walsh discusses a strategy called "scripting for success."[21] Walsh wrote scripts, or contingency plans, for how to respond to all types of game scenarios. He had a plan for what to do if the team was behind by two or more touchdowns after the first quarter; a plan for what to do if a key player got injured; a plan for what to do if the team had 25 yards to go, one play remaining, and needed a touchdown. Walsh realized that it's tough to clear your mind and make effective decisions during critical points of the game, especially when thousands of fans are roaring, hecklers are throwing hot dogs and beer cups at you, and the timer is ticking precious seconds away. Scripting moved the decision-making process away from the distracting and intense emotions of the game. In fact, the first 20 to 25 plays of every 49ers game eventually became scripted, a tree of if-then rules that codified what the team would do in different scenarios. By scripting for success, Walsh led the 49ers to 3 Super Bowl victories and was twice named NFL Coach of the Year. [22]

Like Walsh, we too can script for success and shift our decision-making away from high-stakes and high-pressure situations and into more controlled environments. We can reduce the frequency of situations where emotions cloud our judgments and where time pressure compounds our stress. As engineers, we can even programmatically script our responses and test them to ensure that they're robust. This is particularly important as an engineering organization grows and any infrastructure that can fail will begin to fail.

Like Netflix, other companies have also adopted strategies for simulating failures and disasters, preparing themselves for the unexpected:

- Google runs annual, multi-day Disaster Recovery Testing (DiRT) events. They simulate disasters, like earthquakes or hurricanes, that cut the power for entire data centers and offices. They then verify that teams, communications, and critical systems continue to function. The exercises surface single points of failure, unreliable failovers, outdated emergency plans, and other unexpected errors, allowing teams to deal with them in a controlled setting. [23]
- At Dropbox, the engineering team often simulates additional load for their production systems. Doing so enables them to artificially trigger issues sooner; when they hit a system limit that causes errors, they disable the

simulated load and have ample time to investigate the issue. This is much less stressful than firefighting the same issues when they have to deal with real traffic that they can't just turn off. [24]

Netflix, Google, and Dropbox all assume that the unexpected and the undesired will happen. They practice their failure scenarios to strengthen their ability to recover quickly. They believe that it's better to proactively plan and script for those scenarios when things are calm, rather than scramble for solutions during circumstances outside of their control. While we might not necessarily work at the same scale or have the same scope of responsibility as the engineers at these companies, it's just as important for us to be prepared for whatever failure scenarios we experience. Ask "what if" questions and work through contingency plans for handling different situations:

- What if a critical bug gets deployed as part of a release? How quickly can we roll it back or respond with a fix, and can we shorten that window?
- What if a database server fails? How do we fail over to another machine and recover any lost data?
- What if our servers get overloaded? How can we scale up to handle the increased traffic or shed load so that we respond correctly to at least some of the requests?
- What if our testing or staging environments get corrupted? How would we bring up a new one?
- What if a customer reports an urgent issue? How long would it take customer support to notify engineering? How long for engineering to follow up with a fix?

Practicing our failure scenarios so that we can recover quickly applies more generally to other aspects of software engineering, as well:

- What if a manager or other stakeholder at an infrequent review meeting raises objections about the product plan? What questions might they ask, and how might we respond?
- What if a critical team member gets sick or injured, or leaves? How can we share knowledge so that the team continues to function?

- What if users revolt over a new and controversial feature? What is our stance and how quickly can we respond?
- What if a project slips past a promised deadline? How might we predict the slippage early, recover, and respond?

Just like service downtime, it's hard—indeed, sometimes impossible—to prevent these failure modes. The best that we can do is to "script for success," practice failure scenarios, and work on our ability to recover quickly.

All the strategies in this chapter focus on minimizing the time and energy spent operating and maintaining what we build. Instagram grew and scaled successfully in part because the team didn't spend all their time keeping their app up and running. Minimizing our own operational burden means that we, too, can invest our time in more meaningful ways of driving impact.

Key Takeaways

- **Do the simple thing first.** Simpler systems are easier to understand, extend, and maintain.
- **Fail fast to pinpoint the source of errors.** Make debugging easier by not masking your errors and by not deferring failures until later.
- **Automate mechanics over decision-making.** Aggressively automate manual tasks to save yourself time. At the same time, think twice before trying to automate decision-making, which tends to be hard to get correct.
- **Aim for idempotence and reentrancy.** These properties make it easier for you to retry actions in the face of failure.
- **Plan and practice failure modes.** Building confidence in your ability to recover lets you proceed more boldly.

10

Invest in Your Team's Growth

"SINK OR SWIM." THESE WEREN'T THE MOST ENCOURAGING WORDS THAT Sean Knapp, my new CTO, could have said to me as I was ramping up, but they did set the tone for my onboarding experience at Ooyala, my first foray into the startup world. No life preserver was coming—I had better figure out how to stay afloat, fast.

Knapp and his two other co-founders had brought along much of their Google spirit to Ooyala. They envisioned using superior technology to disrupt the online video space, just as Google had disrupted the online search and advertising spaces. Greens, yellows, reds, and blues—traditional Google colors—were splashed throughout the open-floor office layout, giving visitors the impression that Ooyala could actually be a small Google offshoot. But the founders also shared a Red Bull-chugging intensity that I hadn't seen in Google's laid-back culture, an environment where I hadn't experienced many urgent deadlines or panics.

My first assignment at Ooyala was to build and launch an already-promised feature that would allow video publishers to schedule when their online videos would go on the air.[1] I had two weeks. On my first day, I found myself wading through a confusing codebase laced with technical debt—accumulated in the team's sprint to build a working product—and lacking any documentation or unit tests. Most of the code was also written in a Java-like language called ActionScript that I wasn't familiar with. I needed to learn ActionScript, get comfortable with Ruby on Rails, and familiarize myself with Flash video and graphics libraries before I could even get started building the feature. My eyes glued to my monitor, I traced through code littered with obscure variable names like `qqq` and questionable function names like `load2` and `load3`.

That "sink-or-swim" onboarding program created one of the most tense and intimidating experiences of my career. I ended up pulling two nerve-wracking 80-hour weeks to ship my first feature on schedule, wondering the whole time whether leaving the comforts of Google and joining the startup world had been the right choice. Eventually, I acclimated to the new environment, and over time, the team supplanted the untested and cryptic code with a much stronger foundation. But sending me flailing into the water induced unnecessary stress and was not an effective use of my time and energy. Moreover, for a long time, subsequent new hires had to struggle through a similar experience.

One of the biggest lessons I learned from Ooyala is that investing in a positive, smooth onboarding experience is extremely valuable. That lesson was re-emphasized when I joined the 12-person team at Quora. Onboarding wasn't well-structured; it mainly consisted of haphazard and ad hoc discussions. Neither company was opposed to having a higher quality onboarding process, but creating one also hadn't been prioritized. My desire for something better motivated and informed my subsequent work building Quora's onboarding program, discussed later in this chapter.

Investing in onboarding is just one way to invest in your team's growth. Up until now, most of what you've read have been lessons on how to be a more effective individual contributor. So how did a chapter on team-building find its way into a book about becoming a more effective engineer? It's because the people and the team that you work with have a significant impact on your own effectiveness—and you don't have to be a manager or a senior engineer to influence your team's direction. For some people, developing a team may be less enjoyable than developing software. But if you want to increase your effectiveness, it's important to recognize that building a strong team and a positive culture has a considerable amount of leverage.

The higher you climb up the engineering ladder, the more your effectiveness will be measured not by your individual contributions but by your impact on the people around you. Companies like Google, Facebook, and others all have similar criteria for senior engineers, staff engineers, principal engineers, distinguished engineers, and their equivalent positions: the higher the level, the higher the expected impact. Marc Hedlund, the former Senior VP of Product Development and Engineering at Etsy and now the VP of Engineering at Stripe, offered a succinct description of the different positions. "You're a staff engineer if you're making a whole team better than it would be otherwise. You're a principal engineer if you're making the whole company better than it would be otherwise. And you're distinguished if you're improving the industry." [2] Thinking early in your career about how to help your co-workers succeed instills the right habits that in turn will lead to your own success.

Investing in other people's success is important for another reason: you can get swept up the ladder with them. Yishan Wong, based on his decade of experience leading teams in Silicon Valley, argues this point with a thought experiment. "Imagine that you have a magic wand, and by waving this magic wand, you can make every single person in your company succeed at their job [by] 120%. What would happen?" Wong answers his own question: "[I]f everyone knocked their job out of the park, the company would probably be a huge success and even if you did nothing else, you'd be swept along in the tide of success of everyone around you." [3] Wong firmly believes the secret to your own career success is to "focus primarily on making everyone around you succeed."

And he is not the only one giving that advice. Andy Rachleff co-founded Benchmark Capital, a venture capital firm that's invested in over 250 companies and manages nearly $3 billion in capital. He's accumulated decades of experience in growing companies. [4] Rachleff tells students in his Stanford class, "You get more credit than you deserve for being part of a successful company, and less credit than you deserve for being part of an unsuccessful company." [5] The message is clear: your career success depends largely on your company and team's success, and the success of your company or team depends on more than just your individual contributions. You'll accomplish much more if those around you are aligned with you rather than against you, and you can do that by investing in their success.

In this chapter, we'll go over techniques to invest in different phases of your team's growth. We'll start by walking through why strong engineering companies make hiring a top priority, and what your role should be in the hiring process. We'll talk about why designing a good onboarding process for new members of your team is a high-leverage activity and how to do it. We'll discuss how, once you've assembled your team, sharing ownership of code makes your team stronger. We'll go over how using post-mortems to build collective wisdom leads to long-term value. And we'll close with a discussion of how to build a great engineering culture.

Make Hiring Everyone's Responsibility

Interviewing new engineering candidates can feel bothersome. It interrupts productivity and breaks up our day, and it's time-consuming to write feedback on candidates and debrief with the team. If the recruiting pipeline is not set up well, interviews can feel like hit-or-miss sessions with unqualified candidates who bomb our questions. We can leave interviews feeling like we weren't able to get sufficient signal on a prospective hire. And since it's hard to recruit the best talent, the majority of interviews don't actually result in accepted offers. As a result, individual interviews might not appear to be particularly good time investments.

It's only when we look at interviews in the aggregate do we realize that hiring is an extremely high-leverage activity. The smaller the company—and the more likely that the person you interview will be an immediate co-worker—the greater the leverage of those interviews. When Quora's team was only about 30 people, I had a 20-day stretch where I interviewed one engineer per day. On average, I spent two hours of every day that month talking with a candidate, writing up feedback, and debriefing on whether to make an offer. It was exhausting. But if those 40 hours resulted in even just one additional hire, the 2,000+ hours of output that he or she would contribute per year would more than justify the cost. And, in fact, we struck gold with that particular batch; we ended up hiring five full-time engineers and one intern.

I'm not alone in adopting a mindset that hiring ought to be a top priority. Albert Ni, one of the first ten engineers at the popular file synchronization service Dropbox, also realized that building a great team can be higher-leverage than working on "traditional" software engineering. Ni built out the original analytics and payments code at Dropbox during his first few years at the company. He loved the work, but in October 2011, when the company consisted of 30 engineers, he switched his focus to recruiting. "I became responsible for the engineering hiring problem that we had here," Ni told me. "We were really struggling to hire engineers at the time." A core part of the problem was that engineers simply weren't spending enough time on hiring. There was no standardization across interviews, no organized process for sourcing new candidates, and no formalized campus recruiting efforts. [6]

Focusing on recruiting instead of writing code was difficult. "I'd be lying if I said I was super excited to do it at the time, because I really enjoyed the work I was doing," Ni explained. But he also knew that there weren't enough engineering resources to execute on everything the team wanted to do, so improving the hiring process would have a huge impact. Ni immersed himself in the problem. He started reviewing all the inbound resumes, screening all the interview feedback, and attending the debriefs for every engineering candidate. He did the actual interview scheduling and talked with candidates to understand their perspectives on the process. Over the years, Ni's work paid off. Slowly, interviews became more standardized, and the company built a culture where interviewing was everyone's responsibility. By early 2014, the engineering team at Dropbox had grown to over 150 members, more than 5x its size when Ni began focusing on recruiting.

So how do we design an effective interview process? A good interview process achieves two goals. First, it screens for the type of people likely to do well on the team. And second, it gets candidates excited about the team, the mission, and the culture. Ideally, even if a candidate goes home without an offer, they still leave with a good impression of the team and refer their friends to interview with the company. One of your primary levers as an interviewer is therefore making the interview experience both fun and rigorous.

As an interviewer, your goal is to optimize for questions with high *signal-to-noise* ratios—questions that reveal a large amount of useful information (signal) about the candidate per minute spent, with little irrelevant or useless data (noise). Good, well-executed questions let you confidently differentiate among candidates of varying abilities; bad, poorly managed questions leave you unsure whether to hire the candidate.

The types of questions that generate the most signal depend on the qualities most correlated with success on your team. Traditionally, many large technology companies like Google, Microsoft, Facebook, and Amazon require engineering candidates to answer algorithm and coding questions on a whiteboard. These textbook-style questions evaluate a candidate's computer science knowledge, but they can often fall short in gauging whether an engineer actually gets things done in a work environment.

An increasing number of companies have shifted toward interviews that include a hands-on programming component. At Quora, for example, we augmented our suite of whiteboard interviews with a practical coding exercise on a laptop. Candidates navigated around, debugged, and extended a large, open-source codebase in their favorite text editors, and they used Google, Stack Overflow, or other online resources as needed. The exercise revealed whether someone could effectively use a terminal, invoke basic UNIX commands, dive into unfamiliar libraries, set up a tight development loop, and write clean code—all of which were valuable signals not well captured by the traditional whiteboard interview.

At the payments startup Stripe, the team similarly designed its on-site interviews to simulate the work that their engineers do on a day-to-day basis. Problems included designing and implementing a small end-to-end system, squashing bugs in a popular open-source codebase, refactoring a poorly organized application, and pair programming on a self-contained project. [7] Ooyala tasked candidates with implementing and demoing a functional Tetris game to test their ability to manage a project and trade off different technical choices under time constraints. Dropbox, Airbnb, Uber, Square, and many other companies have also incorporated hands-on or even take-home programming exercises into their interviews. [8] These interview questions do require a larger upfront investment to design and calibrate, but their growing adoption indicates that many teams find the payoffs to be well worth it.

Ample literature exists to help you get started on designing questions. Gayle Laakmann McDowell's book *Cracking the Code Interview*, for example, covers standard interview patterns and questions at some of the larger technology companies. [9] Beware, however, that your interviewees have access to the same question banks.

Perhaps trickier than the choice of questions is how to continuously iterate on improving your interview process. Based on my experience conducting over 500 interviews, here are a few higher-leverage strategies to keep in mind:

- Take time with your team to identify which qualities in a potential teammate you care about the most: coding aptitude, mastery of programming languages, algorithms, data structures, product skills, debugging, communication skills, culture fit, or something else. Coordinate to ensure that all the key areas get covered during an interview loop.
- Periodically meet to discuss how effective the current recruiting and interview processes are at finding new hires who succeed on the team. Keep on iterating until you find ways to accurately assess the skills and qualities that your team values.
- Design interview problems with multiple layers of difficulty that you can tailor to the candidate's ability by adding or removing variables and constraints. Building a fast search interface can, for instance, be made harder by requiring the search query to be distributed across multiple machines. Or, it can be made simpler by assuming size constraints on the items to be indexed. Layered problems tend to provide more fine-grained signals about a candidate's ability than binary ones, where the candidate either gets the answer or he doesn't.
- Control the interview pace to maintain a high signal-to-noise ratio. Don't let interviewees ramble, get stumped, or get sidetracked for too long. Either

guide the interviewee along with hints, or wrap up and move on to a different question.

- Scan for red flags by rapidly firing short-answer questions to probe a wide surface area. Questions like how parameter passing works in a programming language or how a core library works might take a qualified candidate no more than a few seconds or a minute to answer, but can surface any warning areas that you might want to further address.
- Periodically shadow or pair with another team member during interviews. These sessions help calibrate ratings across interviewers and provide opportunities to give each other feedback on improving the interview process.
- Don't be afraid to use unconventional interview approaches if they help you identify the signals that your team cares about. Airbnb, for example, devotes at least two of its interviews to evaluating a candidate's culture fit because they attribute much of their success to everyone's alignment on the company's core values.

As with all skills, the only way that you can become more effective in interviewing and hiring is through iteration and practice. But it's worth the effort: the additional output from adding a strong engineer to your team far exceeds the output of many other investments that you could make.

Design a Good Onboarding Process

Despite my sink-or-swim experience at Ooyala and my ad hoc ramping up at Quora, I was convinced that onboarding could be more organized and less stressful. Sure, I had survived both initiation processes, but they left much to be desired if we wanted to successfully scale our engineering organizations. In a small team, there aren't many places to look or people to consult when you're trying to figure out what's most important. As the team grows and the surface area of new things to explore increases, it becomes harder and harder for a recent hire to figure out what to learn first without any guidance. Employees lay out different subsets of concepts to new people, and it's easy for useful information to be omitted among the scattered explanations. An engineer might not learn a key abstraction because his initial projects deal with peripheral features that don't touch core parts of the codebase. Or, if expectations aren't communicated clearly, a new engineer might spend too much time reading through design documents or programming language guides and not enough time fixing bugs and building features. And so, when we were growing the engineering team at Quora, I volunteered to lead an effort to build an onboarding program for new engineers.

I'd never done anything like this before—it was way outside of my normal software-building comfort zone. So I researched Google's EngEDU training program and Facebook's 6-week Bootcamp onboarding program, and I reached out to engineers at different companies to learn what had and hadn't worked for them. Based on my research, I formally defined the role of engineering mentorship at Quora and organized a recurring series of onboarding talks. Over time, I took on responsibilities for coordinating the creation of training materials, holding mentor-training workshops, and mentoring many of the new hires on the team.

I was motivated by my realization that a quality onboarding process is a powerful leverage point for increasing team effectiveness. First impressions matter. A good initial experience influences an engineer's perception of the engineering culture, shapes her ability to deliver future impact, and directs her learning and activities according to team priorities. Training a new engineer for an hour or two a day during her first month generates much more organizational impact than spending those same hours working on the product. Moreover, the initial time investment to create onboarding resources continues to pay dividends with each additional team member.

Onboarding benefits the team and the company, but if you've already ramped up and become a productive contributor, you might wonder how helping new hires acclimate benefits you personally. Why take time away from your own work? Remember: investing in your team's success means that *you* are more likely to succeed as well. Effectively ramping up new team members ultimately gives you more flexibility to choose higher-leverage activities. A stronger and larger team means easier code reviews, more people available to fix bugs, increased resources for on-call rotations and support, and greater opportunities to tackle more ambitious projects.

As an example, one component of Quora's new onboarding program is pairing each hire with a mentor. Mentors assign small features or bugs from their task lists to do as starter projects. These are great learning opportunities for new hires, since the mentors have context for each project and can provide guidance and answer questions. It also frees mentors to shift their attention from less-interesting tasks to higher-leverage projects that they are better suited to tackle. Onboarding is a win-win situation; the new hires receive valuable training, and the mentors get more things done.

Conversely, a poor onboarding experience reduces a team's effectiveness. Productive output gets lost when a recent hire takes longer to ramp up. Code quality suffers if new team members use abstractions or tools incorrectly, or if they aren't familiar with team conventions or expectations. Insufficient training means it's harder to accurately identify low performers—are they doing poorly because they were bad hires, or do they just need more time to acclimate? Moreover, good engineers undergo unnecessary stress and may even get weeded out because of weak guidance. The impact of low-quality onboarding is far-reaching.

Regardless of your seniority, you can contribute meaningfully to onboarding. If you're a new engineer and have just experienced the process yourself, you can provide the most direct feedback about what worked and what didn't. If there are wikis or internal documents that you used, see if you can directly update and improve them. If you're a more senior engineer, observe what new team members pick up well and what they struggle with, and use that knowledge to improve onboarding for future employees.

So how do you create a good onboarding process for your team? First, identify the goals that your team wants to achieve. Second, construct a set of mechanisms to accomplish these goals. When designing Quora's onboarding program, I outlined four goals that I thought the process should achieve:

1. **Ramp up new engineers as quickly as possible.** Onboarding does require a short-term productivity hit for those leading it. The sooner new employees get ramped up, however, the sooner they'll produce meaningful output—enabling the team to get more done in the long run.

2. **Impart the team's culture and values.** While new engineers may have glimpsed parts of the culture through recruiting, marketing materials, and interviews, the onboarding process helps ensure that they learn the values that the team shares. Those values might include getting things done, being data-driven, working well as a team, building high quality products and services, or something else.
3. **Expose new engineers to the breadth of fundamentals needed to succeed.** What are the key things that every engineer should know? What valuable tips and tricks have you learned since joining the team? A key part of a good onboarding program is ensuring that everyone starts on a consistent, solid foundation.
4. **Socially integrate new engineers onto the team.** This means creating opportunities for them to meet and develop working relationships with other teammates. The sooner that new engineers become full-fledged parts of the team rather than isolated silos, the more effective they will be.

Depending on your team, your own goals may vary. What's important is understanding what you want to achieve so that you can focus your efforts appropriately. Using these goals, we developed the four main pillars for Quora's onboarding program:

1. **Codelabs.** We borrowed Google's concept of *codelabs* to introduce abstractions and tools at Quora. A codelab is a document that explains why a core abstraction was designed and how it's used, walks through relevant parts of its code internals, and supplies programming exercises to validate understanding. We created codelabs for our web framework WebNode, our real-time updating system LiveNode, our caching layer DataBox, and our debugging tools, in order to teach new engineers the fundamentals of how we built Quora. [10]

   I invested extra effort to create the first codelab that others could use as a model; I then scaled the effort by recruiting teammates to pitch in. These investments primarily involved an upfront, one-time cost of creating reusable resources, followed by a small recurring cost of updating any stale materials. The codelabs clarified what abstractions were important to master early on and recommended a particular order for learning them. They enabled new engineers to ramp up more quickly and make product changes sooner.

2. **Onboarding talks.** We organized a series of ten onboarding talks to be delivered during a new hire's first three weeks. These talks, given by senior engineers on the team, introduced the codebase and site architecture, explained and demoed our different development tools, covered engineering expectations and values around topics like unit testing, and introduced Quora's key focus areas—the things we believed were the most important for new hires to learn. They also provided a great opportunity for everyone on the team to get to know each other. The most critical talks, like "Introduction to the Codebase," were scheduled each time a new hire started; others were batched together and given once there were several new people. Together, the onboarding talks and codelabs helped ensure that new hires learned the fundamentals.
3. **Mentorship.** Because each new hire's background is different, onboarding programs can't be one-size-fits-all. Quora paired each new hire with a mentor to provide more personalized training during their first few months. Mentors checked in daily with their mentees during the first week, and then met for weekly 1:1s. Responsibilities included everything from reviewing code, discussing design tradeoffs, and planning work priorities, to introducing new hires to the right people on the team and helping them acclimate to the fast pace of a startup. Quora also held mentoring workshops and meetings to exchange tips and help mentors improve.

As a team, we built a shared understanding that it was acceptable—and, in fact, strongly encouraged—for mentors to spend time away from their regular work to train new employees. On their first day, I would explicitly tell my mentees that getting them ramped up had higher priority than getting my other work done. We even took physical space into consideration; we placed mentees close to their mentors so it was easy for them to ask questions. All of this helped establish the shared goal of ramping up new hires as quickly as possible, and set the expectation that they shouldn't hesitate to seek guidance.

4. **Starter tasks.** New engineers pushed commits to add themselves to the team page on their first day, and we aimed for each of them to complete a starter task—whether it be deploying a bug fix, a small new feature, or a new experiment—by the end of the first week. This aggressive target conveyed the value of getting things done and moving fast. It also meant that the team needed to remove enough onboarding friction for new hires to build momentum quickly. For example, we had to reduce overhead sufficiently for them to be able to set up a development environment, make a simple change, run tests, commit the code, and deploy it—all on their first day.

    Mentors were responsible for identifying starter tasks of increasing complexity for their mentees. These tasks could be bugs, features, or experiments that the mentors needed to get done and that provided a valuable learning opportunity. I generally advised mentors to pick a project that would take them a day to finish, so that even if ramping up took longer than expected and the project slipped, there would still be a high probability that the new hire could ship it in the first week.

These goals and implementations are just some examples of what to consider when designing the onboarding process for your own team. It's important to realize that building a good onboarding program is an iterative process. Maybe you simply start with a document on how to set up a development environment, with the goal of getting a new engineer ready to write code on day one. Perhaps you realize later that not all starter projects provide the same ramp-up benefit, and decide to articulate a set of guiding principles for how to pick good ones. Maybe you notice that you're giving the same codebase or architecture walkthrough over and over again, and realize that it would be more efficient to prepare a talk or even record a video on the topic.

Wherever you are in designing an onboarding process, think about your own experience and survey others on the team to get a sense of what worked well and what could use some improvement. Reflect on where new hires struggled and what things you can do to help them ramp up more quickly. Enumerate key concepts, tools, and values that you wish you had learned earlier. Implement your most valuable ideas, and then survey new hires and their mentors to see if the changes helped. Rinse and repeat.

Share Ownership of Code

The entire engineering team at Ooyala had been sprinting to launch a rewrite of our video player. We had pulled 70-hour weeks for months, and I was exhausted. But finally, I was able to take a much-needed vacation in Hawaii. One day, I was hiking the Crater Rim Trail on Mauna Loa, the world's largest volcano, enjoying the welcome respite from my office routine. Suddenly, my phone buzzed. I pulled it out of my pocket and read the text message from Ooyala's CTO: "Logs processor down."

The logs processor. I had inherited this particular piece of software when we were still growing Ooyala's analytics team. It ingested all the raw data we collected from millions of online video viewers and crunched out analytics reports for our business customers. The continuously-updated reports showed customers how their viewers engaged with online videos and provided detailed metrics segmented by viewer demographics. And at that moment on Mauna Loa, I was the sole person who knew how to run it.

Since my CTO had paged me, I knew that the problem was non-trivial. I also knew that no one else at the office understood the system well enough to debug the issue. Unfortunately, since neither my laptop nor Wi-Fi were readily accessible, all I could do was reply, "Hiking on a volcano. Can't look at it until tonight." The problem loomed over my head for the rest of the day.

When I finally got back to my hotel, I investigated the problem and revived the logs processor. But it was clear that our process was far from ideal. The situation wasn't great for me; my vacation was disrupted. It wasn't great for my team; they depended on me, and I wasn't available. And it wasn't great for our customers; they didn't have access to any new analytics reports for almost an entire day.

There's a common misconception that being the sole engineer responsible for a project increases your value. After all, if fewer people know what you know, then the scarcity of your knowledge translates into higher demand and value, right? What I've learned, however, is that sharing code ownership benefits not only yourself but your entire team as well. As you increase in seniority, your responsibilities as an engineer also grow. You become the point-person for more projects, and other engineers consult with you more frequently. While that can feel good and may even increase your job security, it also comes with a cost.

When you're the bottleneck for a project, you lose your flexibility to work on other things. High-priority bugs get routed to you more frequently because your expertise enables you to fix them faster. When you're the only one with complete knowledge of a working system and it goes down, you find yourself as the first (or only!) line of defense. When a good chunk of your time is spent responding to issues, performing maintenance, tweaking features, or fixing bugs in a system simply because you're the most knowledgeable person, it's harder for you to find free time to learn and build new things. Identifying others on your team who can relieve some of those demands gives you more freedom to focus on other high-leverage activities. That's a key reason why investing in your team, particularly by teaching and mentoring, helps you in the long run.

From a company's perspective, sharing ownership increases the *bus factor* to more than one. The quirky term refers to the number of key people who can be incapacitated (for example, by getting hit by a bus) before the rest of the team is no longer able to keep the project going. [11] A bus factor of one means that if any member of the team gets sick, goes on vacation, or leaves the company, the rest of the team suffers. It also means that it's harder for engineers on the team to be *fungible*. When engineers are fungible, "nobody is uniquely positioned to do one thing," explains Nimrod Hoofien, Director of Engineering at Facebook. "Any one thing can be done by multiple people, and that allows you more degrees of freedom, more flexibility in development, and fewer constraints for on-call and support." [12] Shared ownership eliminates isolated silos of information and enables an engineer to step in for another teammate, so that everyone can focus on whatever produces the most impact. Moreover, since engineering often involves grinding through unpleasant tasks, shared ownership also means that everyone participates in maintenance duties and one person doesn't carry the entire burden.

To increase shared ownership, reduce the friction that other team members might encounter while browsing, understanding, and modifying code that you write or tools that you build. Here are some strategies:

- Avoid one-person teams.
- Review each other's code and software designs.
- Rotate different types of tasks and responsibilities across the team.
- Keep code readable and code quality high.
- Present tech talks on software decisions and architecture.
- Document your software, either through high-level design documents or in code-level comments.
- Document the complex workflows or non-obvious workarounds necessary for you to get things done.
- Invest time in teaching and mentoring other team members.

The engineering organization at Ooyala has adopted an increasingly stronger emphasis on shared code ownership. Anyone on a given team can be on-call and responsible for issues that arise. This gives senior engineers more free time to work on other projects and junior engineers an opportunity to ramp up on the infrastructure and the codebase. Share ownership and remove yourself from the critical path to give yourself more opportunities to grow.

Build Collective Wisdom through Post-Mortems

In our haste to get things done, we often move from task to task and project to project without pausing to reflect on how effectively we spent our time or what we could have done better. Developing the habit of regular prioritization, covered in Chapter 3, provides one opportunity for retrospection. Another valuable opportunity comes from debriefing after incidents and projects and sharing lessons more widely across other teams.

After a site outage, a high-priority bug, or some other infrastructure issue, effective teams meet and conduct a detailed *post-mortem*. They discuss and analyze the event, and they write up what happened, how and why it happened, and what they can do to prevent it from happening in the future. The goal of the post-mortem is not to assign blame, which can be counterproductive to the discussion, but to work together to identify better solutions. If the situation is not preventable, the post-mortem may prompt the team to build new tools to make recovery easier or compile a step-by-step document that explains how to deal with similar situations. The post-mortem write-up generally gets shared across teams, since many people in the organization want to know what happened.

It's less common to dedicate the same healthy retrospection to projects and launches. Your team might launch a feature to a favorable press write-up. You clink champagne glasses to celebrate a job well done, and then move onto the next project. But how effectively did your feature actually accomplish your team's goals? Or say your team rewrites the infrastructure code, making it 5% faster after a few months of work. Was that actually the best use of your team's time? Without pausing to debrief and review the data, it's hard to know. Moreover, even when post-mortems do get conducted on projects, their results often are not widely distributed, and every team has to re-learn the same lessons on their own.

There's some friction to doing this better. If your team hasn't defined a clear goal or metric for a launch, it's difficult to assess its success. If your team doesn't want to publicly declare months of work to be a failure, it's tempting to close discussions. Or if your team is overwhelmed with new projects, it's hard to make time for reflection. As a result, opportunities for building collective wisdom get lost. Lessons might not get learned; or if they do, they are isolated in a few people's heads. Costly mistakes are repeated. And when people leave, collective wisdom decreases.

Contrast this typical experience with how knowledge is collected at NASA. NASA astronauts debrief with their supporting teams after every simulation and every mission to extract all the lessons they can about what went wrong and what they could do better. Debriefs are intense. Experts fire barrages of questions, and every decision and action is dissected carefully. A 4-hour simulation might be followed by a 1-hour debrief. A space flight might be followed by a month or more of all-day debriefs. Participants have to steady themselves for critical feedback, keeping in mind that the goal is not to levy blame but to maximize collective wisdom.

The mission debriefs are time-consuming but invaluable, and the cumulative lessons from 200+ space flights are captured in NASA's comprehensive tome, *Flight Rules*. Chris Hadfield describes *Flight Rules* in his book *An Astronaut's Guide to Life on Earth*, writing, "NASA has been capturing our missteps, disasters and solutions since the early 1960s, when Mercury-era ground teams first started gathering 'lessons learned' into a compendium that now lists thousands of problematic situations, from engine failure to busted hatch handles to computer glitches, and their solutions."

The compendium describes in minute detail what to do in a myriad of different circumstances—and why you should do it. Have a cooling system failure? *Flight Rules* tell you how to fix it, step by step, supplementing with the rationale for each step. Fuel cell issue? *Flight Rules* tell you whether the launch needs to be postponed. The playbook contains "extremely detailed, scenario-specific standard operating procedures," all the lessons ever learned and distilled from past missions. Mission control consults *Flight Rules* every time they run into an unexpected issue; they add to it whenever they tackle a new problem. Given that each space shuttle launch costs $450 million, [13] it's not hard to understand why NASA spends so much time preparing for and debriefing after missions.

Most of us aren't launching spacecraft or coordinating moonwalks, but NASA's practice of conducting project post-mortems to build the team's collective wisdom is still extremely valuable for our work. We certainly can compile step-by-step operational guides like NASA's *Flight Rules* for different procedures. MySQL database failure? *Flight Rules* tell you how to fail over from the master to the slave. Servers overloaded from traffic overload? The playbook tells you which scripts to run to bring up extra capacity.

These lessons and rules also apply at the project level. Project falling behind schedule? *Flight Rules* tells you what happened in the past when different project teams worked overtime, what those teams believed were the main contributors to their eventual success or failure, and whether team members burned out. Have an idea for a new ranking algorithm? *Flight Rules* contains a compilation of all past A/B tests, what their hypotheses were, and whether the experiments confirmed or rejected those hypotheses.

To build their own version of *Flight Rules*, companies like Amazon and Asana use methodologies like Toyota's "Five Whys" to understand the root cause of operational issues.[14] [15] For instance, when the site goes down, they might ask, "Why did the site crash?" Because some servers were overloaded. "Why were they overloaded?" Because a disproportionately high fraction of traffic was hitting a few servers. "Why wasn't traffic more randomly distributed?" Because the requests were all coming from the same customer, and their data is only hosted on those machines. By the time the fifth why is asked, they've moved from the symptom to the root cause. A similar methodology can be used to facilitate productive discussion about a project's success or failure.

Ultimately, compiling team lessons is predicated upon honest conversation—and holding an honest conversation about a project can be uncomfortable. It requires acknowledging that months of effort may have resulted in failure, and viewing the failure as an opportunity for growth. It requires aligning behind a common goal of improving the product or team, and not focusing on where to assign blame. It requires being open and receptive to feedback, with the goal of building collective wisdom around what went wrong and what could've been done better. But if a difficult hour-long conversation can increase the chances that your next month-long team project succeeds, it's high-leverage and well worth both the time and the emotional investment.

It's difficult to instill a culture of collective learning into an entire organization. However, consistent applications of effort can go a long way. Start with small projects that you're working on with your immediate team; gradually establish the practice of doing post-mortems after larger projects as well. The more you learn from each experience, the more you'll take with you into your next project, and the more you'll succeed. Optimize for collective learning.

Build a Great Engineering Culture

Throughout my career, I've reviewed thousands of resumes and interviewed over five hundred candidates. Many of them were engineers from top technology companies like Facebook, Google, Amazon, Dropbox, Palantir, and Apple. Interviewers tend to develop a set of questions that they've calibrated against multiple candidates. For example, I always asked, "What is one thing that you like and one thing that you dislike about the engineering culture at __________?" I'd fill in the blank with the name of the company the engineer was leaving or, if the candidate was a fresh college graduate, a company where she had previously interned.

Initially, I just wanted to make sure that a candidate shared good engineering hygiene for best practices. But I kept tallies of the responses, and, over time, they painted evocative pictures of different engineering cultures. Some responses illustrated toxic culture—the elements that pushed some of the best engineers to leave their teams. Others revealed great culture—the characteristics engineers actually look for when deciding whether to join a new organization. I used my tallies to visualize what our own team culture should look like.

Engineering culture consists of the set of values and habits shared by people on the team, and a great culture provides a number of benefits. Engineers feel empowered to get things done, which makes them happier and more productive. Happy and productive engineers in turn translate to higher employee retention. The culture provides a shared context and a framework for making decisions, which helps teams and organizations adapt more quickly to problems they encounter. And because the best engineers look for a strong engineering culture, it becomes a useful tool for recruiting talent. Hiring those engineers further strengthens the culture and creates a positive feedback loop.

So what do the best engineers look for in a prospective company? Based on my hundreds of interviews and conversations, I've found that great engineering cultures:

1. Optimize for iteration speed.
2. Push relentlessly towards automation.
3. Build the right software abstractions.
4. Focus on high code quality by using code reviews.
5. Maintain a respectful work environment.
6. Build shared ownership of code.

7. Invest in automated testing.
8. Allot experimentation time, either through 20% time or hackathons.
9. Foster a culture of learning and continuous improvement.
10. Hire the best.

You'll notice that most of these topics have already been covered in this book. This shouldn't be a surprise. The best engineers enjoy getting things done, and the high-leverage investments we've been discussing empower them to get things done faster. The best engineers want to build on top of high-quality and well-tested codebases. They want to have short iteration and validation cycles so that they learn quickly and aren't wasting effort. They believe in relentlessly automating processes to relieve their operational burden so that they can keep learning and building new things. They know the value of leverage, and they want to work at places where they can create meaningful impact.

A great engineering culture isn't built in a day; nor is it already in place when a company first starts. It begins with the values of the initial team members, and it's a continual work-in-progress that every engineer helps to shape. It evolves over time with the decisions we make, the stories we tell, and the habits we adopt. It helps us make better decisions, adapt more quickly, and attract stronger talent. And when we focus on high-leverage activities, we not only become more effective engineers, we also lay the groundwork for a more effective engineering culture.

Key Takeaways

- **Help the people around you be successful.** The high rungs of an engineering ladder are reserved for those who make their co-workers more effective. Moreover, the success of those around you will also carry you along.
- **Make hiring a priority.** Keep a high hiring bar and play an active role in growing your team.
- **Invest in onboarding and mentoring.** The more quickly you can ramp up new team members, the more effective your team will be. The more effective your team, the more freedom you have to tackle different projects.
- **Build shared ownership of code.** Increase your bus factor to be greater than one so that you're not a bottleneck for development. This will give you the flexibility to focus on other high-leverage activities.
- **Debrief and document collective wisdom.** Reflect on projects with team members, learn what worked and what didn't work, and document and share the lessons so that valuable wisdom doesn't get lost.
- **Create a great engineering culture.** This will help you be more productive, streamline decisions, and recruit other strong engineers. You build a great culture by fostering the same habits you need to effectively deliver impact.

Epilogue

I began this book with a search. How could I create meaningful impact without pulling the 70- to 80-hour work weeks characterizing my early startup days? How could I cut out the hours building products and features that customers didn't use, the hours maintaining infrastructure that software could automate, and the hours stuck on tasks where I was the bottleneck? How could I have worked less and accomplished more?

In this book, I've shared what I learned in my journey to be a more effective engineer. We've covered a broad range of topics and lessons. At the same time, we've only barely scratched the surface of the problems that we face as engineers. When should we use one technology over another? Which programming languages or paradigms are worthwhile to learn? Should we work on side projects or focus on skills directly relevant to our jobs? How much time should we spend improving our communication or presentation techniques? The list of questions could go on and on, and distilling the best advice to tackle each one would take volumes. Moreover, the best answer varies based on our circumstances, our personal preferences, and our goals.

The good news is that the same operating principle—leverage—that we've used throughout *The Effective Engineer* can help us navigate these waters. If there's one idea that I want you to take away from this book, it's this: **Time is our most finite asset, and leverage—the value we produce per unit time—allows us to direct our time toward what matters most.** We should always ask ourselves: Does the work I'm doing provide the highest leverage for my current goal? If not, why am I doing it? Moreover, when we make the wrong choice—which is bound to happen over the course of our careers—a growth mindset allows us to view each failure as an opportunity to learn and do better next time.

Leverage is the lens through which effective engineers view their activities. And, as you might have realized, most of the advice in this book applies beyond engineering. The limitations of time apply just as much in life as it does in work. The principle of leverage can guide us toward those life activities that provide the highest impact for our efforts.

When we're planning our finances, we should spend significantly more time on negotiating our salaries and setting up our investment asset allocations—both of which could lead to tens or hundreds of thousands of dollars down the line—than on agonizing over the tens of dollars that we might save by changing a coffee habit. When planning trips or events, we should focus on the parts that matter most to us—whether it's the location, the food, the activities, the invitees, or something else—before sweating the smaller details. We should make similar calculations about the best use of our time when we're debating whether to hire a virtual assistant, outsource a task to a remote team, or call Uber or Lyft instead of waiting for public transportation. Even when I was writing this book, I needed to overcome the risks of a one-person team and consciously remind myself that an hour spent collecting feedback would frequently provide higher leverage than a siloed hour spent writing and editing.

Does this perspective mean that we should be pursuing only high-leverage activities? No; that would be exhausting. We enjoy plenty of leisure activities like traveling, hiking, salsa dancing, and spending time with family and friends without giving any thought to whether they're high-impact or represent the optimal use of our time—and that's how it should be. But when it comes to achieving our work and life goals, leverage is a powerful framework for helping us focus on the right things.

Appendix

MANY RESOURCES HAVE GUIDED AND INSPIRED MY JOURNEY. THE following books have significantly shaped my way of thinking about what it means to be an effective engineer. In addition, you may wish to follow the listed blogs to continue your own learning.

10 Books Every Effective Engineer Should Read

- *Peopleware: Productive Projects and Teams* by software consultants Tom De-Marco and Timothy Lister. First published in 1987, this book discusses the many dynamics within projects and teams, presenting ideas backed up by actual research. Though somewhat dated, the book provides many pearls of wisdom, like how imposing overtime can destroy a team's ability to gel and how listening to music while programming can interfere with our ability to focus. *Peopleware* started me on my path toward thinking about how to build effective engineering teams and great engineering cultures.
- *Team Geek: A Software Developer's Guide to Working Well with Others* by Brian W. Fitzpatrick and Ben Collins-Sussman. In this book, two Googlers who founded Google's Chicago engineering office share stories and insights about how to work well with your fellow engineers. Covering strategies on how to deal with managers or poisonous team members, and discussing both patterns and anti-patterns on how to lead teams, it's a worthwhile book for any growing engineer to read.

- *High Output Management* by Andrew S. Grove. Grove, the former CEO of Intel, introduced me to the language of leverage and provided me with the lens that I now use to allocate my time. Don't be turned off by the word "management" in the title. His advice on how to increase your output is relevant to both people managers as well as to those he calls "know-how managers"—people like senior engineers who hold much of the valued knowledge within an organization.
- *Getting Things Done: The Art of Stress-Free Productivity* by David Allen. This book thoroughly describes a concrete implementation of how to manage to-dos and task lists. While I don't subscribe to all of Allen's ideas, it was eye-opening to read about one possible way of doing things. If you don't have a good workflow for prioritizing and getting things done, this book can provide you with a baseline.
- *The 4-Hour Workweek: Escape 9-5, Live Anywhere, and Join the New Rich* by Timothy Ferriss. Regardless of whether you actually choose to subscribe to the type of extreme lifestyle that Ferriss advocates, this book will teach you two things. First, it shows what's possible if you relentlessly prioritize your work and focus on the 10% of effort that produces most of your gains. Second, it drives home the importance of creating sustainable systems with low maintenance. That's a lesson that's often underemphasized in engineering, where our inclination to build new features with the latest sexy technologies doesn't necessarily take into account the cost of future maintenance.
- *The 7 Habits of Highly Effective People: Powerful Lessons in Personal Change* by Stephen R. Covey. I'm not actually a fan of Covey's writing style—much of it is a little too abstract and fluffy—but the lasting impact of the ideas in the book compensate for it. From Covey's third habit of "putting first things first," I learned that people tend to neglect important but non-urgent activities and spend a lot of time dealing with tasks like emails, phone calls, and meetings that may be urgent but ultimately unimportant. A key takeaway from this habit is to explicitly budget time to invest in yourself, whether it's by learning new skills, maintaining relationships, reading, etc.

- *Conscious Business: How to Build Value Through Values* by Fred Kofman. Kofman taught leadership seminars at companies like Facebook and Google, and his book transformed how I approach difficult conversations with others. Through simple language and well-constructed hypotheticals, Kofman demonstrates that we often conflate the facts of a situation and our own interpretations, resulting in unproductive conversations. Only by separating fact from story can we actually have those difficult conversations where we achieve our goals.
- *Your Brain at Work: Strategies for Overcoming Distraction, Regaining Focus, and Working Smarter All Day Long* by David Rock. In this easy-to-read book, Rock combines research on the brain's functions with actionable advice on how to work more effectively around the brain's limitations. For instance, this book taught me that because prioritization is a difficult but high-leverage activity that requires substantial cognitive effort, it's best done at the beginning of the day.
- *Flow: The Psychology of Optimal Experience* by Mihály Csíkszentmihályi. In this book, Csíkszentmihályi, a Hungarian professor and the world's leading researcher on positive psychology, summarizes years of research on what's required to make someone feel fulfilled and motivated. Criteria include a quick feedback loop, an appropriate level of challenge, and an absence of interruptions. Given how much time we spend working, being conscious of these requirements as we go from job to job and from project to project is very valuable.
- *Succeed: How We Can Reach Our Goals* by Heidi Grant Halvorson. Halvorson discusses different frameworks for thinking about goals and how to best frame a goal to increase our chances of success. When is it helpful to be optimistic versus pessimistic in a goal? Is it better to think about why you want to achieve a certain goal, or to think about what steps are necessary to achieve it? Should you visualize what you might gain from achieving a goal or what you might lose by failing to achieve it? It turns out that depending on the type of goal, different ways of mentally framing the goal can significantly affect your chances for success.

Recommended Blogs To Follow

- http://www.theeffectiveengineer.com/. The Effective Engineer is my personal blog, where I write about engineering habits, productivity tips, leadership, and culture.
- http://www.kalzumeus.com/. Patrick McKenzie runs his own software business and has written many excellent long-form articles on career advice, consulting, SEO, and software sales.
- http://katemats.com/. Kate Matsudaira, who has worked at large companies like Microsoft and Amazon as well as at startups, shares advice about tech, leadership, and life on her blog.
- http://randsinrepose.com/. Michael Lopp has worked for many years in leadership positions at Netscape, Apple, Palantir, and Pinterest, and writes about tech life and engineering management.
- http://softwareleadweekly.com/. Oren Ellenbogen curates a high-quality weekly newsletter on engineering leadership and culture.
- http://calnewport.com/. Cal Newport, an assistant professor of computer science at Georgetown, focuses on evidence-based advice for building a successful and fulfilling life.
- http://www.joelonsoftware.com/. Joel Spolsky, the co-founder of Stack Exchange, provides all sorts of programming pearls of wisdom on his blog.
- http://martinfowler.com/. Martin Fowler, author of the book *Refactoring*, writes about how to maximize the productivity of software teams and provides detailed write-ups of common programming patterns.
- http://pgbovine.net/. Philip Guo, a computer science professor, has written extensively and openly about his graduate school and work experiences.

Acknowledgments

I am grateful to the many people who helped make writing and publishing *The Effective Engineer* possible.

A huge thank you to my wife, Chen Xiao, for her patience and support as I took a personal sabbatical away from work to follow my dream of writing a book. She beta tested many of my early book drafts and really helped me to figure out a unifying structure for the book.

My editor, Emily M. Robinson, brought the quality of my writing to another level, and it was a joy to iterate with her on the drafts on Quip. As a first-time author, I couldn't have hoped for a better editor.

Many thanks to Philip Guo, Leo Polovets, Phil Crosby, Zach Brock, Xiao Yu, Alex Allain, Ilya Sukhar, Daniel Peng, Raffi Krikorian, Mike Curtis, Jack Heart, Tamar Bercovici, Tracy Chou, Yiren Lu, Jess Lin, Annie Ding, Ellis Lau, and Jessica Lau for reading drafts of the book and providing valuable feedback.

Many people contributed to the stories in the book: Mike Krieger, Marc Hedlund, Sam Schillace, Tamar Bercovici, Bobby Johnson, Albert Ni, Nimrod Hoofien, Kartik Ayyar, Yishan Wong, Jack Heart, Joshua Levy, and Dan McKinley. Thank you all for taking the time to sit down for interviews. The stories and lessons you shared were invaluable.

Thanks to Bret Taylor for taking the time to write the foreword and for starting a company around a product that made the collaborative writing and project management aspects of this book so much more enjoyable.

Thank you to the team at Quora for building a knowledge-sharing platform that re-inspired my passion for writing, and particularly to Charlie Cheever, who empowered me to create meaningful impact at the company.

Notes

Chapter 1: Focus on High-Leverage Activities

1. Kah Keng Tay, "The Intern Experience at Quora," *Quora*, November 4, 2013, https://blog.quora.com/The-Intern-Experience-at-Quora.

2. Peter F. Drucker, *The Effective Executive* (HarperBusiness 2006).

3. "Pareto principle," *Wikipedia*, http://en.wikipedia.org/wiki/Pareto_principle.

4. "Archimedes," *Wikipedia*, http://en.wikiquote.org/wiki/Archimedes.

5. Assuming a 40–60 hour work week, 2 weeks of federal holidays, and 3 weeks of personal vacation.

6. Andrew S. Grove, *High Output Management* (Vintage 1995), p53–54.

7. Yishan Wong, interview with the author, March 14, 2013.

8. Yishan Wong, "Engineering Management," October 22, 2009, http://algeri-wong.com/yishan/engineering-management.html.

9. Yishan Wong, "Engineering Management - Hiring," October 23, 2009, http://algeri-wong.com/yishan/engineering-management-hiring.html.

10. "Company Info | Facebook Newsroom," http://newsroom.fb.com/company-info/.

11. Bill & Melinda Gates Foundation, "Foundation Fact Sheet," http://www.gatesfoundation.org/Who-We-Are/General-Information/Foundation-Factsheet.

12. Bill Gates, "Bill Gates: Here's My Plan to Improve Our World—And How You Can Help," *Wired*, November 12, 2013, http://www.wired.com/business/2013/11/bill-gates-wired-essay/.

Chapter 2: Optimize for Learning

1. "Protocol Buffers: Developer Guide," https://developers.google.com/protocol-buffers/docs/overview.
2. Fay Chang et al., "Bigtable: A Distributed Storage System for Structured Data," *Operating Systems Design and Implementation*, 2006, http://research.google.com/archive/bigtable-osdi06.pdf.
3. Jeffrey Dean and Sanjay Ghemawat, "MapReduce: Simplified Data Processing on Large Clusters," *Operating Systems Design and Implementation*, 2004, http://research.google.com/archive/mapreduce-osdi04.pdf.
4. Carol Dweck, *Mindset: The New Psychology of Success* (Ballantine Books 2007), p6.
5. Dweck, *Mindset*, p6–7.
6. Dweck, *Mindset*, p17–18.
7. Dweck, *Mindset*, p218–224.
8. Dweck, *Mindset*, p23.
9. Dweck, *Mindset*, p57.
10. The formula for compounding interest is V = P(1+r/n)^nt, where V = the future value of the investment, P = the principal investment amount, r = the annual interest rate, n = the number of times that interest is compounded per year, and t = the number of years the money is invested for.
11. Blake Masters, "Peter Thiel's CS183: Startup - Class 5 Notes Essay," April 20, 2012, http://blakemasters.tumblr.com/post/21437840885/peter-thiels-cs183-startup-class-5-notes-essay.
12. Reid Hoffman and Ben Casnocha, *The Start-up of You: Adapt to the Future, Invest in Yourself, and Transform Your Career* (Crown Business 2012).
13. Tony Hsieh, *Delivering Happiness: A Path to Profits, Passion, and Purpose* (Business Plus 2010), p173–175.
14. 1.01^365 = 37.78.
15. Hsieh, *Delivering Happiness*, p163–165.
16. Sheryl Sandberg, *Lean In: Women, Work, and the Will to Lead* (Knopf 2013), p58.

17. Andrew Bosworth, "Facebook Engineering Bootcamp," *Facebook Notes*, November 19, 2009, https://www.facebook.com/notes/facebook-engineering/facebook-engineering-bootcamp/177577963919.

18. Ryan Tate, "Google Couldn't Kill 20 Percent Time Even if It Wanted To," *Wired*, August 21, 2013, http://www.wired.com/2013/08/20-percent-time-will-never-die/.

19. Ryan Tate, "LinkedIn Gone Wild: '20 Percent Time' to Tinker Spreads Beyond Google," *Wired*, December 6, 2012, http://www.wired.com/2012/12/llinkedin-20-percent-time/.

20. John Rotenstein, "Atlassian's 20% Time now out of Beta," *Atlassian Blogs*, March 23, 2009, http://blogs.atlassian.com/2009/03/atlassians_20_time_now_out_of_beta/.

21. Steven Sinofsky, "The path to GM – some thoughts on becoming a general manager," *Steven Sinofsky's Microsoft TechTalk*, September 19, 2005, http://blogs.msdn.com/b/techtalk/archive/2005/09/18/471121.aspx.

22. Peter Brown et al., *Make It Stick: The Science of Successful Learning* (The Belknap Press of Harvard University Press 2014), p19.

23. Peter Brown et al., *Make It Stick: The Science of Successful Learning* (The Belknap Press of Harvard University Press 2014), p46–66.

24. Bobby Johnson, interview with the author, December 17, 2013.

25. Philip Moeller, "Why Learning Leads To Happiness," *Huffington Post*, April 10, 2012, http://www.huffingtonpost.com/2012/04/10/learning-happiness_n_1415568.html.

26. Aden Hepburn, "Infographic: 2013 Mobile Growth Statistics," *Digital Buzz*, October 2013, http://www.digitalbuzzblog.com/infographic-2013-mobile-growth-statistics/.

27. Benedict Evans, "Mobile is Eating the World," *Slideshare*, November 2013, http://www.slideshare.net/bge20/2013-11-mobile-eating-the-world.

28. Bill Gates, "The Best Books I Read in 2013," *gatesnotes*, December 12, 2013, http://www.thegatesnotes.com/Personal/Best-Books-2013.

29. "Junto (club)," *Wikipedia*, http://en.wikipedia.org/wiki/Junto_(club).

30. "Google Tech Talks," *YouTube*, http://www.youtube.com/user/GoogleTechTalks/videos.

31. "Talks at Google," *YouTube*, http://www.youtube.com/user/AtGoogleTalks/featured.

32. "TED: Ideas Worth Spreading," https://www.ted.com/.

33. Richard Wiseman, *The Luck Factor: The Four Essential Principles* (Miramax 2004), p38.

34. Scott H. Young, "Learn Faster with the Feynman Technique," *Scott H Young Blog*, http://www.scotthyoung.com/blog/2011/09/01/learn-faster/.

35. Karlyn Adams, "The Sources of Innovation and Creativity," *National Center on Education and the Economy (NCEE) Research Summary and Final Report*, July 2005, p4, http://www.ncee.org/wp-content/uploads/2010/04/Sources-of-Innovation-Creativity.pdf.

36. "State of the Media Trends in TV Viewing—2011 TV Upfronts," *Nielsen*, 2001, http://www.nielsen.com/content/dam/corporate/us/en/newswire/uploads/2011/04/State-of-the-Media-2011-TV-Upfronts.pdf.

37. Martin E. P. Seligman, *Authentic Happiness: Using the New Positive Psychology to Realize Your Potential for Lasting Fulfillment* (Free Press 2002), p176.

Chapter 3: Prioritize Regularly

1. Greg Buckner, "Andy Johns' 'The Case for User Growth Teams,'" *Quibb*, 2012, http://quibb.com/links/andy-johns-the-case-for-user-growth-teams.

2. Alexia Tsotsis, "Quora Grew More Than 3X Across All Metrics In The Past Year," *TechCrunch*, May 28, 2013, http://techcrunch.com/2013/05/28/quora-grows-more-than-3x-across-all-metrics-in-the-past-year/.

3. Atul Gawande, *The Checklist Manifesto: How to Get Things Right* (Picador 2011).

4. David Allen, *Getting Things Done: The Art of Stress-Free Productivity* (Penguin Books 2002).

5. George Miller, "The Magical Number Seven, Plus or Minus Two: Some Limits on Our Capacity for Processing Information," *The Psychological Review*, 1956, vol. 63, .81–97, http://www.musanim.com/miller1956/.

6. "Pi World Ranking List," http://pi-world-ranking-list.com/lists/memo/index.html.

7. Joshua Foer, *Moonwalking with Einstein* (Penguin Books 2012).

8. Daniel Kahneman, *Thinking, Fast and Slow* (Farrar, Straus and Giroux 2011).

9. Baba Shiv and Alexander Fedorikh, "Heart and Mind in Conflict: The Interplay of Affect and Cognition in Consumer Decision Making," *Journal of Consumer Research*, December 1999, Vol. 26, https://5aeed477-a-62cb3a1a-s-sites.googlegroups.com/site/xiaoliangtushuguanfenguan3/gm934xing-wei-jue-ce-zhi-ding/Shiv%26Fedorikhin1999.pdf.

10. Samuele M. Marcora, Walter Staiano, and Victoria Manning, "Mental fatigue impairs physical performance," *Journal of Applied Physiology*, 2009, 106: 857–864, http://jap.physiology.org/content/106/3/857.full.pdf.

11. Yishan Wong, "What are some ways to 'work smart' rather than just working hard?," *Quora*, June 30, 2010, https://www.quora.com/What-are-some-ways-to-work-smart-rather-than-just-working-hard/answer/Yishan-Wong.

12. Stephen. R. Covey, *7 Habits of Highly Effective People* (Simon & Schuster 2013).

13. Mihály Csíkszentmihályi, *Flow: The Psychology of Optimal Experience* (Harper Perennial Modern Classics 2008).

14. Paul Graham, "Maker's Schedule, Manager's Schedule," July 2009, http://www.paulgraham.com/makersschedule.html.

15. Shamsi T. Iqbal and Eric Horvitz, "Disruption and Recovery of Computing Tasks: Field Study, Analysis, and Directions," *ACM CHI Conference*, 2007, http://research.microsoft.com/en-us/um/people/horvitz/chi_2007_iqbal_horvitz.pdf.

16. Jennifer Robison, "Too Many Interruptions at Work?," *Gallup Business Journal*, June 8, 2006, http://businessjournal.gallup.com/content/23146/too-many-interruptions-work.aspx#1.

17. David Rock, *Your Brain at Work* (HarperCollins Publishers 2009).

18. Tonianne DeMaria Barry and Jim Benson, *Personal Kanban: Mapping Work | Navigating Life* (Modus Cooperandi Press 2011).

19. Frank Wieber and Peter Gollwitzer, *Overcoming Procrastination through Planning in C. Andreou, M. D. White (Eds.), The Thief of Time. Philosophical Essays on Procrastination* (New York: Oxford University Press 2010), p 185–205.

20. Elizabeth J. Parks-Stamm, Peter M. Gollwitzer, and Gabriele Oettingen, "Action Control by Implementation Intentions: Effective Cue Detection and Efficient Response Initiation," *Social Cognition*, 2007, Vol. 25, No. 2, . 248–266, http://webapp7.rrz.uni-hamburg.de/files/u130/Action_Control_by_Implementation__Intentions.pdf.
21. Heidi Grant Halvorson, *Succeed: How we can reach our goals*, p177–180.
22. Halvorson, *Succeed*, p14–20.
23. Halvorson, *Succeed*, p175–177.
24. Allen, *Getting Things Done*.
25. Tonianne DeMaria Barry and Jim Benson, *Personal Kanban*.
26. Francesco Cirillo, "The Pomodoro Technique," 2007, http://pomodorotechnique.com/book/.
27. Nick Cernis, *todoodlist*.
28. On any Linux-based system (like a Mac), you can add a line like `127.0.0.1 www.facebook.com` to route network requests to that domain to localhost, effectively blocking the site.
29. "focus booster," http://www.focusboosterapp.com/.

Chapter 4: Invest in Iteration Speed

1. Martin Michelsen, "Continuous Deployment at Quora," *Quora*, https://engineering.quora.com/Continuous-Deployment-at-Quora.
2. Alexia Tsotsis, "Quora Grew More Than 3X Across All Metrics In The Past Year," *TechCrunch*, May 28, 2013, http://techcrunch.com/2013/05/28/quora-grows-more-than-3x-across-all-metrics-in-the-past-year/.
3. George Neville-Neil, "Merge Early, Merge Often," *ACM Queue*, October 29, 2009, vol. 7, no. 9, http://queue.acm.org/detail.cfm?id=1643030.
4. Erik Kastner, "Quantum of Deployment," *Code as Craft*, May 20, 2010, http://codeascraft.com/2010/05/20/quantum-of-deployment/.
5. Timothy Fitz, "Continuous Deployment at IMVU: Doing the impossible fifty times a day," February 10, 2009, http://timothyfitz.com/2009/02/10/continuous-deployment-at-imvu-doing-the-impossible-fifty-times-a-day/.

6. David Fortunato, "Deployment Infrastructure for Continuous Deployment," *Wealthfront Engineering Blog*, May 2, 2010, http://eng.wealthfront.com/2010/05/deployment-infrastructure-for.html.
7. Jake Douglas, "Deploying at GitHub," https://github.com/blog/1241-deploying-at-github.
8. Brett G. Durrett et al., "What are best examples of companies using continuous deployment?," *Quora*, https://www.quora.com/What-are-best-examples-of-companies-using-continuous-deployment.
9. Haydn Shaughnessy, "Facebook's 1 Billion Users: Why The Sky Is Still The Limit," *Forbes*, October 4, 2012, http://www.forbes.com/sites/haydnshaughnessy/2012/10/04/facebooks-1-billion-users-why-the-sky-is-still-the-limit/.
10. Andrew Bosworth, "How does Facebook Engineering's 'Bootcamp' program work?," *Quora*, October 11, 2011, https://www.quora.com/How-does-Facebook-Engineerings-Bootcamp-program-work/answer/Andrew-Boz-Bosworth.
11. Chuck Rossi, "Ship early and ship twice as often," *Facebook Notes*, August 3, 2012, https://www.facebook.com/notes/facebook-engineering/ship-early-and-ship-twice-as-often/10150985860363920.
12. "Facebook Beacon," *Wikipedia*, http://en.wikipedia.org/wiki/Facebook_Beacon.
13. Josh Constine, "Facebook's S-1 Letter From Zuckerberg Urges Understanding Before Investment," *TechCrunch*, February 2012, http://techcrunch.com/2012/02/01/facebook-ipo-letter/.
14. Robert Johnson, "More Details on Today's Outage," *Facebook Notes*, September 23, 2010, https://www.facebook.com/notes/facebook-engineering/more-details-on-todays-outage/431441338919.
15. "$1 Billion. Two and a Half Years.," *Wealthfront*, https://www.wealthfront.com/one-billion.
16. David Fortunato, "Deployment Infrastructure for Continuous Deployment," *Wealthfront Engineering Blog*, May 2, 2010, http://eng.wealthfront.com/2010/05/deployment-infrastructure-for.html.
17. Pascal-Louis Perez, "Continuous Deployment in an SEC-Regulated Environment," *Wealthfront Engineering Blog*, May 25, 2011,

http://eng.wealthfront.com/2011/05/continuous-deployment-in-sec-regulated.html.

18. Bobby Johnson, interview with the author.

19. Raffi Krikorian, conversation with the author.

20. Nils Klarlund, "distcc's pump mode: A New Design for Distributed C/C++ Compilation," *Google Open Source Blog*, http://google-opensource.blogspot.com/2008/08/distccs-pump-mode-new-design-for.html.

21. Ian Lance Taylor, "gold: Google Releases New and Improved GCC Linker," *Google Open Source Blog*, http://google-opensource.blogspot.com/2008/08/distccs-pump-mode-new-design-for.html.

22. Research by Prechelt that compares 80 implementations of the same set of requirements across 7 different languages shows that solutions written in C.

23. Joshua Levy, et al., "What are the most useful 'Swiss army knife' one-liners on Unix?," *Quora*, https://www.quora.com/What-are-the-most-useful-Swiss-army-knife-one-liners-on-Unix.

24. Phil Crosby, "Live CSS - Making the browser dance to your CSS," *GitHub*, https://github.com/ooyala/livecss.

25. "LiveReload," http://livereload.com/.

26. Nicholas Carlson, "The Truth About Marissa Mayer: An Unauthorized Biography," *Business Insider*, August 24, 2013, http://www.businessinsider.com/marissa-mayer-biography-2013-8.

Chapter 5: Measure What You Want to Improve

1. Steven Levy, "Exclusive: How Google's Algorithm Rules the Web," *Wired*, February 22, 2010, http://www.wired.com/2010/02/ff_google_algorithm/all/1.

2. "Algorithms - Inside Search - Google," http://www.google.com/intl/en_us/insidesearch/howsearchworks/algorithms.html.

3. Daniel Russell, "Daniel Russell's Home Page," https://sites.google.com/site/dmrussell/.

4. Eric Savitz, "Google's User Happiness Problem," *Forbes*, April 12, 2011, http://www.forbes.com/sites/ciocentral/2011/04/12/googles-user-happiness-problem/.

5. Emil Protalinski, "comScore: Google is once again the most-trafficked US desktop site, ends Yahoo's seven-month streak," *TheNextWeb*, March 25, 2014, http://thenextweb.com/google/2014/03/25/comscore-google-breaks-yahoos-seven-month-streak-trafficked-us-desktop-site/.

6. Steven Levy, "Exclusive: How Google's Algorithm Rules the Web," *Wired*, February 22, 2010, http://www.wired.com/2010/02/ff_google_algorithm/all/1.

7. Peter Fleischer, "Why does Google remember information about searches?," *Google Official Blog*, May 11, 2007, http://googleblog.blogspot.com/2007/05/why-does-google-remember-information.html.

8. Steven Levy, *In The Plex: How Google Thinks, Works, and Shapes Our Lives* (Simon & Schuster 2011), p47.

9. Levy, *In the Plex*, p49.

10. Levy, *In the Plex*, p57–59.

11. "Algorithms - Inside Search - Google," http://www.google.com/intl/en_us/insidesearch/howsearchworks/algorithms.html.

12. Peter F. Drucker, *The Effective Executive*.

13. Tom DeMarco and Timothy Lister, *Peopleware: Productive Projects and Teams*.

14. Steven Levy, *In The Plex*.

15. Jake Brutlag, "Speed Matters," *Google Research Blog*, June 23, 2009, http://googleresearch.blogspot.com/2009/06/speed-matters.html.

16. Stoyan Stefanov, "YSlow 2.0," *CSDN Software Development 2.0 Conference*, December 6, 2008, http://www.slideshare.net/stoyan/yslow-20-presentation.

17. Zizhuang Yang, "Every Millisecond Counts," *Facebook Notes*, August 28, 2009, https://www.facebook.com/note.php?note_id=122869103919.

18. Kit Eaton, "How One Second Could Cost Amazon $1.6 Billion in Sales," *Fast Company*, March 15, 2012, http://www.fastcompany.com/1825005/how-one-second-could-cost-amazon-16-billion-sales.

19. Tony Hsieh, *Delivering Happiness*, p145–146.

20. Jim Collins, *Good to Great: Why Some Companies Make the Leap... And Others Don't* (HarperBusiness 2001), p104–105.

21. Eric Ries, *The Lean Startup: How Today's Entrepreneurs Use Continuous Innovation to Create Radically Successful Businesses* (Crown Business 2011), p128–143.

22. "Flight Instruments," *Wikipedia*, http://en.wikipedia.org/wiki/Flight_instruments.

23. Paul Mulwitz, "What do all the controls in an airplane cockpit do?," *Quora*, March 6, 2012, https://www.quora.com/What-do-all-the-controls-in-an-airplane-cockpit-do/answer/Paul-Mulwitz.

24. Sharon Begley, "Insight - As Obamacare tech woes mounted, contractor payments soared," *Reuters*, October 17, 2013, http://uk.reuters.com/article/2013/10/17/uk-usa-healthcare-technology-insight-idUKBRE99G06120131017.

25. Paul Ford, "The Obamacare Website Didn't Have to Fail. How to Do Better Next Time," *Businessweek*, October 16, 2013, http://www.businessweek.com/articles/2013-10-16/open-source-everything-the-moral-of-the-healthcare-dot-gov-debacle.

26. Adrianne Jeffries, "Obama defends Healthcare.gov despite massive tech problems: 'there's no sugarcoating it,'" *The Verge*, October 21, 2013, http://www.theverge.com/2013/10/21/4862090/obama-defends-healthcare-gov-despite-massive-tech-problems-theres-no.

27. Steven Brill, "Obama's Trauma Team," *Time*, February 27, 2014, http://time.com/10228/obamas-trauma-team/.

28. Jeffrey Young, "Obamacare Sign-Ups Hit 8 Million In Remarkable Turnaround," *Huffington Post*, April 17, 2014, http://www.huffingtonpost.com/2014/04/17/obamacare-sign-ups_n_5167080.html.

29. Ian Malpass, "Measure Anything, Measure Everything," *Code as Craft*, February 15, 2011, http://codeascraft.com/2011/02/15/measure-anything-measure-everything/.

30. "Graphite Documentation," http://graphite.readthedocs.org/en/latest/.

31. "StatsD," *GitHub*, https://github.com/etsy/statsd/.

32. Mike Brittain, "Tracking Every Release," *Code as Craft*, December 8, 2010, http://codeascraft.com/2010/12/08/track-every-release/.

33. "We are the Google Site Reliability team. We make Google's websites work. Ask us Anything!," *Reddit*, January 24, 2013, http://www.reddit.com/r/IAmA/comments/177267/we_are_the_google_site_reliability_team_we_make/c82y43e.
34. Cory G. Watson, "Observability at Twitter," *Twitter Engineering Blog*, September 9, 2013, https://blog.twitter.com/2013/observability-at-twitter.
35. Greg Leffler, "A crash course in LinkedIn's global site operations," *LinkedIn Engineering Blog*, September 18, 2013, http://engineering.linkedin.com/day-life/crash-course-linkedins-global-site-operations.
36. "Percona," http://www.percona.com/.
37. "MySQL Performance Audits," http://www.percona.com/products/mysql-consulting/performance-audit.
38. Baron Schwarz, "How Percona does a MySQL Performance Audit," *MySQL Performance Blog*, December 24, 2008, http://www.mysqlperformanceblog.com/2008/11/24/how-percona-does-a-mysql-performance-audit/.
39. Jeffrey Dean, "Google Research Scientists and Engineers: Jeffrey Dean," http://research.google.com/people/jeff/.
40. Jeffrey Dean, "Building Software Systems At Google and Lessons Learned," *Stanford EE380: Computer Systems Colloquium*, November 10, 2010, https://www.youtube.com/watch?v=modXC5IWTJI.
41. Jeffrey Dean, "Software Engineering Advice from Building Large-Scale Distributed Systems," http://static.googleusercontent.com/media/research.google.com/en/us/people/jeff/stanford-295-talk.pdf.
42. "Snappy, a fast compressor/decompressor.," *Google Project Hosting*, https://code.google.com/p/snappy/source/browse/trunk/README.
43. "Average Email Campaign Stats of MailChimp Customers by Industry," *MailChimp*, http://mailchimp.com/resources/research/email-marketing-benchmarks/.
44. Eric Colson, "Growing to Large Scale at Netflix," *Extremely Large Databases Conference*, October 18, 2011, http://www-conf.slac.stanford.edu/xldb2011/program.asp.

45. Edmond Lau, "What A/B testing platform does Quora use?," *Quora*, November 10, 2012, https://www.quora.com/What-A-B-testing-platform-does-Quora-use/answer/Edmond-Lau.

Chapter 6: Validate Your Ideas Early and Often

1. Anthony Ha, "Cuil might just be cool enough to become the Google-killer in search," *VentureBeat*, July 27, 2008, http://venturebeat.com/2008/07/27/cuil-might-just-be-cool-enough-to-become-the-google-killer-in-search/.
2. Michael Arrington, "Cuill: Super Stealth Search Engine; Google Has Definitely Noticed," *TechCrunch*, September 4, 2007, http://techcrunch.com/2007/09/04/cuill-super-stealth-search-engine-google-has-definitely-noticed/.
3. Anthony Ha, "Cuil might just be cool enough to become the Google-killer in search," *VentureBeat*, July 27, 2008, http://venturebeat.com/2008/07/27/cuil-might-just-be-cool-enough-to-become-the-google-killer-in-search/.
4. Joseph Tartakoff, "'Google Killer' Cuil Looks To Make Money—Perhaps Via Google," *GigaOm*, June 24, 2009, http://gigaom.com/2009/06/24/419-google-killer-cuil-looks-to-make-money-perhaps-via-google/.
5. Danny Sullivan, "Cuil Launches—Can This Search Start-Up Really Best Google?," *Search Engine Land*, June 28, 2008, http://searchengineland.com/cuil-launches-can-this-search-start-up-really-best-google-14459.
6. Saul Hansell, "No Bull, Cuil Had Problems," *The New York Times Bits*, June 29, 2008, http://bits.blogs.nytimes.com/2008/07/29/no-bull-cuil-had-problems/.
7. John C. Dvorak, "The New Cuil Search Engine Sucks," *PC Magazine*, July 28, 2008, http://www.pcmag.com/article2/0,2817,2326643,00.asp.
8. Rafe Needleman, "Cuil shows us how not to launch a search engine," *CNET*, July 28, 2008, http://www.cnet.com/news/cuil-shows-us-how-not-to-launch-a-search-engine/.
9. Anita Hamilton, "Why Cuil Is No Threat to Google," *Time*, July 28, 2008, http://content.time.com/time/business/article/0,8599,1827331,00.html.

10. Dave Burdick, "Cuil Review: Really? No Dave Burdicks? This Search Engine Is Stupid," *Huffington Post*, August 5, 2008, http://www.huffingtonpost.com/dave-burdick/cuil-review-really-no-dav_b_115413.html.
11. "BloomReach Customers," http://bloomreach.com/customers/.
12. John Constine, "BloomReach Crunches Big Data To Deliver The Future Of SEO and SEM," February 22, 2012, http://techcrunch.com/2012/02/22/bloomreach/.
13. MASLab stood for Mobile Autonomous Systems Laboratory.
14. Zach Brock, conversation with the author.
15. Eric Ries, "Minimum Viable Product: a guide," *Startup Lessons Learned*, August 3, 2009, http://www.startuplessonslearned.com/2009/08/minimum-viable-product-guide.html.
16. Eric Ries, "The Lean Startup," p98.
17. Drew Houston, "DropBox Demo," *YouTube*, September 15, 2008, http://www.youtube.com/watch?v=7QmCUDHpNzE.
18. Alex Wilhelm, "Dropbox Could Be A Bargain At An $8 Billion Valuation," *TechCrunch*, November 18, 2013, http://techcrunch.com/2013/11/18/dropbox-could-be-a-bargain-at-an-8-billion-valuation/.
19. Darren Nix, "How we test fake sites on live traffic," *42Floors Blog*, November 4, 2013, http://blog.42floors.com/we-test-fake-versions-of-our-site/.
20. Jackie Bavaro, "Have you tried a fake buy button test, as mentioned in Lean UX, on your website?," *Quora*, August 30, 2013, https://www.quora.com/Product-Management/Have-you-tried-a-fake-buy-button-test-as-mentioned-in-Lean-UX-on-your-website-How-did-it-turn-out-Were-your-customers-unhappy?share=1.
21. Joshua Green, "The Science Behind Those Obama Campaign E-Mails," *Businessweek*, November 29, 2012, http://www.businessweek.com/articles/2012-11-29/the-science-behind-those-obama-campaign-e-mails.
22. Adam Sutton, "Email Testing: How the Obama campaign generated approximately $500 million in donations from email marketing," *MarketingSherpa*, May 7, 2013, http://www.marketingsherpa.com/article/case-study/obama-email-campaign-testing.

23. "Inside the Cave: An In-Depth Look at the Digital, Technology, and Analytics Operations of Obama for America," *engage Research*, http://engagedc.com/download/Inside%20the%20Cave.pdf.
24. Alexis C. Madrigal, "When the Nerds Go Marching In," *The Atlantic*, November 16, 2012, http://www.theatlantic.com/technology/archive/2012/11/when-the-nerds-go-marching-in/265325/?single_page=true.
25. Jeremy Ashkenas, et al., "The 2012 Money Race: Compare the Candidates," *The New York Times*, 2012, http://elections.nytimes.com/2012/campaign-finance.
26. Alexis C. Madrigal, "Hey, I Need to Talk to You About This Brilliant Obama Email Scheme," *The Atlantic*, November 9, 2012, http://www.theatlantic.com/technology/archive/2012/11/hey-i-need-to-talk-to-you-about-this-brilliant-obama-email-scheme/265725/.
27. Jaclyn Fu, "The New Listing Page: Better Shopping, More Personality," *Etsy News Blog*, July 24, 2013, https://blog.etsy.com/news/2013/the-new-listing-page-better-shopping-more-personality/.
28. Frank Harris and Nellwyn Thomas, "Etsy's Product Development with Continuous Experimentation," *QCon*, November 8, 2012, http://www.infoq.com/presentations/Etsy-Deployment.
29. Sarah Frier, "Etsy Tops $1 Billion in 2013 Product Sales on Mobile Lift," *Bloomberg*, November 12, 2013, http://www.bloomberg.com/news/2013-11-12/etsy-tops-1-billion-in-2013-product-sales-on-mobile-lift.html.
30. Edmond Lau, "What A/B testing platform does Quora use?," *Quora*, November 10, 2012, https://www.quora.com/Quora-company/What-A-B-testing-platform-does-Quora-use/answer/Edmond-Lau?share=1.
31. "Feature API," *GitHub*, https://github.com/etsy/feature.
32. "Vanity: Experiment Driven Development," http://vanity.labnotes.org/metrics.html.
33. "Welcome to the home of genetify," *GitHub*, https://github.com/gregdingle/genetify/wiki.
34. "Benefits of Experiments - Analytics Help," https://support.google.com/analytics/answer/1745147?hl=en.
35. "Optimizely," https://www.optimizely.com/.

36. "Apptimize," http://apptimize.com/.
37. "Unbounce," http://unbounce.com/.
38. "Visual Website Optimizer," http://visualwebsiteoptimizer.com/.
39. Alex Hern, "Why Google has 200m reasons to put engineers over designers," *The Guardian*, February 5, 2014, http://www.theguardian.com/technology/2014/feb/05/why-google-engineers-designers.
40. Laura M. Holson, "Putting a Bolder Face on Google," *The New York Times*, February 28, 2009, http://www.nytimes.com/2009/03/01/business/01marissa.html?_r=0.
41. "Steve Wozniak," *Wikipedia*, http://en.wikipedia.org/wiki/Steve_Wozniak.
42. research on teaching for learning.
43. Brian Fitzpatrick and Ben Collins-Sussman, *Team Geek: A Software Developer's Guide to Working Well with Others* (O'Reilly Media 2012).

Chapter 7: Improve Your Project Estimation Skills

1. "Ooyala Launches 'Swift,' Version 2.0 of the Ooyala Player," http://www.ooyala.com/about/press/ooyala-launches-swift-version-20-ooyala-player.
2. "Ooyala Video Technology," http://www.ooyala.com/resources/video-technology.
3. Philip Su, "Broken Windows Theory," *The World As Best As I Remember It*, June 14, 2006, http://blogs.msdn.com/b/philipsu/archive/2006/06/14/631438.aspx.
4. "Windows Vista," *Wikipedia*, http://en.wikipedia.org/wiki/Windows_Vista.
5. Joel Spolsky, "Painless Software Schedules," *Joel on Software*, March 29, 2000, http://www.joelonsoftware.com/articles/fog0000000245.html.
6. Jamie Zawinski, "resignation and postmortem," March 31, 2009, http://www.jwz.org/gruntle/nomo.html.
7. "CHAOS Summary 2009," *The Standish Group*, 2009, http://emphasysbrokeroffice.com/files/2013/04/Standish-Group-CHAOS-Summary-2009.pdf.

8. Steve McConnell, "Software Estimation: Demystifying the Black Art," *Microsoft Press*, 2006.
9. Cyril Northcote Parkinson, "Parkinson's Law," *The Economist*, November 19, 1955.
10. Tom DeMarco (1982), *Controlling Software Projects: Management, Measurement, and Estimates* (Prentice Hall 1986).
11. "Anchoring," *Wikipedia*, http://en.wikipedia.org/wiki/Anchoring.
12. Frederick Brooks, *The Mythical Man-Month: Essays on Software Engineering*, p20.
13. Quadratic growth is proportional to the square of the input. With communication the number of distinct channels of pairwise communication among N people is described by N choose 2 = N (N + 1) / 2 = O(N^2).
14. Joel Spolsky, "Evidence Based Scheduling," *Joel on Software*, October 26, 2007, http://www.joelonsoftware.com/items/2007/10/26.html.
15. Frederick Brooks, *The Mythical Man-Month*, p154.
16. Jack Heart, interview with the author, March 21, 2014.
17. Alex Allain, conversation with the author, October 15, 2014.
18. Tamar Bercovici and Florian Jourda, "One to Many: The Story of Sharding at Box," *Percona Live MySQL Conference & Expo*, 2012, http://www.percona.com/files/presentations/percona-live/PLMCE2012/PLMCE2012-Sharding_At_Box.pdf.
19. The "tragedy of the commons" is an economic term describing the situation where individuals acting independently and rationally according to their own self-interest deplete a shared resource despite knowing that the depletion is contrary to the group's long-term interests.
20. Tamar Bercovici, "Scaling MySQL for the Web," *MySQL Conference & Expo*, 2013, http://www.percona.com/live/mysql-conference-2013/sites/default/files/slides/Scaling%20MySQL.pdf.
21. Martin Fowler et al., *Refactoring: Improving the Design of Existing Code* (Addison-Wesley Professional 1999).
22. Sam Schillace, interview with the author, April 8, 2014.
23. Sara Robinson, "Bring back the 40-hour week," *Salon*, March 14, 2012, http://www.salon.com/2012/03/14/bring_back_the_40_hour_work_week/.

24. Evan Robinson, "Why Crunch Modes Doesn't Work: Six Lessons," *International Game Developers Association*, 2005, http://www.igda.org/why-crunch-modes-doesnt-work-six-lessons.

25. "Sidney Chapman," *Wikipedia*, http://en.wikipedia.org/wiki/Sydney_Chapman_(economist).

26. Samuel Crowther, "Henry Ford: Why I Favor Five Days' Work With Six Days' Pay," *World's Work*, October 1926, p613–616, http://web.archive.org/web/20040826063314/http://www.worklessparty.org/timework/ford.htm.

27. "Ford factory workers get 40-hour week," *History*, http://www.history.com/this-day-in-history/ford-factory-workers-get-40-hour-week.

28. Roundtable Report, "Scheduled Overtime Effect on Construction Projects," *Business Roundtable*, 1980, http://trid.trb.org/view.aspx?id=206774.

29. Tom DeMarco and Timothy Lister, *Peopleware*, p15.

30. Tom DeMarco and Timothy Lister, *Peopleware*, p179.

Chapter 8: Balance Quality with Pragmatism

1. "Style guides for Google-originated open-source projects," https://code.google.com/p/google-styleguide/.

2. Ben Maurer and Kevin X. Chang, "What is Google's internal code review policy/process?," *Quora*, June 7, 2010, https://www.quora.com/What-is-Googles-internal-code-review-policy-process.

3. "2014 Financial Tables," *Google Financial Tables*, https://investor.google.com/financial/tables.html.

4. "Ten things we know to be true," *Google*, http://www.google.com/about/company/philosophy/.

5. "List of public corporations by market capitalization," *Wikipedia*, http://en.wikipedia.org/wiki/List_of_public_corporations_by_market_capitalization.

6. Robert Johnson, "Right and Wrong," *Facebook Notes*, October 9, 2009, https://www.facebook.com/notes/robert-johnson/right-and-wrong/148275708485.

7. Evan Priestley, "How did Evan Priestley learn to program?," *Quora*, November 20, 2013, https://www.quora.com/How-did-Evan-Priestley-learn-to-program/answer/Evan-Priestley.
8. Capers Jones, "Software Quality in 2008: A Survey of the State of the Art," *Software Productivity Research LLC*, January 30, 2008, p52, http://www.jasst.jp/archives/jasst08e/pdf/A1.pdf.
9. Albert Ni, interview with the author, October 9, 2013.
10. Josh Zelman, "(Founder Stories) How Dropbox Got Its First 10 Million Users," *TechCrunch*, January 2011, http://techcrunch.com/2011/11/01/founder-storie-how-dropbox-got-its-first-10-million-users/.
11. Victoria Barret, "Dropbox: The Inside Story Of Tech's Hottest Startup," *Forbes*, October 18, 2011, http://www.forbes.com/sites/victoriabarret/2011/10/18/dropbox-the-inside-story-of-techs-hottest-startup/.
12. There's a small exception. Experimental code checked in within certain directories don't need to be reviewed.
13. Mike Krieger, interview with the author, October 2, 2013.
14. Allen Cheung, "Why We Pair Interview," *The Corner - Square Engineering Blog*, October 5, 2011, http://corner.squareup.com/2011/10/why-we-pair-interview.html.
15. Raffi Krikorian, conversation with the author.
16. "Pylint - code analysis for Python," http://www.pylint.org/.
17. "cpplint.py," https://code.google.com/p/google-styleguide/source/browse/trunk/cpplint/cpplint.py.
18. "Barkeep - the friendly code review system," http://getbarkeep.org/.
19. Jeffrey Dean and Sanjay Ghemawat, "MapReduce: Simplified Data Processing on Large Clusters," *OSDI*, 2004, http://static.googleusercontent.com/external_content/untrusted_dlcp/research.google.com/en/us/archive/mapreduce-osdi04.pdf.
20. Edmond Lau, "HARBOR : an integrated approach to recovery and high availability in an updatable, distributed data warehouse," *Massachusetts Institute of Technology*, 2006, http://dspace.mit.edu/bitstream/handle/1721.1/36800/79653535.pdf?sequence=1.

21. Jeffrey Dean and Sanjay Ghemawat, "MapReduce: Simplified Data Processing on Large Clusters," *Communications of the ACM*, January 2008, Vol. 51, No. 1, 107–113, https://files.ifi.uzh.ch/dbtg/sdbs13/T10.0.pdf.

22. Rob Pike et al., "Interpreting the Data: Parallel Analysis with Sawzall," *Scientific Programming Journal*, 13:4, . 227–298, http://research.google.com/archive/sawzall.html.

23. Daniel Jackson, *Software Abstractions: Logic, Language, and Analysis* (The MIT Press 2012).

24. "Don't repeat yourself," *Wikipedia*, http://en.wikipedia.org/wiki/Don't_repeat_yourself.

25. "Protocol Buffers - Google's data interchange format," *GitHub*, https://github.com/google/protobuf/.

26. Fay Chang et al., "Bigtable: A Distributed Storage System for Structured Data," *OSDI*, 2006, http://research.google.com/archive/bigtable.html.

27. "Apache Thrift," http://thrift.apache.org/.

28. "Apache Hive," http://hive.apache.org/.

29. Mark Marchukov, "TAO: The power of the graph," *Facebook Notes*, June 25, 2013, http://www.facebook.com/notes/facebook-engineering/tao-the-power-of-the-graph/10151525983993920.

30. Shreyes Shesasai, "Tech Talk - webnode2 and LiveNode," *Quora*, May 25, 2011, https://www.quora.com/Shreyes-Seshasai/Posts/Tech-Talk-webnode2-and-LiveNode.

31. Justin Rosenstein, "Asana Demo & Vision Talk," *YouTube*, February 15, 2011, 34:38, https://www.youtube.com/watch?v=jkXGEgTnUXk&t=34m38s.

32. Jack Heart, "Why is Asana developing their own programming language (Lunascript)?," *Quora*, December 9, 2010, https://www.quora.com/Why-is-Asana-developing-their-own-programming-language-Lunascript/answer/Jack-Lion-Heart?share=1.

33. Joshua Bloch, "How To Design A Good API and Why it Matters," *YouTube*, January 24, 2007, http://www.youtube.com/watch?v=aAb7hSCtvGw.

34. Joshua Bloch, "How To Design A Good API and Why it Matters," *Library-Centric Software Design*, 2005, http://lcsd05.cs.tamu.edu/slides/keynote.pdf.

35. Rich Hickey, "Simple Made Easy," *InfoQ*, October 20, 2011, http://www.infoq.com/presentations/Simple-Made-Easy.

36. Jiantao Pan, "Software Reliability," *Carnegie Mellon University 18-849b Dependable Embedded Systems*, 1999, http://www.ece.cmu.edu/~koopman/des_s99/sw_reliability/.

37. Kartik Ayyar, interview with the author, October 28, 2013.

38. "Cityville," *Wikipedia*, http://en.wikipedia.org/wiki/CityVille.

39. Ward Cunningham, "The WyCash Portfolio Management System," *OOPSLA*, 1992, http://c2.com/doc/oopsla92.html.

40. Martin Fowler, "Technical Debt," October 2003, http://martinfowler.com/bliki/TechnicalDebt.html.

41. Matt Cutts, "Engineering grouplets at Google," *Matt Cutts: Gadgets, Google, and SEO*, October 22, 2007, http://www.mattcutts.com/blog/engineering-grouplets-at-google/.

42. Ryan Tate, "The Software Revolution Behind LinkedIn's Gushing Profits," *Wired*, April 10, 2013, http://www.wired.com/business/2013/04/linkedin-software-revolution/.

Chapter 9: Minimize Operational Burden

1. "Instagram," http://www.instagram.com/.

2. MG Siegler, "Instagram Launches With the Hope of Igniting Communication Through Images," *TechCrunch*, October 6, 2010, http://techcrunch.com/2010/10/06/instagram-launch/.

3. Christine Lagorio-Chafkin, "Kevin Systrom and Mike Krieger, Founders of Instagram," *Inc.*, April 9, 2012, http://www.inc.com/30under30/2011/profile-kevin-systrom-mike-krieger-founders-instagram.html.

4. Kim-Mai Cutler, "From 0 To $1 Billion In Two Years: Instagram's Rose-Tinted Ride To Glory," *TechCrunch*, April 9, 2012, http://techcrunch.com/2012/04/09/instagram-story-facebook-acquisition/.

5. "Pinterest beats Facebook in number of users per employee," *Pingdom*, February 26, 2013, http://royal.pingdom.com/2013/02/26/pinterest-users-per-employee/.

6. "What Powers Instagram: Hundreds of Instances, Dozens of Technologies," *Instagram Engineering Blog*, 2012, http://instagram-engineering.tumblr.com/post/13649370142/what-powers-instagram-hundreds-of-instances-dozens-of.

7. Instagram recently switched over to using Cassandra after they hired someone who had actually worked on Cassandra internals.

8. Steven Levy, "Good for the Soul," *Alt+Tabs of an Open Mind*, October 16, 2006, https://ashim.wordpress.com/2006/10/16/49/.

9. Kevin Systrom, "What is the genesis of Instagram?," *Quora*, January 11, 2011, https://www.quora.com/Instagram/What-is-the-genesis-of-Instagram/answer/Kevin-Systrom?share=1.

10. Todd Hoff, "Scaling Pinterest - From 0 To 10s Of Billions Of Page Views A Month In Two Years," *High Scalability*, April 15, 2013, http://highscalability.com/blog/2013/4/15/scaling-pinterest-from-0-to-10s-of-billions-of-page-views-a.html.

11. Yashwanth Nelapati and Marty Weiner, "Scaling Pinterest," *QCon*, 2012, http://www.infoq.com/presentations/Pinterest.

12. Yashwanth Nelapati and Marty Weiner, "Scaling Pinterest," *QCon*, 2012, 5:56, http://www.infoq.com/presentations/Pinterest.

13. Jim Shore, "Fail Fast," *IEEE Computer Society*, 2004, p21–25, http://martinfowler.com/ieeeSoftware/failFast.pdf.

14. "Memcached," https://code.google.com/p/memcached/wiki/NewProgramming#Expiration.

15. "Tragedy of the commons," *Wikipedia*, http://en.wikipedia.org/wiki/Tragedy_of_the_commons.

16. Shlomo Priymak, "Under the hood: MySQL Pool Scanner (MPS)," *Facebook Notes*, October 22, 2013, https://www.facebook.com/notes/facebook-engineering/under-the-hood-mysql-pool-scanner-mps/10151750529723920.

17. Rajiv Eranki, "Scaling lessons learned at Dropbox, part 1," *Rajiv's blog*, July 12, 2012, http://eranki.tumblr.com/post/27076431887/scaling-lessons-learned-at-dropbox-part-1.

18. John Ciancutti, "5 Lessons We've Learned Using AWS," *The Netflix Tech Blog*, December 16, 2010, http://techblog.netflix.com/2010/12/5-lessons-weve-learned-using-aws.html.

19. Cory Bennett and Ariel Tseitlin, "Chaos Monkey Released into the Wild," *The Netflix Tech Blog*, July 30, 2012, http://techblog.netflix.com/2012/07/chaos-monkey-released-into-wild.html.

20. Adrian Cockroft, Cory Hicks, and Greg Orzell, "Lessons Netflix Learned from the AWS Outage," *The Netflix Tech Blog*, April 29, 2011, http://techblog.netflix.com/2011/04/lessons-netflix-learned-from-aws-outage.html.

21. Bill Walsh, *The Score Takes Care of Itself: My Philosophy of Leadership* (Portfolio Trade 2010), p51.

22. "Bill Walsh (American football coach)," *Wikipedia*, http://en.wikipedia.org/wiki/Bill_Walsh_(American_football_coach).

23. Kripa Krishan, "Weathering the Unexpected," *ACM Queue*, September 16, 2012, http://queue.acm.org/detail.cfm?id=2371516.

24. Rajiv Eranki, "Scaling lessons learned at Dropbox - part 1," http://eranki.tumblr.com/post/27076431887/scaling-lessons-learned-at-dropbox-part-1.

Chapter 10: Invest in Your Team's Growth

1. Mark R. Robertson, "Ooyala Video Scheduling – New Flight Time Feature," *ReelSEO*, June 29, 2008, http://www.reelseo.com/ooyala-video-scheduling/.

2. Marc Hedlund, interview with the author, October 9, 2013.

3. Yishan Wong, "The Secret to Career Success," April 23, 2009, http://algeri-wong.com/yishan/the-secret-to-career-success.html.

4. "Benchmark (venture capital firm)," *Wikipedia*, http://en.wikipedia.org/wiki/Benchmark_(venture_capital_firm).

5. Andy Rachleff, "48 Hot Tech Companies To Build A Career," *Wealthfront Knowledge Center*, October 25, 2012, https://blog.wealthfront.com/hot-mid-size-silicon-valley-companies/.

6. Albert Ni, interview with the author, October 9, 2013.

7. Greg Brockman, "What is the engineering interview process like at Stripe?," *Quora*, August 27, 2013, https://www.quora.com/What-is-the-engineering-interview-process-like-at-Stripe/answer/Greg-Brockman?share=1.

8. Parth Upadhyay, "Pair Programming Interviews," *The Corner: Square Engineering Blog*, September 11, 2013, http://corner.squareup.com/2013/09/pair-programming-interviews.html.

9. Gayle Laakmann McDowell, *Cracking the Coding Interview: 150 Programming Questions and Solutions* (CareerCup 2011).

10. Tommy MacWilliam, "What is the on-boarding process for new engineers at Quora?," *Quora*, November 5, 2013, https://www.quora.com/What-is-the-on-boarding-process-for-new-engineers-at-Quora/answer/Tommy-MacWilliam?share=1.

11. "Bus Factor," *Wikipedia*, http://en.wikipedia.org/wiki/Bus_factor.

12. Nimrod Hoofien, interview with the author, October 29, 2013.

13. "Kennedy Space Center FAQ," *NASA*, http://www.nasa.gov/centers/kennedy/about/information/shuttle_faq.html#10.

14. Pete Abilla, "Jeff Bezos and Root Cause Analysis," *Shmula.com*, January 23, 2009, http://www.shmula.com/jeff-bezos-5-why-exercise-root-cause-analysis-cause-and-effect-ishikawa-lean-thinking-six-sigma/987/.

15. Sara Himeles and Joey Dello Russo, "5 powerful tactics we use to achieve great teamwork," *Asana Blog*, December 16, 2013, http://blog.asana.com/2013/12/culture-practices/.

About the Author

Edmond Lau is an engineer at Quip, where he's building a productivity suite to make teams more effective.

Previously, he was an early engineer at Quora, where he led the engineering team on user growth and built the onboarding and mentoring programs for new engineers. Before Quora, he worked as the tech lead of analytics at Ooyala and as an engineer on search quality at Google. He earned his Bachelor's and Master's Degree in Computer Science at MIT.

He lives in Palo Alto, CA. Visit him at www.theeffectiveengineer.com, where he shares more lessons, stories, and habits to help engineers be more productive and effective.

He's passionate about helping engineering teams build strong cultures, and his writing has been featured on *Forbes*, *Slate*, *Fortune*, *Inc.*, and *Times*. He's guest lectured at MIT and Stanford, and he also speaks at startups about building great engineering culture.

The Effective Engineer is his first book. He'd love to get your thoughts and feedback over Twitter (@edmondlau) or over email (edmond@theeffectiveengineer.com).

Made in the USA
Coppell, TX
21 March 2021